Illusion in Art

Botticelli. *St. Augustine in His Study*

Illusion in Art

Trompe l'Oeil

A History of Pictorial Illusionism

by M.L. d'Otrange Mastai

ABARIS BOOKS • NEW YORK

Copyright © 1975 by Abaris Books, Inc.
International Standard Book Number 0-913870-03-X
Library of Congress Card Number 74-6501
First published 1975 by Abaris Books, Inc.
200 Fifth Avenue, New York, New York 10010
Printed in the United States of America

To my husband, Boleslaw Mastai

—— "prime mover," as always.

Contents

ACKNOWLEDGEMENTS

My thanks go first of all to Walter L. Strauss: without his ready understanding and enthusiasm, this project could never have matured. Next, to Sara E. Pyle, for sympathy and interest well above and beyond the call of editorial duty—as well as, more specifically, for painstaking and minutious copyediting and for bringing to completion the mammoth task of obtaining and organizing the illustrative material.

I am thankful for this opportunity to express my personal thanks to all owners, institutional and private, who have generously granted permission to reproduce the works in their possession.

Although I trust that my indebtedness to many art scholars in their respective fields is plainly evidenced in references throughout the text, as well as by inclusion of their works in the bibliography, I am eager to acknowledge here once more my deep obligation. Their labors furnished unfailing inspiration and immeasurably eased my own task.

Over the course of many years, and more specially in connection with the present work, I owe deep gratitude to that noble institution, the Frick Art Reference Library, and its staff, headed by Miss Mildred Steinbach.

For numerous helpful suggestions, information volunteered, and various other highly valued courtesies, my special thanks are due to the following: James W. Alsdorf; Ms. Francesca Barran, The National Trust, London; Baroness Gabriele Bestinck-Thyssen; A. Berkes, Curator, Thyssen-Bornemisza Collection, Lugano; Mrs. Lois Blomstrann, The New Britain Museum of American Art, Conn.; Prof. Dr. Zbigniew Bochénski, Vice-Director, National Museum, Cracow; Aaron Bohrod; Mlle. Béatrice Brinicombe, Fondation Custodia, Institut Néerlandais, Paris; Berthe Bülow-Jacobson, Royal Museum of Fine Arts, Copenhagen; Irving F. Burton, M.D.; Margaret Chalfant; Marie-Lucie Cornillot, Conservateur des Musées de Besançon; Deanna Cross (Mrs. John D. Cross), Library, The Metropolitan Museum of Art; Mr. Peter Day, Devonshire Collections, Chatsworth; Mr. Lawrence Di Carlo, Fischbach Gallery, New York; Leonard K. Firestone; Alfred Frankenstein; Charles B. Furguson, Director, The New Britain Museum of American Art; J. Hellemans, General Consul of Belgium, New York; Herr Hess, Öffentliche Kunstsammlung, Basel; John D. Kilbourne, Curator, The Historical Society of Pennsylvania; Dr. Rudiger Klessmann, Staatliche Museum Preussischer Kulturbesitz; Inge Koch, Royal Museum of Fine Arts, Copenhagen; Ms. Irene Konefal, John G. Johnson Collection, Philadelphia; Herr Krüger, Staatliche Kunstsammlungen, Dresden; Francis S. McIlhenny, Jr.; Henry P. McIlhenny; Ms. Priscilla E. Muller, Curator of Paintings, The Hispanic Society, New York; Clyde Newhouse; Ms. Mary Beth O'Brian, The Supreme Court Historical Society, Washington, D. C.; James Ogelsby Peale; Dr. M. Poch-Kalous, Director, Gemäldegalerie der Akademie der bildenden Künste, Vienna; Andrew Poggenpohl, Art Editor, *National Geographic Magazine*; A. Poljakov, The Hermitage, Leningrad; Mrs. Samuel Register; Mr. Oscar Salzer, Los Angeles; Dr. Sheila Schwartz; Laurie Sucher; Le Directeur du Musée Marmottan, Paris; Ms. Wendy J. Shadwell, Curator, The Middendorf Collection; H. R. Bradley Smith, Assistant to the Director, Shelburne Museum, Mass.; Dr. George Szabo, The Robert Lehman Collection, The Metropolitan Museum of Art; Michiko Okaya Taylor, Registrar-Librarian, The Museum at Stony Brook, Stony Brook, N. Y.; Max Terrier, Conservateur en Chef du Musée National du Château de Compiègne; Jacques Wilhelm, Conservateur en Chef, Musée Carnavalet, Paris; W. E. Woolfendel, Director, Archives of American Art; Mr. Rudolf Wunderlich, Kennedy Galleries, New York; finally, Hermann Strohbach and Ewa A.M. Pietkewicz for design.

COLOR PLATES

The color plates follow page 205

OPVS·KAROLI·CRIVELLI·VENETI

1

Illusionism

Definitions and Limitations

A significant but frequently neglected aspect of the development of Western art is the persistence of an unmistakable element of illusionism that meanders, like an unbroken thread in a tapestry, throughout the entire fabric of painting from antiquity to the present day—at times prominent, in a coherent pattern; at times elusive, a mere glinting filament in the underweave. Because of this pervasiveness, a comprehensive history of illusionism might well expand into an entire history of painting. The more modest purpose here is to furnish a schematic synthesis, indicating the major manifestations, with emphasis on the continuity of the phenomenon. Our goal is to present a panorama rather than a map.

The guidelines given below are admittedly personal and pragmatic, primarily because the principles of illusionism—and its deriviative, trompe l'oeil—have never been formally enunciated by their practitioners. The subject has generally been treated not in and of itself, but in relation to other topics. Some of the most valuable thoughts on trompe l'oeil in particular have been part of recent treatises on still-life painting. But most of the information has been found in a number of articles and essays, highly stimulating but fragmentary in scope.[1]

At times the approach has been rather abstruse, dealing with scientific aspects of illusionism, and delving deeply into projective geometry and the laws of optics. The public has been far more intrigued, however, by the lingering aura of an arcane art within art; mysterious, faintly occult—if not ac-

7

tually partaking of sorcery—vestiges of an ancient tradition. Whatever one's orientation, what is beyond doubt is the lack of a definition in reasonably lucid language of the meaning and repertory of illusionism, starting with the essential terms.

Illusionism and trompe l'oeil are words that have become so closely related in modern times that one must make a conscious effort to recall that they are by no means synonymous. Illusionism appeals predominantly to the imagination, as its magic is always in some measure "in the eye of the beholder," and it might even be defined as poetic illusion in visual form. On the contrary, trompe l'oeil, i.e., "that which deceives the eye," strives relentlessly to achieve perfect duplication of reality to the point of *de*lusion. Illusionism is ancient; trompe l'oeil is a relative newcomer. Illusionism is wide, deep, and all-embracing; trompe l'oeil is a mere tributary.

Ideally, the expression trompe l'oeil should be applied only to the specific art form it was coined to identify: a very special kind of precisionistic still-life painting that first became popular in the seventeenth century. The term itself is not found in print in its country of origin until the first decade of the nineteenth century—more exactly in 1803, according to the authoritative *Petit Robert* dictionary. However, it is likely that it was in use in ateliers considerably earlier. But it appears that the term was not familiar to the public as late as the first decade of the eighteenth century. On June 15, 1707, a notarized appraisal was drawn of the estate of the late Antoine Simonin, who had been a goldsmith in the city of Beauvais, presumably a man of means, and evidently a collector of art works. The list of paintings in his possession includes several that were unmistakably trompe l'oeil but are not referred to by that convenient name. Instead, they are painstakingly described as "two paintings representing boards of pine wood upon which are landscapes and engravings in red" (i.e., *sanguine*), and "a plank upon which are painted some books." [2a]

At the present time, the term trompe l'oeil forms part of the international glossary of art and has become thoroughly naturalized in English-speaking countries, although it is not yet listed in all English dictionaries. This is not due solely to its foreign origin, for even the word illusionism is still restricted by lexicographers to its philosophical meaning, although it too has long been in widespread use in the literature of art. *Webster's Third New International Dictionary* does include trompe l'oeil and defines it as follows:

Deception of the eye, especially by a painting as (a) the intensification of the reality of component objects in an unnaturally arranged still life through the use of minute detail and the careful rendition of tactile and tonal values; (b) the use in mural and ceiling decoration of painted detail suggestive of architectural or other three-dimensional elements but often characterized by exaggerated perspective, abrupt contrast of light and shade, or general stylization which stresses artificiality.

Acceptance of this definition must be conditional upon several important reservations. There can be no doubt, for instance, that the effect of intensified reality came about unsought. As one authority put it, "The old masters of trompe l'oeil, while they thought that they were reproducing reality with slavish faithfulness, actually intensified it far beyond all accepted conventions, whether mental or optical."[3] In fact, their vision was totally impartial; they neither minimized nor magnified what they saw, which is of itself unnatural, for the human eye does make a choice. The result in such works is an overall heightening of values, described here as "intensification," but perhaps only the viewer's subconscious and faintly disquieting awareness of an unbalance (pl. 1).

1. *Jacopo de'Barbari.* Dead Partridge, *1504. Munich, Alte Pinakothek*

It is evident that if a still life, for example, seems to have been "unnaturally arranged," this would be a grievous fault automatically invalidating the trompe l'oeil effect. The same holds true for "stylization" and "artificiality." One might also object that it is logically impossible for perspective to be "exaggerated." Realistic perspective must obey the laws of projective geometry, and if it does so, regardless of how *unusual* the angle of vision chosen by the artist may be, the perspective is not subject to criticism *per se*. And "abrupt contrast of light and shade," like any other dramatic excess, has always been shunned by illusionists, whose goal was to lull the eye into complacent acceptance rather than to shock and bewilder their audience.

The most serious misconception is the indiscriminate equation of illusionism and trompe l'oeil. "Mural and ceiling decoration" properly falls under the heading of illusionism, more specifically architectural illusionism. There are at least two reasons for this. First, such decorations, of their very nature, always form part of a larger, preexistent whole from which they cannot be separated, whereas trompe l'oeil stands by itself as a self-contained rendering of objects in their entirety. Second, mural and ceiling decorations are part of a large category that calls for several subdivisions, widely different in scope and mood, ranging from uninspired duplication of the actual architectural features (generally to give the permanent effect of enlarged space) to grandiose imaginative visions by such artists as Mantegna, Tiepolo, or Veronese (which can only "deceive" momentarily). Trompe l'oeil, on the other hand, is necessarily restricted and limited in area.

However, scale alone cannot be the standard for differentiating illusionism and trompe l'oeil. Illusionism is make-believe, very like a theatrical spectacle. It invariably requires of the viewer a willing participation, amounting to complicity with the artist. The famous ceiling decoration on the theme of "The Apotheosis of St. Ignatius" (pl. 2) can be viewed at best advantage from a specific point that is marked on the floor below. No deception is attempted or achieved. More importantly, the viewer is thus made aware that the painted scene is merely an incentive to his own imagination. Far from being passive, he must place himself not only in the right spot, but in the right frame of mind. This covenant between artist and viewer has always been implicit, whether or not the public was directed to a special vantage point. No great illusionistic scheme ever truly deceived, or attempted to deceive. The artist's function was to fling open the illusionistic portals into the domain of imagination, that those who were worthy might enter.

Possibly the deepest meaning of pictorial illusionism is found in an Oriental parable, the beautiful tale of the Chinese painter, Wu Tao-tzu, who "entered a grotto in a landscape he had painted, after which the picture

11

2. *Andrea Pozzo.* The Apotheosis of St. Ignatius, *1691–94. Rome, S. Ignazio*

faded from the whitening wall."[4] An occidental counterpart is the famous tale of "*Le Chef-d'Oeuvre Inconnu,*" one of Balzac's *Etudes Philosophiques,* in which Frenhofer, an imaginary Northern painter of the early seventeenth century, is driven mad by his endless search for perfect pictorial translation of reality. He finally destroys all his works, including his masterwork, a formless daub, built up of countless superimposed coats of paint, all different versions of the same subject. Below, in a forgotten corner of the canvas, lies one exquisite bare foot, the only bit remaining of his original creation, painted as no painter ever dared dream of painting. All else is invisible to the two artists, Pourbus and Poussin, whom Frenhofer has invited to view the painting. Only the aged artist can see, with his mind's eye, the chef-d'oeuvre forever "*inconnu.*"

The victim of "the search for the absolute" does not win our sympathy, nor, significantly, did Balzac intend that he should. Frenhofer's ambition, it is implied, was unholy: he longed for the divine gift of creation. Something of this aversion did, in early days, become attached to practitioners of pictorial illusionism. The magic of the art was not considered entirely white: legends of pagan antiquity recounting impressive feats of illusionism had not been forgotten, and the Church's eventual approval of religious images never quite exorcised the memory of those practices in the public mind. One is reminded of the Judaic and Moslem restrictions on the making of images; or of the even more ancient fear, prevalent among primitive peoples, that portrayal drains the subject's life essence. From the romantic era, E. T. A. Hoffmann's and Edgar Allen Poe's fantastic tales of live puppets or artist's models whose souls left their bodies to migrate into their painted semblances recall those very superstitions and ancient dreads. Similarly, an aura of the occult hovered about trompe l'oeil, and with it the lingering suspicion that the objects portrayed had exacted the life spirits of their "creators."

Significantly, trompe l'oeil reached its zenith during the troublous time of transition between the Renaissance and the Age of Reason, the seventeenth century. It continued to be held in favor as late as the Victorian era, when moral considerations began to intrude. The odium of "trickery" applied to trompe l'oeil came as the result of a censure not only narrow and ungenerous but completely insensitive to either the artistic merit or the true purpose of illusionism in any form. Some of this odium may have been due to the appellation itself which is certainly not entirely satisfactory—even to the French, who have similarly failed to find a substitute for that even worse misnomer, "*la nature morte.*" For want of a better term, Sir Joshua Reynolds described a trompe l'oeil painting as "one of the best *deceptions* I have ever seen."[5] The literal translation of only half of the phrase is even less satisfactory, and the subsequent unfavorable attitude towards trompe l'oeil—reflected even, as we have seen, in dictionary definitions—may be largely the result of this unfortunate name. Two fairly recent quotations from essays dealing with trompe l'oeil should suffice to demonstrate that the misconception endures to the present:

> It should be borne in mind that trompe l'oeil is less a picture than
> a feat of trickery. In short, it is to the still life what a waxwork
> figure is to a statue.[6]

> A trompe l'oeil picture is one which is essentially a piece of trickery, where the artist consciously strives to deceive the spectator
> rather than to impress him with a demonstration of technical virtuosity.[7]

Two fallacies of reasoning should be immediately apparent: first, from the nature of things, the delusion or "trickery" cannot endure very long, so that the ultimate result will indeed be precisely "to impress . . . with a demonstration of technical virtuosity"; second, it is difficult to believe that any artist with the talent to perpetrate such masterly "trickery" should be willing to lavish so much effort on either of these goals: to impress the viewer or even to deceive him by trickery. When the writer spontaneously makes a subtle distinction by terming the viewer a "spectator," he unconsciously grants trompe l'oeil its right status. It is after all an offspring of illusionism and therefore also a spectacle of sorts.

It is a truism that any worthy portraitist portrays himself while his followers keep on portraying him; and that a landscape is never merely a topographical survey, but also a pretext for the expression of a personal mood. There is no reason why a trompe l'oeil painting should prove an exception in that regard. All great realists, or "naturalists"—including the practitioners of trompe l'oeil on the highest level—have been also great visionaries, who sought perfection in the duplication, even the delusion, of reality.

It had been said that "a painting begins to become a book at the very moment it uses lines and colors to tell a story or to describe human emotions, human passions, human thoughts—in short, whatever could be expressed as well as by means of words."[8] Trompe l'oeil never "tells a story," for its sole purpose is precisely to mirror those aspects of reality that cannot "be expressed as well by means of words." Thus, trompe l'oeil is revealed as the most scrupulous of all forms of artistic expression.

13

Ciuitas syrie que nunc tyrus dicit. olim serra uocabat a pisce quodam qui illic abundabat. quem sua lingua sar apellat ex quo diriuatū est huiᵒ similitudinis pisciculos sardas. sardinas q̄ uocari.

3. *English artist.* The Flying Fish of Tyre, *c. 1170.*
New York, Pierpont Morgan Library, Ms. 81

14

Trompe l'oeil, then, is devoted not to "trickery" but to the representation of pure visual experience with utmost objectivity. In another sense, it represents the culmination of pictorial realism; under ideal conditions, the result is one of totally convincing visual delusion. But, as this is early, traceable even in such unlikely eras as the Byzantine (pl. 30) and the Romanesque (pl. 3), the question must inevitably arise of why there came a time when artists suddenly felt the need to differentiate between a type of painting that "fooled the eye" and another type that by implication did not. The differentiation is meaningful, for it coincided with the important and definite assertion of the artist as personal creator instead of as recorder or at best interpreter, however genial. This was, in modern photographic terms, a change of focus: from "infinity," a wide but somewhat passive and unquestioning vision (indeed the vision of the ages of Faith) to "close-up," with a new freedom of choice for the artists who could now arbitrarily emphasize certain elements to the detriment of others.

Approximately with the beginning of the eighteenth century, technical competence had become a matter of academic training, available with relative ease to any aspiring painter with a modicum of natural aptitude. Even the *camera obscura* and the *camera lucida,* those forerunners of the familiar Kodak of modern times, had not weakened the prestige of realism. Instead, they were gladly welcomed as helpful tools, although now, with the wisdom of hindsight, we realize that they did prophesy an abasement of realism.

In the nineteenth century, the practitioners of trompe l'oeil were not swept away by the new Romantic current; rather, they were among the "conservative" minority of artists, who remained unconvinced that their emancipation from the necessity merely to record reality was actually a genuine liberation. They did not give up the quest for reality, that "loftier reality" of Goethe, known successively in our own day as heightened realism, magic realism, surrealism, and presently, hyper-realism. This is the reality by which Juan Gris has defined painting itself: "Certain private relationships between the elements of an imaginary reality."[9]

Illusionism has been called "basically an applied science rather than an art." This description is true only in the sense that a combination of scientific knowledge with artistic feeling is called for. It remains an art nevertheless, and as such is governed by intuition rather than theorems. A man may possess profound knowledge of the laws of optics and projective geometry, but he will be unable to create a painting embodying all these, unless, like Leonardo, he is an artist as well as a scientist.

The development of the essential laws of perspective—the work of Alberti, and of Pélérin, called "Viator"—led to the establishment of *"construzione legittima,"* a theory that has been of inestimable worth to generations of illusionists. The celebrated schema of Viator's living room (pl. 4) helped make possible the great architectonic painting of the Renaissance and all following ages. The third great name associated with the rationalization of sight during the Renaissance is that of Dürer, who is thought to have done for the Northern lands what Alberti did for Italy, and Pélérin for France (pl. 5). In fact, it has been demonstrated that Dürer oddly misapplied in his own works the theories of the two geometricians.[10] He owned at least one literary work of Leone Battista Alberti,[11] and he certainly knew—if not the original edition (Toul, 1505), then the pirated version (Nuremberg, 1509)—of *De Artificiali Perspectiva* by Viator. As Ivins has observed, it seems as if Dürer looked at figures from below, and at buildings from above, the result being a pyramid in the first instance and an inverted pyramid in the second. He then combined the two sets of studies, so that he actually had not one but two vanishing points. Both were right, but taken together, both were wrong.

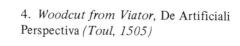

4. *Woodcut from Viator,* De Artificiali Perspectiva *(Toul, 1505)*

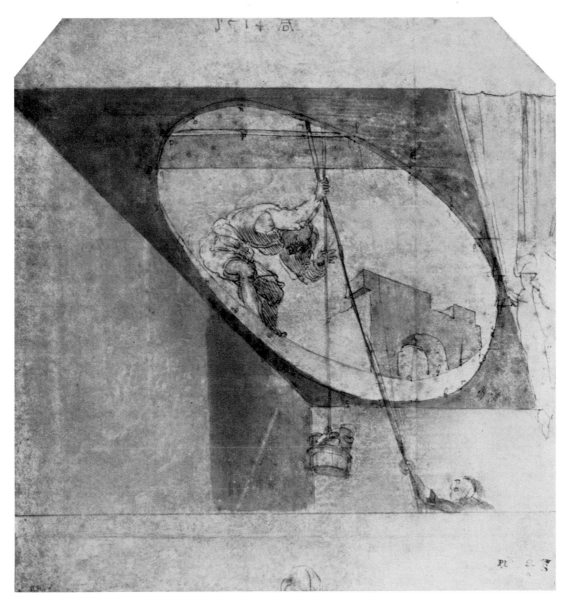

5. *Albrecht Dürer.* Perspective Study, *1514. Vienna, Albertina*

Yet, Dürer did not actually fail. "This fundamental contradiction of one of the great intuitive bases of experience produces a subtle psychological malaise in the beholder of his work that, not being readily traceable to an obvious cause, is doubtless one of the principal reasons for the peculiar fascination that his work has always exercised over the mind of man."[12]

Had Dürer's purpose been purely illusionistic, he could not have thus flaunted the rules. The "subtle psychological malaise" would have verged on optical insecurity for the viewer. This is the one risk no illusionist dares take, to arouse suspicion by extravagance. On this foundation of solid common sense, the entire edifice of illusionism rests.

6. *Samuel van Hoogstraten (1627–1678).* Vide-Poche. *Vienna, Akademie*

Essentially, a work of illusionism is part of, or related to, a greater whole into which it is integrated, and separation from which weakens, if not entirely destroys, its significance. On these terms, it is apparent that both the huge ceiling decorations of the churches of the Baroque era and the *devant de cheminée* (the temporary screens that hid the empty hearth in summer) of the eighteenth century belong to the domain of illusionism. This is true regardless of scale: a ceiling may be a gigantic project (pl. 2), and a chimney screen may be as small as "La Chaufferette aux Oeufs" (color pl. 15), a mere fifteen by eighteen inches. Therefore, the link between these examples is not their size, nor even their decorative purpose, but the fact that both were designed for integration into a preexisting scheme.

18

9. *Samuel van Hoogstraten (1627–1678).* Perspective Box of a Dutch Interior. *Detroit, Courtesy of the Detroit Institute of Arts*

In theory, a painting of a cathedral or of any large edifice, if properly rendered according to the laws of perspective and then viewed in a box or through a pinhole, can be trompe l'oeil. This is actually the principle of the perspective box (pl. 9) or peep show (pls. 197—197a), and it is clear that if one is willing to include performances of this kind, the field would be extended immeasurably. Any realistically painted subject presented in this manner could then become a trompe l'oeil, although the artist did not intend it as such. This establishes another limitation in defining trompe l'oeil: a trompe l'oeil must have been conceived with the specific purpose in mind of convincing visual delusion.

21

In both illusionism and trompe l'oeil, whatever is depicted must be shown in original coloring. For example, there can be no such thing as a grisaille trompe l'oeil, unless the object depicted, such as a stone bas-relief (pl. 10) is itself of that coloring. As very few objects in nature are monochromatic —and even then they generally reflect some measure of additional coloring from their surroundings, or even merely receive it from the ambient light— it follows that there really should be no such thing as an absolutely monochrome illusionistic painting. Therefore media such as pen, pencil, and charcoal are inherently disqualified: a drawing may be a brilliant schema, but never a convincing duplication of reality. Even certain polychrome media, such as pastel and watercolor, are inadequate with respect to body, luster, and flexibility.

10. *Constantino Brumidi.* Frieze of the Dome of the Capitol, Washington, D. C. *Courtesy of the U. S. Capitol Historical Society*

Illusionism, it is true, may at times make use of distemper. But as a general rule—and invariably in trompe l'oeil—only oil colors make possible the subtle shading, imperceptible gradation of tones, and effortless transition from light to dark that are essential for deception at close quarters. Occasionally, when depicting a grouping of papers on a flat surface, fairly satisfactory results were achieved in other media because of the near two-dimensionality of the subject and the coolness of the color scheme, but there can be no doubt that the use of oil colors would have brought even greater success.

Experience has proven that cool, even lighting is most favorable for purposes of pictorial illusionism in general, and especially for trompe l'oeil. One encyclopedia of art defines it as "a positively established unilateral illumination, equivalent to a perspective of light."[13] Not only this requirement but also those indicated earlier can be summarized in a simple statement that extremes of any kind unduly tax the optical credulity of the viewer. There is no reason why dramatic chiaroscuro should be an exception to this rule. One

A trompe l'oeil, on the contrary, is of its very nature independent and self-contained. Because it is unrelated to any particular setting, it can effect visual illusion wherever displayed. As to its "component objects," to use Webster's phrase, they should, without exception, be contained within the picture plane. Theoretically, what that plane may be is unlimited: anything from a purely geometric shape to such an extreme of asymmetry as Forbera's "Easel" (pl. 220). But within that chosen space, whatever is shown must be shown whole and complete. This is what separates genuine trompe l'oeil from precisionistic still life, where objects are placed on the corner of a table, or on a ledge cut off at both ends by the limits of the canvas, the viewer being expected to supply the missing part through imagination (pls. 6–7). Illusion-ism may on occasion show part of an object, but only when the remainder of the object can plausibly be supposed to be hidden by an existing feature extraneous to the painting, such as a protruding cornice, a baluster, or the like. The special character of trompe l'oeil is that it deals not in suggestion but in "fact." It goes without saying that the objects *within* the trompe l'oeil can overlap and mask each other in part, but they cannot trespass the edges of the canvas, board, or whatever the painting surface may be. If the eye must roam beyond the boundaries of the frame to seek the continuation of

7. *William Harnett.* Philadelphia Letter, Books, Writing Plume, *1879. New York, Kennedy Galleries*

a partially depicted object, the viewer is immediately made aware that he is dealing with a conventional depiction on a flat, two-dimensional surface, and all hope of any "deception," delusion, trickery, or whatever else one may wish to call it, is instantly and irretrievably lost.

In a large illusionistic scheme involving great depth, the objects diminish in size as they seemingly recede from the spectator. The question does not arise in trompe l'oeil, which deals only with subjects in the foreground, near the viewer's plane of vision. Apparent tridimensional projections into the viewer's own plane, although not absolutely essential, are both dramatically effective and an actual help to the viewer for the unconscious but unavoidable physical adjustment in focusing that he is called upon to make.

Extreme proximity is of course the test that neither an illusionistic painting nor even a trompe l'oeil can withstand. In its very brief listing devoted to trompe l'oeil, the popular *Petit Larousse* dictionary nevertheless manages to bring out this most important point: "Trompe l'oeil is painting of a sort that gives at a distance the illusion of reality." *At a distance*—which naturally varies with the circumstances. For instance, there is the well-documented story of the banknote portrayed in an American trompe l'oeil of the late nineteenth century (cf. pl. 8): the work was examined under a magnifying glass by a renowned artist of the period (an opponent of illusionism), who firmly declared it to be an original pasted to the canvas. He was proven wrong and had to present his apologies to the artist (see p. 298).

8. *William Harnett.* Five-Dollar Bill, *1877. Philadelphia Museum of Art, Alex Simpson, Jr. Collection*

ought to distinguish, however, between chiaroscuro and the use of a dark background against which forms stand out sharply silhouetted, as if viewed by candlelight. One might even contend that Georges de La Tour and the Dutch Luminists were striving for nocturnal illusionism. The use of a very dark, sometimes actually night-black background, as in Floris van Schouten's "Dessert Table" (pl. 165), or Sebastian Stosskopf's "Basket of Glasses and Pâté" (pl. 11), does effect "an intensification of reality" to the extent of bringing works of this kind to the borderline between trompe l'oeil and still life. As a result of the exaggerated contrast of light and dark, the middle distance is to all effects abolished. The bright objects in the foreground are depicted in relief, and we almost feel as if we could reach over and touch them. The dark void beyond, on the contrary, cannot easily be gauged, and the suggestion of considerable depth naturally contributes to the impression of three-dimensionality.

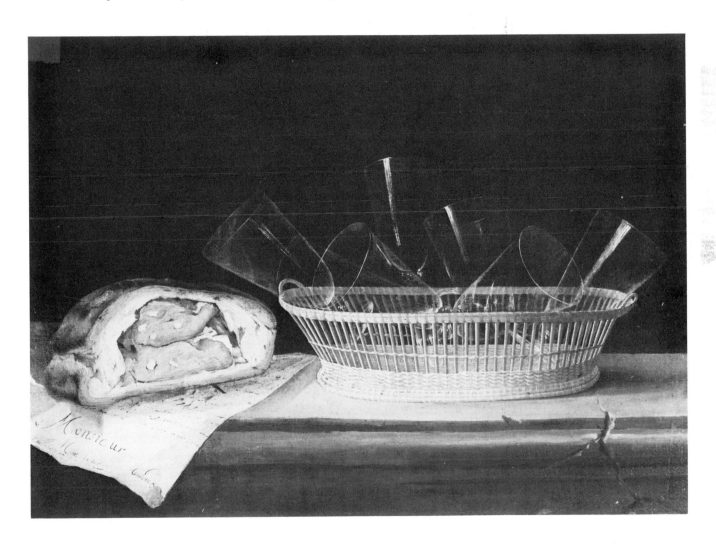

11. *Sebastian Stosskopf (1597–1657).* Basket of Glasses and Pâté. *Strassburg, Musée des Beaux-Arts*

A kindred example is the *devant de cheminée* in which the painter also indicates a dark indeterminate space—in this example the recessed niche of the hearth, where the forms depicted in the foreground are abruptly swallowed by the penumbra (pl. 12).

12. *Jean-Baptiste Oudry.* Dog with a Porcelain Bowl (devant de cheminée), *1751. Paris, Musée du Louvre*

Trompe l'oeil is not only a form of still life but indeed "still" life in the most literal meaning of the term, as any suggestion of unnaturally arrested movement immediately destroys the illusion. Conceivably, to the purist, inclusion of even the smallest life forms (insects, butterflies, mice, lizards, and the like), permissible in still life, should not be tolerated in trompe l'oeil. This stricture is perhaps too extreme. A number of medieval and Renaissance paintings included an illusionistic fly (pls. 13–14), and it is also encountered in an American portrait of the Colonial era (pl. 298). The depiction of such small life forms is so natural a conceit that it has always proven entirely credible, because of the insect's habit of alternating pauses of immobility with sudden rapid movement. The same is true of other small animals: a moth remains motionless throughout the daylight hours; a mouse or a lizard "freezes" for considerable periods of time. But no justification is truly necessary, because of the ephemeral nature of the "deception." In the end, one might conclude, it is really up to the taste and common sense of the artist, the essential requirement being that he does not overburden our willing credulity to the point of disbelief.

Contrary to what might have been expected, the advent of photography brought trompe l'oeil "moral support." It was soon found out that while the camera does not lie and tells "nothing but the truth," it does not, however, tell "the whole truth." The dissemination of photographic illustrations has made it evident how much was left unsaid that might have been said beautifully, subtly, and eloquently—and above all, with the personal voice of an artist—in a fine trompe l'oeil. At last came the realization that the element of "trickery" was the very least, and true artistry the most important, component of trompe l'oeil.

After the serious setback inflicted on illusionism in general and trompe l'oeil in particular by the rise of Impressionism—to which trompe l'oeil was profoundly alien because of its analytical approach and quality of detachment—trompe l'oeil has once more come into favor in our age.

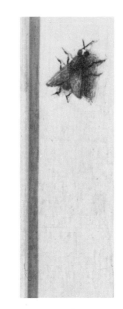

14. *Detail of pl. 13*

13. *Carlo Crivelli (attrib.).* Sts. Catherine of Alexandria and Mary Magdalene, *c. 1480–85.* London, Courtesy of the Trustees of the National Gallery

25

Mosaic Pavement from the House of the Mysteries of Isis, Antioch, early 3d century A.D.

2

Classical Antiquity

Egypt to Byzantium

Of all modes of painting, pictorial illusionism makes the greatest demands on the proficiency of the artist. Since it presupposes technical excellence at the start, there can be no period of trial or of groping for the desired effect; nor can there be such a thing as "primitive illusionism"; the terms are mutually contradictory.

It is not then surprising that the first instances of what we now call trompe l'oeil should appear only at a comparatively late date: the period from the fifth to the third century before the Christian era, during the "Golden Age" of Greece. We may well believe—although only from a persistent tradition, for no actual examples survive—that the skill of the painters of Hellas fully rivalled that of her sculptors, enabling the practitioners of illusionism to perform the legendary feats with which they are credited.

Yet, whereas these constitute an artistic zenith, not to be attained again for many centuries, the imitation of life had nonetheless been given tangible and eloquent expression considerably earlier, although in another form. The seeds of this illusionism had originally been planted in the fertile soil of the Nile.

In an age that was already remote antiquity when the Greek painters first undertook illusionism, sculptural and pictorial elements had been conjoined in perfect harmony in the polychrome statuary of Egypt. These extraordinary simulacra recreate for us the entire gamut of national life, from the formal stylized elegance of the royal portraits to the more lively realism

27

of plebeian countenances, scribes, overseers, and other petty officials of the Pharaonic court. The fidelity of these depictions received unexpected confirmation when the famed statue known as the "Sheik-el-Beled," now in the Cairo Museum, was unearthed at Sakkarah.

The incident was recorded by the Egyptologist Gaston Maspero, who was present when the "Sheik" was removed from the hypogeum: "By a curious coincidence, the statue of this ancient Egyptian was the exact portrait of one of the *Sheik-el-Beled,* or headman, of the village of Sakkarah; our Arab workmen, always quick to seize on a likeness, straightway dubbed it 'Sheik-el-Beled,' and the name has stuck to it."[1]

No other testimony than that of our own eyes, however, is necessary to convince us of the verisimilitude reflected in the sarcophagus of Queen Meritamun (pl. 15). Not only is this the ideal of the aristocratic Egyptian type, but we sense also that the personal touches are so just and precise that only the breath of life is missing. In Théophile Gautier's *Le Roman de la Momie,* those who view the sarcophagus of the fictional Queen Tahoser experience precisely the same sensations:

> the long Egyptian eyes, outlined with black and enamel; the delicate winged nose, rounded cheeks and full lips, smiling still with the indescribable smile of the Sphinx; the chin with its short curve—all offered to the beholder an example of the purest type of the ideal Egyptian, and by many little characteristic details that art had not invented, an individual portrait was clearly indicated. A multitude of fine curls, tightly knotted, fell upon each side of the mask in opulent masses.

Gautier's description corresponds perfectly to the image of Queen Meritamun, whose flower face and slender neck emerge amazingly lifelike from the monumental royal headdress and the sumptuously imbricated sheath of gold and turquoise scales. If the effect produced even in the impersonal setting and cold light of a conventional museum is of a brooding presence, somewhat melancholy in its exquisite grace, how much more dramatically illusionistic the statue must have appeared in its original setting: set upright during the mourning ceremonies at home, reposing on a couch for the crossing of the Nile to the City of the Dead, and finally as the stellar, if silent, performer in the hypogeum, under the fitful glow of torches held by family members and friends tendering their last farewells. Maspero commented in precisely this way of another polychrome statue of a man standing in the niche of the

28

stela in his tomb (which itself was certainly architectural illusionism, since it was meant to feign the facade and entrance of a house):

> The statue of Mruruka-Mari is seen in it, its face turned outwards, its left foot advanced, preparing to descend a flight of four steps into the chapel. The movement is so true and lifelike that, in the dim lamp-light, those present at the funeral service must have had the sensation of the actual presence of the dead man among them.[2]

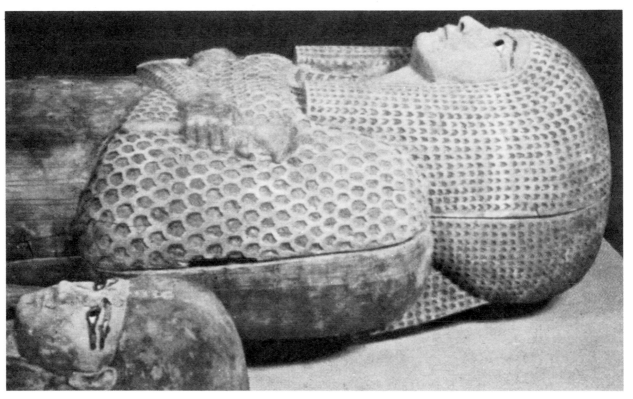

15. *Anthropoid Coffin of Queen Meritamun, early XVIIIth dynasty. Tomb of the Queen, Deir-el-Bahari. Cairo, Egyptian Museum*

The most famous and the most splendid of all such semblances is certainly the mask of beaten gold of the Pharaoh Tutankhamun (pl. 16). If it seems unusual to link this golden image to illusionism, one should recall that it was conceived as a *portrait*—in this instance, not of a man but of a god. The Pharaoh, son of the Sun God, had gone to join his father, and already partook of the splendor of divinity. The perfection of plastic form reinforced the plausibility of the divine metamorphosis.

Masterworks of such superlative quality, executed in precious gold, were necessarily the exception rather than the rule, even in the land of the Pharaohs, since they were reserved solely for the royal house.

16. *Beaten Gold Mask of Pharoah Tutankhamun, late XVIIIth dynasty. Cairo, Egyptian Museum*

The illusionistic mask, however, corresponding in value to the relative rank and wealth of the patron, was used widely by every level of society. Examples of it are found from as late as the second century of our era. By then, the illusionism had become entirely two-dimensional, as in the remarkable paintings discovered at El Faiyum (pl. 17): the masks are now actual portraits, painted in encaustic on small wooden panels, but still they are life-sized and it is clear that utmost realism remained the goal.

17. *Portrait of a Lady from El Faiyum, 2d century A.D. Berlin, Staatliche Museen*

Illusionism, whatever greater heights it attained in other times and civilizations, would never again be charged with the profoundly religious earnestness and solemn significance of the Egyptian works. Even statues created for purposes other than the perpetuation of the afterlife were believed to be endowed with a measure of magical existence, brought about by the creative force of the image.

> Just as uttering the name of a god brought him into one's presence, so by the representation of a man or an object one diverted into the new image part of the spiritual personality of that man or that object; from another point of view, it provided a means of control over him, or it. To the first of these principles belonged all the magical rites which made use of formulae; and the second included everything which attempted to bring about reality by representation.[3]

Dread of the power of graphic representation extended even to hieroglyphs because these signs originally stood for the thing represented and only later for a sound—i.e., they were first symbolic and then became phonetic. Not surprisingly, therefore, hieroglyphs continued to be looked upon as portraits of a sort, and proper pecautions were taken against any latent malignancy.

> An indication of the Egyptians' belief in magic is provided by the custom of mutilating hieroglyphic signs representing dangerous animals or insects, or showing them as pierced with knives when they occured in tomb insciptions; it was a precaution against these potentially dangerous signs coming to life.[4]

The importance of such beliefs in relation to illusionism can hardly be overestimated, regardless of whether they stemmed from official religious dogma or from popular superstition. Nothing less than universal credence in the transfer of spiritual attributes to material artifacts can explain the meticulous care bestowed on portrayals of the humblest as well as the most exalted personages. As a result, the burden of responsibility placed on the artist as creator was considerable. The artist who carved the "Seated Scribe" (pl. 18) does not appear to have shirked this responsibility: he strove for a lifelike aspect to the extent of inserting slivers of highly polished stone to suggest the gleam of the pupils.

18. *Seated Scribe from Sakkara, Vth dynasty. Paris, Musée du Louvre*

Turning now to ancient Greece: Hellenic mythology inspired men to strive for a kind of naturalistic perfection in very emulation of the gods themselves. Hephaestos (or Vulcan), god of fire and patron of all the arts and industries, fashioned the dread aegis as well as the imperial scepter of Zeus, father of the gods. For himself, this most subtle artificer created two live golden statues to assist him on his way because he was lame. In the *Iliad*, Homer further recounts how this supreme artist, this divine practitioner of "deception," forged and then ornamented the marvellous shield of Achilles— upon which he depicted the entire heavens and the earth, with the respective denizens of both realms engaged in every imaginable activity, from weddings and dances, agriculture and the hunt, to great combats in full sway. The gods, in all their Olympian splendor and might, were shown presiding over this dazzling cosmic pageant, assisted by the full choir of the Muses, who "seemed indeed like live women full-throatedly singing."[5]

From the start, then, Greek artists were not likely to run short of suitable inspiration. Variations abounded on the theme of man's impious but incurable longing for the gift of divine creation: there was Prometheus, the benign Titan who stole the spark of sacred fire for mankind; Daedalus, architect of the labyrinth and maker of man's first wings, who, though but an ordinary mortal, nevertheless had the power to fashion live statues of gold; and, perhaps best remembered, Pygmalion, the sculptor who fell in love with his own beautiful creation and won for it the breath of life from Aphrodite, goddess of love.

We are what we dream, and legend has it that the artists of Greece eventually came within respectable distance of these mythical achievements. They could do so not only because they were undoubtedly in full command of an exceedingly rich and complex artistic idiom, but also because their myths permitted them to approach the challenge of illusionism in a mood of emulation that had not been possible in earlier civilizations.

According to Vitruvius' *De Architectura*,[6] written in the first century A.D. and dedicated to the Emperor Augustus, the first recorded Greek illusionistic painting was conceived as a piece of stage scenery to serve as a backdrop for a tragedy by Aeschylus. (It was probably a mock curtain like the one painted by Jean Louis Charles Garnier in 1874 for the Paris Opera House.) Created by the famous painter Agatharcos, it caused a sensation. For us Agatharcos' painting has a significant place in the history of illusionism; his curtain must ever retain the supreme merit of being the first display of its kind, and if the Aeschylus play was acted in front of it, the entire shadowy pageant of pictorial illusionism lay beyond. For curtains eventually became part of the repertory not only of illusionism but even of trompe l'oeil, there to be viewed at a much closer range, and therefore all the more critically, as in the

Gerard Dou curtain (pl. 191)

Other incidents relating to Greek illusionism, principally in the form of anecdotes, have been recounted by Pliny the Elder. Only a decade or so later than Vitruvius, this Roman chronicler undertook to record the history and traditions of antiquity. In Pliny's review of Greek painting of the "Age of Pericles"—approximately five hundred years before his own time—he included an anecdote about one of the most renowned artists, the painter Zeuxis, who depicted grapes so convincingly that birds attempted to pick at the clusters.[7]

Whether we presume that the grapes were displayed in some receptacle or in a natural setting, perhaps with leafy twigs still attached, there is nothing fundamentally implausible about this incident. As every hunter and fisherman knows, animals can be lured by surprisingly crude decoys.[8] The history of illusionism abounds in variations of the Zeuxis grape anecdote, citing cases of other deluded animals—pheasants, cats, dogs, horses. These tales are always recounted as great wonders in their own time, and as incontrovertible evidence of the superlative skill of the artists. But that the application of this skill went far beyond the delusion of animals is affirmed in the sequel to the tale of Zeuxis. Parrhasios, a rival painter, envious of Zeuxis' fame, challenged him to a contest, claiming that his own skill would go even beyond Zeuxis' vaunted achievement. When Zeuxis was summoned at last to view the results of his competitor's efforts, he eagerly reached out to pull aside the folds of the drapery which, he believed, concealed the masterwork of Parrhasios. At that moment he knew himself defeated, for the curtain itself was the "deception." Parrhasios was awarded the laurel, "for Zeuxis had deceived only the birds of heaven, but Parrhasios had deceived Zeuxis."[9] A second defeat, this one self-inflicted, was also in store for Zeuxis: he painted the figure of a child standing next to the famous grapes, but the birds passed summary judgment on it by refusing to be frightened away from the fruit.[10]

Clearly related to the tale of the Zeuxian birds is the story of the live horses who neighed in greeting to their counterparts painted by the famous Apelles.[11] Apelles' most renowned achievment, however, was an extraordinarily lifelike representation of the goddess Aphrodite. Another anecdote tells how an ingenious artist (the first impresario?) placed trumpet players in back of his canvas of a great battle scene, with instructions to sound alarums, calls to the charge, and other martial sound effects.[12]

But these sensational effects of illusionism are only the lighter part of the subject. There were other very different and more serious applications of illusionism; for example, in architecture, the rectification of optical irregularities by entasis—the slight convexity of horizontal planes and of columns—to make them appear, respectively, mathematically even and gradually tapered.

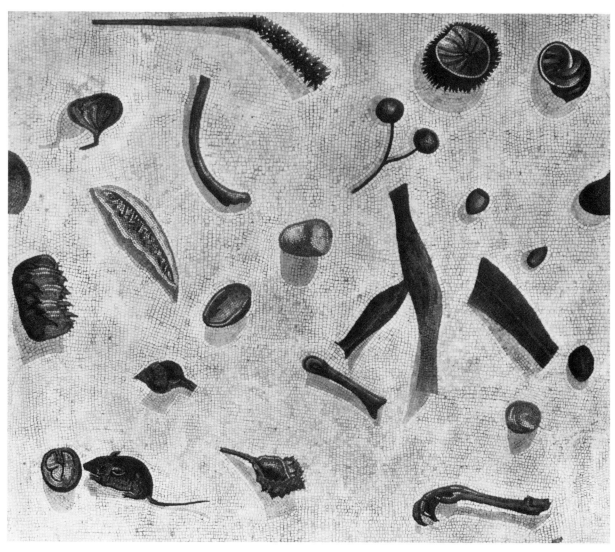

19. *Roman Mosaic.* The Unswept Floor, *2d century A.D. (copy of a 2d–3d century B.C. Greek original by Sosos of Pergamum). Rome, Lateran Museum*

If these effects seem related more to the study of optics than to esthetics, they cannot be entirely bypassed; for they affected the result of an artist's work very materially indeed: without the subtle but significant assistance of entasis, the beauty of the Pantheon would fall unaccountably short of its perfect harmony.

More relevant to the present theme of illusionism is the subject matter in Greek painting, which was divided into two categories: megalography, the painting of great things, and rhyparography, the painting of small things. The categories were based not on size but on style and subject. To the first group belonged mythological and historical scenes, with emphasis on the human figure amid architectural settings and in landscapes of suitable grandeur and beauty. The second group comprised what is now known as still life, "genre," flower pieces, and other related, ostensibly minor themes. While both types of painting enjoyed equal popularity—and the practitioners of each, equal financial success—the devotees of the "grand" school eventually expressed their disapproval of the more familiar mode by dubbing it "rhyparography," literally, the painting of vile, sordid objects. In this category, however, we find the oldest extant example of two-dimensional trompe l'oeil, the renowned mosaic pavement called "The Unswept Floor" (pl. 19).[12a] The fact that this is a second-century A.D. Roman copy after a second- or third-century B.C. Greek original by Sosos of Pergamum proves that its popularity remained undiminished for at least four, and perhaps five hundred years. Quite an enviable record for a "vile and sordid" subject. It is difficult for the modern eye to find even the slightest suggestion of these negative qualities in this delightful conceit of a floor still casually littered with debris scattered haphazardly on the white ground. The miscellany includes the carapace of a crayfish, empty shells of snails, random pea pods, filberts in their shells and chestnuts still in their burs, the claws of some small fowl and other less easily identifiable fragments. In any event, these are clearly the leftovers of a very recent feast, and hardly strike us as repulsive unless one chooses so to consider the small mouse in the corner, about to start its own belated feast, now that the guests have vacated the hall, on half of a large walnut meat. (This last detail, incidentally, became a favorite theme in the repertory of trompe l'oeil painting both in Europe and in America. By an odd coincidence, one of the most charming interpretations is the famous "Dessert Piece with Mice" by a near homonym of Sosos, Lodovico de Susio [pl. 20].) Each min-

20. *Lodovico de Susio.* Dessert Piece. with Mice, *1619. St. Louis, Mo., City Art Museum*

ute object on the mosaic floor is shown with its precisely delineated shadow, achieving a convincing effect of relief. Why, one wonders, was this tour de force carried out in the rather unbending medium of mosaic? We may assume that, despite its beauty, the mosaic is only a crude copy of what must have been a far finer original.

Mosaic decoration of this kind was undoubtedly carried out by craftsmen after a cartoon prepared by an artist (this practice was later followed for tapestry weaving in Europe). The mosaicists would faithfully duplicate the delicate gradations of colors and values on a design prepared by some able pupil of Agatharcos or Apollodorus. According to Plutarch, the title of *skiagraphos*—"painter of shadows"—was bestowed on the latter in tribute to his discovery and mastery of chiaroscuro at the end of the fifth century B.C.[13] Pliny records that as technical prowess increased, the painter Pausias in turn gained fame for his rendering of a figure drinking from a transparent goblet, the face clearly visible through the glass.[14] Certainly great technical skill was necessary to achieve such an effect, and one regrets that yet another display of painterly virtuosity is known only by a reference of Petronius,[15] who recalls that Protogenes (a contemporary of Apelles) depicted to perfection the foam on the lips of a dog and the startled look in the eye of a pheasant.

At times, painters and sculptors joined forces. The abstract monochrome beauty of Grecian marble sculpture is largely a figment of modern imagination. The painter Nicias was entrusted with the task of bestowing the blush of life on some of the works of his contemporary Praxiteles.[16] Even in giant chryselephantine statuary, the effect of life was striven for, ivory being reserved for the flesh tones, and precious stones for the pupils of the eyes. Clearly, the masterpieces of statuary we now know solely in the whiteness of marble were originally polychromed. The much-vaunted Parian marble served merely as a base for brilliant tints duplicating as closely as possible the color of flesh and vestments. Unadorned, its candid whiteness, which later taste extols so highly, would have seemed palely anemic to the robust Hellenes, lovers of the ruddy glow of life.

After the conquest of Greece, Greek art continued to inspire, and Greek artists to execute, imaginative decorations for the palaces and villas of the Latin conquerors. Many of the remaining examples are from the doomed towns of Pompeii and Herculaneum. One of the dwellings that escaped total devastation is the House of the Faun in Pompeii, where one of the most charming decorative features is a mosaic pavement depicting aquatic life along an African waterway with various kinds of flora and fauna. Its chief motif is the head of a hippopotamus shown as if it had just emerged from the water, soon to be followed by the great cumbrous body. Perhaps

Pliny, who often visited in Pompeii, had on occasion "tread water" on this humorous trompe l'oeil, when paying a visit to some superannuated proconsul, for whom the decoration was conceived as a souvenir of his sojourn in a Nilotic province. In the Temple of Primigenia in Palestrina we find a more complex waterscape, with hunting boats and figures looking on from the shore (pl. 21).

21. *Mosaic from the Temple of Primigenia.* Aquatic Life on the Nile, *1st century A.D. Palestrina, Palazzo Baronale*

In the Villa of Livia (pl. 22) the illusionistic decoration on the wall suggests instead the calm and disciplined loveliness of a well-ordered garden: along the floor line, a rank of simulated planters, and beyond them a low garden wall, forming at regular intervals rectangular bays, each planted with a slender young tree. The tiering of the several planes opens pleasant vistas in the otherwise rather small room. In other instances, only a delicate floral border is suggested at ground level, with vases, perching birds, cast-off scarves, ribbons, and other minute implements of daily life. In the frigidarium of the Thermes in Pompeii, however, an impressive illusionistic view is presented as if from a terrace overlooking town and sea (pl. 23). The general mood of all these illusionistic decorations is uniformly estival and idyllic, highly suitable for these "pleasure domes."

22. *Fresco in the Villa of Livia Primaporta, 1st century B.C. Rome*

23. *Frescoes in the Antechamber of the Frigidarium of the Thermes, 1st century B.C. (reconstruction). Pompeii*

24. *Frescoes in the Bedroom from Boscoreale, 1st century B.C. New York, The Metropolitan Museum of Art, Rogers Fund*

In the delightful cubicle from Boscoreale installed at the Metropolitan Museum of Art, New York (pl. 24; color pl. 1), the scenes painted beyond the simulated columns of red marble depict not landscapes or gardens, but terraces, porticoes, arches, and colonnades—all the pride and pomp of statuary and stonework that delighted the Roman heart. The foreground details, masks, golden bucklers, and the deeply carved decoration of the capitals are frankly illusionistic and seem to project into the room. It is evident that the decorator lavished all his art and care on this one small chamber; but for this, how dark and somber it must have appeared. Eventually, a window was cut out of the rear wall; forbiddingly barred, it must have opened onto a street passage. The change irretrievably damaged the decorative scheme and did away with the illusion. Only an awkward truncated base remains of one of the four columns originally shown on the rear wall, and much of the painted blue sky is also gone.

41

25. *Roman Fresco.* Still Life
with Partridge and Pomegranate
(xenion). *Naples, Museo Nazionale*

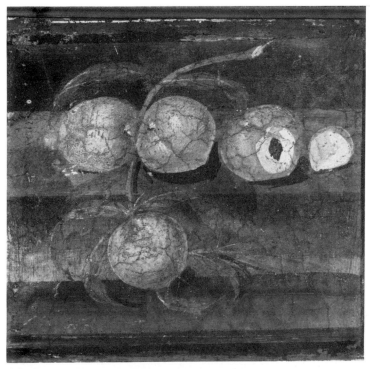

26. *Roman Fresco.* Still Life
with Branch of Peaches (xenion).
Naples, Museo Nazionale

42

Small easel paintings, originally called *xenia,* appear to have come in a direct line from Greece to the Roman households (pls. 25—26). They generally depicted what we would now call still-life subjects—displays of foodstuffs with kitchen utensils, table vessels, and small animals, alive or dead. It is thought that the subjects alluded to hospitality received, and that the paintings themselves, therefore, were ancient equivalents of the weekend "bread-and-butter" gift. As a folding shutter was provided on either side of the painting proper, a *xenion* was a kind of triptych, although the shutters do not seem to have been decorated, as they would have been in a medieval triptych. The tripartite *xenion* may originally have been displayed standing with half-opened wings on a narrow shelf or cornice along the ceiling. In the House of the Vestals in Pompeii, however, *xenia* are depicted illusionistically on the walls of the room, each hanging on a string from a nail (pl. 27). The inclu-

27. *Engraving after Frescoes in the House of the Vestals, Pompeii, 1st century B.C.*

28. *Frescoes in the Villa of Lucrezio Frontone, 1st century A.D. Pompeii*
29a. *Frescoes in the House of the Gladiators, 1st century B.C. Pompeii*

44

sion of this realistic detail fulfilled an essential part of the illusionistic scheme, for had it been omitted, the small paintings within the larger decorative plan might have appeared to be placed within recessed niches, or even as cabinets with parted doors. Note also the pair of miniature triptychs seemingly attached to the mock columns. In a sense, the illusionistic *xenia* in the mural frescoes of the House of the Vestals foreshadowed the "cabinet de curiosité" trompe l'oeil theme of the sixteenth century (pl. 149), which remained popular and has even occasionally been revived in our own days (pl. 427).

In the villa of Lucrezio Frontone in Pompeii (pl. 28), the walls are no longer decorated with feigned *xenia* painted as if hanging on the walls. Instead, a complex figural scene is shown in the middle wall, as if it were a framed painting centered within a rectangular panel outlined with slender, light-colored molding on the darker ground. To the right and left of this, a pair of small framed landscapes are apparently upheld on narrow illusionistic tripodal stands—a unique and graceful way of presenting the miniature works of art.

The illusionistic mural decorations of the Greco-Roman villas have been classified in four groups: the First, Second, Third, and Fourth Styles. These correspond to the degree of complexity and elaboration of the illusionistic technique, which ranges all the way from mere imitation of textures (stippling and marbling) to imaginative compositions involving groups of figures and ambitious vistas of gardens or city views. This latter type reveals that the ancient artist sometimes overreached himself, his knowledge of the laws of perspective being inferior to his mastery of human anatomy. But what concerns us here is not wherein these precursors of architectural illusionism failed, but on the contrary, the measure of their success. This is best exemplified in the renowned frescoes of the House of the Gladiators in Pompeii (pl. 29a). Here, in spite of the damage they have suffered, one can still trace and admire the skill of the artist in depicting plastic elements, delicate yet robust, and in plausibly suggesting considerable depth. Even more important perhaps is the harmonious orchestration of this wealth of diverse elements into a coherent compositional whole. In its soberly sculptural, yet chiselled elegance, the tableau foretells with uncanny accuracy the achievements of the Renaissance masters. But if the frescoes foreshadow a long history to come, they also bear witness to the long tradition that preceded them. From even a summary survey of the body of illusionistic decoration preserved in Pompeii and other antique sites, we must conclude that this refined and masterly technique was conceived by artists and carried out by artisans who were in no sense newcomers to it, who were the inheritors of a centuries-old tradition of pictorial illusionism.[17]

45

To the mute but irrefutable testimony of the surviving works, one may, with proper caution, add the corroborative evidence found in the work of three Greek rhetoricians of the late Hellenistic period: Philostratus the Elder, who in the middle of the third century wrote two books of essays entitled *Imagines,* describing paintings and sculpture; his grandson and homonym, Philostratus the Younger, born in the first year of the fourth century, and author of the third, similarly titled opus; and finally, Callistratus, who may have compiled his *Descriptiones* as late as the fifteenth century.

All three books are fascinating evocations of the life and culture of the late classical period—and it was primarily for this reason that the works of Philostratus the Elder attracted the attention of Goethe. Yet their value as historical documentation is, to say the least, questionable. They are actually tardy examples of a literary mode highly appreciated in the ancient world but puzzling and often alien to the modern mind: description and interpretation of works of art in which the demarcation between fact and fiction is not always clearly discernible. Using this literary device, the rhetoricians passed with complete freedom "from the actual description of a work of art to elements of the story which presumably could not be or were not included in the painting or statue they were describing."[18] But we can assume that the writers were describing what they knew to be possible.

> There is little or nothing to indicate any inconsistency between the paintings existing in his [Philostratus'] day and the paintings he describes. The student of late Greek painting is fully justified in treating these examples as data for his study, whether or not they were actual paintings.[19]

If we add to this the categorical statement Philostratus makes at the very beginning of his *Imagines*, "Painting is imitation by the use of colors."[20] We cannot escape the conclusion that what we now call illusionism was the ideal and the goal of ancient art. But this can be taken only in the most general sense. It does not help us to distinguish actual paintings from literature. The modern reader is bewildered and wonders whether these works of art were real or imaginary, and where the artist's contribution ended and the essayist's began. Callistratus, the latest of the three writers, is the worst offender, but he is also the most easily convicted. It is comparatively simple in his case, since he begins with the exaggerated claim for pictorial and sculptural trompe l'oeil that would have rivalled, if not surpassed, the mythical buckler of Achilles. Describing a statue of Narcissus, he tells us that the marble

29b. *Keraklitos (attrib.). Fragment of a Mosaic. Rome, Lateran Museum*

was so delicate, and imitated a mantle so closely that the color of the body shone through the whiteness of the drapery, permitting the gleam of the limbs to come through.[21]

Elsewhere, it is bronze; the statue of Dionysus

though it was really bronze, . . . nevertheless blushed, and though it had no part in life, . . . sought to show the appearance of life and would yield to the very finger-tip if you touched it, for though it was really compact bronze, it was so softened into flesh by art that it shrank from the contact of the hand. . . . The thyrsus [held by the figure] deceived the beholder's vision; for while it was wrought of bronze it seemed to glisten with the greenness of young growth.[22]

47

The painter's magic is no less than the sculptor's. In a seascape, it "beguiled the senses . . . and wax [i.e., encaustic] seemed to become wet in imitation of the sea, assuming the sea's own qualities."[23]

In contrast to Callistratus stands Philostratus the Elder who has been called with justification "the first art critic." There are scattered hints in his *Imagines* that his comments were not merely the personal impressions of a particularly sensitive connoisseur, but that they were based on knowledge of the techniques of the craft, perhaps even on professional experience. Philostratus is at his most effective in his descriptions of intimate and homely subjects, whereas the grand constructions of megalography afforded a better scope to litterateurs like Callistratus. Not that Philostratus ever loses his winning grace of expression; he wrote "in very pure Attic Greek, and with extreme beauty and force,"[24] as his grandson put it, in his tribute to him in the introduction to his later work. But when he describes such *xenia* as we may still see on the walls of Pompeii and Herculaneum, milk and honey flow from his lips.

> It is a good thing to gather figs and also not to pass over in silence
> the figs in this picture. Purple figs dripping with juice are heaped
> on vine-leaves; and they are depicted with breaks in the skin, some
> just cracking open to disgorge their honey, some split apart, they
> are so ripe. . . . On the tip of the branch a sparrow buries its bill
> in what seems the very sweetest of the figs. . . . and the most
> charming point of all this is: on a leafy branch is yellow honey
> within the comb and ripe to stream forth if the comb is pressed;
> and on another leaf is cheese new-curdled and quivering; and there
> are bowls of milk not merely white but gleaming, for the cream
> floating upon it makes it seem to gleam.[25]

Was the painting that inspired this delightful eclogue only an illusionistic still life or a trompe l'oeil by the strictest standards? All we know is that it was a *xenion*, and generally in *xenia* objects were depicted set on shelves within a niche. It is regrettable that Philostratus did not indicate here the role of artistic skill and therefore "deception" as clearly as he did in the "Singers"—the first essay of Book II of the *Imagines*—where he specifies that

> the artistry of the painting must be praised, first because the artist,
> in making the border of precious stones, has used not only colors
> but light to depict them, putting a radiance in them like the pupil
> in an eye. . . .[26]

48

Whether or not this particular painting was illusionistic, we know at least what the frame around it was. (One thinks of similar feigned jewelled borders in illuminated manuscripts, or of Seurat's pointilliste surrounds.) In another place, Philostratus speaks directly of "deception." To the young man whom he addresses in his essays he declares:

> How I have been deceived! I was deluded by the painting into thinking that the figures were not painted but were real beings . . . and you [were] as much overcome as I was, and unable to free yourself from the deception and the stupefaction induced by it.[27]

And taking up the issue raised by his grandfather, Philostratus the Younger comments:

> The deception inherent in [the painter's] work is pleasurable and involves no reproach; for to confront objects which do not exist as though they existed and to be influenced by them, to believe that they do exist, is not this, since no harm can come of it, a suitable and irreproachable means of providing entertainment?[28]

The information offered by either Philostratus is never as specific or as technical as we would wish. By an odd coincidence, the one reference that comes closest to the modern view of painting as pure painting has to do with a subject that must, of its very nature, have been an exercise in pictorial illusionism. Philostratus' essay "Looms" can hardly have described anything but a bona fide trompe l'oeil:

> Look also at the spider weaving in a picture nearby, and see if it does not excel in weaving both Penelope and the Seres too, though the web these people make is exceedingly fine and scarcely visible. . . . Now the painter has been successful in these respects also: that he has wrought the spider itself in so painstaking a fashion, has marked its spots with fidelity to nature, and has painted its repulsive fuzzy surface and its savage nature—all this is the mark of a good craftsman and one skilled in depicting the truth. And he has also woven these delicate webs for us, . . . and the weavers travel across them, drawing tight such of the threads as have become loose. But they win a reward for their weaving and feed on the flies whenever any become enmeshed in the webs. Hence, the painter has not omitted their prey either; for one fly is caught by the feet, another by the tip of its wing, the head of another is being eaten, and they squirm in their efforts to escape, yet they do not disarrange or break the web.[29]

29c. *Wall Painting with Bird and Vase, from Herculaneum, 1st century A.D. Naples, Museo Nazionale*

This is very likely the first record of the depiction of insects in a work of pictorial illusionism. Coincidentally, a contemporary Chinese artist, Tsao Pu-Ying,[30] is said to have created a trompe l'oeil on precisely the same subject. Having completed the painting of a screen for the Emperor, Tsao Pu-Ying, in the third century A.D., diverted himself by adding several painted flies so realistically that when the Son of Heaven came to view the finished work, His Celestial Majesty attempted to brush them away.

After a lapse of many centuries, European artists would again undertake the depiction of the lowly household insect, but in a widely different mood (cf. pl. 14). The fly, however realistically portrayed, would be charged with a profound symbolic message: it would serve to indicate the taint of mortal corruption inherent in all flesh. This was the outcome of the momentous change that came about with the establishment of Christianity as the state religion throughout the Roman empire: symbolism, not realism, became the new artistic ideal.

29d. *Decoration from a Roman House. Rome, Antiquarium del Palatino*

30. The Empress Theodora and Her Retinue, *6th-century mosaic. Ravenna, S. Vitale*

3

The Rebirth of Illusionism

The Fifteenth Century

After the fall of Rome and the shifting of the center of the Empire to the Eastern capital, Constantinople, a tidal wave of Asian mysticism engulfed the Latin world. One can hardly say that the art of classical antiquity decayed, or that it suffered a blight—it merely ceased to exist because it was not wanted anymore. The requirements of the new religious imagery had become too transcendental to accept classical naturalism. Not only did the polytheist creed that had informed that naturalism become anathema, but the worship of nature and of physical beauty that it had expressed was abandoned as well. Earthly reality being fundamentally evil, the art that had rendered it so lovingly became a pagan abomination—the more naturalistic, the more sinful. For the Christian world, the function of art was instead to extoll only spiritual truth and spiritual beauty.

By the sixth century of our era, the shift had been accomplished. The new ideal is best expressed in the splendid mosaics of Ravenna (pl. 30), where any realism or plasticity still lingering from the two centuries preceding has finally been eliminated. The hieratic figures acting out their symbolic roles are literally bodiless; their absolutely flat, elongated forms have become an ideogram, a mystical calligraphy spelling out the sacred dogma for the illiterate worshippers. They even appear detached from the very earth, hovering above it in the golden or cerulean glaze of the Heavenly Jerusalem. Yet it is noteworthy that at least one of the participants in this solemn pageant conveys by an unguarded gesture a sense of ordinary humanity: in the train of

53

the Empress Theodora, the last courtier's hand still lingers on the looped curtain which he has presumably raised but a moment ago for the silent cortege. This suggestion of arrested movement assumes extraordinary visual eloquence in the context of the otherwise severely stylized scene.

The motif may have been inspired by the reminiscences of the Roman sarcophagi on which it also appears, the influence of classical statuary never being entirely discountable. However motivated, such instances remained the exception. But, while the religious abhorrence of earthly reality did lead to a basic rejection of pagan art, vestiges of the ancient illusionistic tradition persisted. The mosaic decorations of a chapel in the Orthodox Baptistery in Ravenna include trompe l'oeil niches, each depicting an altar upon which rests an open volume of the sacred scriptures. This is more understandable if we look upon these examples as a new species of abstract or spiritual illusionism, wholly congruent with Christian attitudes, and at the same time providing a revealing glimpse at the submerged bedrock of Greco-Roman rationality.

Upwards of seven hundred years would elapse before its next emergence. Yet, in the West, the intervening "dark ages" were by no means unrelievedly somber. The nadir was reached with the fateful year one thousand—the millennium anticipated with universal fear as the coming of the world's end, the Judgment Day. But when it passed without the sound of the trumpet of doom, all Christendom felt reprieved (perhaps for another millennium), and slowly the breath of life began to quicken in the great sluggish body. The Franciscan canticle, written in the thirteenth century, was a hymn to life: "My brother Sun; my sister Moon; my small brothers, birds of the air. . . ." Its echoes were all-pervading, all-vivifying, and artists once more dared to let their eyes turn toward earthly beauty. In gradual, almost imperceptible stages, artists rediscovered volumetric painting and spatial perspective, the two factors that in turn would make possible the eventual rebirth of illusionism. The rediscovery may be traced through such slight but telling indices as those found in the Romanesque illumination "The Flying Fish of Tyre," executed at Lincoln, England, circa 1170 (pl. 3).[1] The illustrator neither attempted nor achieved what might be properly considered illusionism. But the wings of the legendary fish go beyond the limits of the square frame of the composition, so that the fish seems to leap out of the picture plane and into the space of the text. It might be logically predicted that the next stage would be an attempt to intrude into the viewer's own plane.

But first, the two worlds—the real and the imaginary—would draw ever nearer, until nothing separated them but the invisible "space curtain."[2] In the Basilica of St. Francis at Assisi (late thirteenth century), the Isaac Master's "Esau before Isaac" is set within a kind of painted alcove framed by tall slen-

54

31. *The Isaac Master.* Esau before Isaac, *late 13th century. Assisi, S. Francesco, Upper Church*

der painted columns and hedged with a low painted balustrade in the foreground (pl. 31). In front of this niche, at either side, fictive curtains on a rod have been drawn and looped up to reveal the patriarch reclining on a couch in the pose of an ancient river god.[2a] The attendant figures of Esau and Rebecca are marked with the same timeless monumentality and dignity. Nothing, except the halo around Isaac's head, would disqualify the fresco from serving as a wall decoration in some Pompeiian villa.

It will probably never be known whether the inspiration for such works occured simultaneously to a number of artists, each reacting individually to the pervading mood of classical revival, or whether, as was once believed, the initial impulse proceeded from the strongly dominant personality of the great Florentine, Giotto (d. 1337). At any event, Giotto was among the earliest modern exponents of architectural illusionism and of grisaille trompe l'oeil.

55

The buildings in his frescoes are adorned with representations of reliefs in monochrome (pl. 32) and occasionally with simulated marble plinths; grisaille statues of the Seven Virtues and Seven Vices are painted on the dado of the Arena Chapel in Padua.

In addition to visual evidence, what one historian has termed "the scent of oral tradition" also suggests Giotto as the originator of trompe l'oeil proper in our era.[3] An anecdote told of Giotto's youth identifies him unmistakably with illusionism as well as with the ancient literary tradition: while still a pupil in Cimabue's studio, the young artist painted a fly on the nose of a portrait so realistically that his master was deceived and attempted to brush away the insect. Whether or not the story is apocryphal, it remains the first recorded attempt by an occidental artist to pierce through the picture plane by thrusting an element of the painting forward into the viewer's own plane.

32. *Giotto.* The Annuciation to St. Anne, *1304–06. Padua. Arena Chapel*

33. *Taddeo Gaddi.* Niche with Cruets.
Florence, S. Croce, Baroncelli Chapel

A highly significant step was taken in a totally different direction by a pupil of Giotto, Taddeo Gaddi. In the second quarter of the fourteenth century, he painted for the church of Santa Croce in Florence two small panels depicting the implements of the mass as if on the shelves of trompe l'oeil niches—a conceit already nascent in the Orthodox Baptistery at Ravenna. One of the Santa Croce panels (pl. 33) depicts the paten and cruets, and what appears to be a cannister for incense; the other shows a symbolic candlestick, a lavabo, and a prayer book or missal. Both are actually Christian *xenia,* symbolizing thanksgiving for spiritual gifts instead of material ones, although they have also been cited as the first examples of independent still-life painting. Other commentators have held that, as Giotto depicted similar niches somewhat earlier on the altar wall of the Arena Chapel in Padua, he might also have painted the same subjects by themselves slightly in advance of Gaddi.[5] What weakens this assumption, however, is that in the Gaddi panels, the objects cast faint but discernible shadows. This is a degree of pictorial sophistication that Giotto had not yet attained. (One sees in the "Annunciation to St. Anne," pl. 32, that the utensils hanging on the wall in front of St. Anne have no shadows.) It seems likely therefore that if Gaddi found the idea for the niches in Giotto's fresco, his own contribution was at least of equal importance.

57

(detail)

34. *Domenico Ghirlandaio (1449–1494).* Giovanna Tornabuoni. *Lugano, Tyssen-Bornemisza Collection*

Perfect mastery of light and shadow ("chiaroscuro," as it would come to be known) is essential for pictorial illusionism. Chiaroscuro is the *sine qua non* of illusionism. But to achieve it, painting must transcend its own assigned bounds and usurp the privileges of sculpture. The two media had once been closely and intimately connected, and although a tradition of polychrome sculpture continued into the Renaissance, centuries of two-dimensional painting had not only drawn them far apart conceptually, but had made the imitation of sculptural effects in painting seem unnatural. To reverse the process—to do away with a barrier that was psychological as well as material, to raise the invisible but adamant "space curtain" that stood between the viewer and the painted scene—could have proved a slow and arduous task. That it was accomplished within a single century is perhaps the greatest wonder of the Renaissance.

Much of the credit for this was due to the *bottega* (literally, the shop) where a recognized artist-craftsman produced and sold his own works and also trained his artistic family of apprentices. There the aspiring young tyros were exposed to all the various media, and the results were spectacular. A Ghirlandaio, for instance, could design what is perhaps the most beautiful of all Renaissance jewels, seen on the bottom shelf of the niche in his portrait of Giovanna Tornabuoni (pl. 34). If called upon to do so, he could have made it with his own hands, and activities of this kind did not interfere with his development as a great painter.

35. *Masaccio.* Holy Trinity, *1427.*
Florence, S. Maria Novella

There can be little doubt that the most fruitful influence was exerted
by architects. Had not the genial Brunelleschi spelled out his profound knowledge of linear perspective and foreshortening, his contemporary, the painter
Masaccio, would not have been provided with the stable and harmonious foundation necessary to execute his "Holy Trinity" of 1427, one of the great milestones of illusionism (color pl. 5). Against the grandiose setting inspired by ele-

59

36. *Paolo Uccello.* Sir John Hawkwood, *1436. Florence, Cathedral*

ments of Brunelleschi's own work in the Pazzi Chapel, nothing could be simpler or more dramatically effective than the figures of the two kneeling donors in the foreground. The most remarkable illusionistic element is the placement of the two figures and the simulated architectural setting of pilasters and columns, in front of the image of God the Father and the dead Christ. Thus they appear *outside* of the pictorial space, as if within the church itself, and on our own side of the "space curtain." The illusionistic setting creates a superlative "framing" for the symbolic representation.

Paolo Uccello's use of illusionism appears antithetical to Masaccio, whose intense study of perspective served to strengthen and enrich his volumetric style. Uccello, perhaps an even more devoted student of the same subject, never went beyond a linear or graphic rendition into an aerial perspective; his paintings are rather like beautiful colored drawings with the intricate surface design that betrays a *horror vacui.* Uccello's artistic temperament seems to have been unsuited to true illusionism. Although he is often included among its exponents, he actually furnishes proof that the study of perspective alone, other ingredients lacking, may result only in works that might be called glorified blueprints. The one work by Uccello that comes within measurable distance of illusionism is his representation of Sir John Hawkwood, an English soldier of fortune in the service of the city of Florence (pl. 36), as a simulated equestrian statue.

The study of perspective was put to good use by Fra Filippo Lippi in the architectural settings for his major religious paintings, but this is a characteristic which he admittedly shares with almost all the preeminent artists of his time. His special interest in illusionism is more telling in other, comparatively minor, aspects of his work, such as the illusionistic presentation of two books on the wide step in the foreground of the great "Madonna and Child with Four Saints" (in the Uffizi Gallery). But the smaller and more intimate "Madonna and Child with Two Angels" (also at the Uffizi) is completely illusionistic in treatment (color pl. 6). The entire group of four figures trespasses the frame of the depicted space. The delicate nimbus of the Madonna is a thread-thin ring of light apparently floating in midair in the space intervening between the viewer and the framed landscape, and the wings of the cherub at right jut over the carved rectangular border.

Essentially, the device of presenting the figures in front of a fictive frame was by no means new. We have already seen it in Romanesque illumination (pl. 3), and it continually recurs in the later manuscript tradition; it is a common feature of the portraits in the border frames of the late thirteenth and fourteenth century Italian fresco decoration. In panel painting the Umbrian painter Alegretto Nuzi (late fourteenth century) had placed his still iconlike

37. *Fra Filippo Lippi (c. 1406–1469).* Madonna and Child with Two Angels. *Florence, Uffizi*

38. *Alegretto Nuzi.* Madonna and Child. *Philadelphia Museum of Art, Courtesy John G. Johnson Collection, Philadelphia*

Madonna and Child in front of a "frame" figured by a large tooled border in the gold background (pl. 38), Filippo Lippi takes up the same theme but endows it with utmost sophistication. His "frame" is a window and the figures are dramatically detached from the far-off vista.

Piero della Francesca, with effortless grandeur, elected to present his portrait figures against a sweep of territory so vast that only the eye of the eagle could well survey it. The Duke and the Duchess of Urbino are portrayed in profile, as if gazing out upon their dominions from the loftiest terrace (pls. 39—40). The spatial illusion is echoed in the allegorical scenes on the reverse, which are supported by rampartlike elements: great stone tablets carved with lengthy inscriptions in classical lettering (pls. 41—42). The reverse landscapes are also abruptly limited by a rocky crevasse, an antique illusionistic device encountered in Greco-Roman and Byzantine art.[6]

In Northern landscapes the figures in the foreground as much as those in the background seem somehow to become absorbed in the setting: man is dwarfed by nature. Here, on the contrary, he towers above it as lord of all life, animate as well as inanimate. The great pair of Urbino portraits is not

39–40. *Piero della Francesca.* Federigo da Montefeltro and Battista Sforza, Duke and Duchess of Urbino, *c. 1465. Florence, Uffizi*

only a milestone in the history of illusionism but a humanistic manifesto as well.

The same brooding monumentality of the Urbino portraits, together with a distant vista and rocky ledge in the foreground, is encountered, though

41–42. *Piero della Francesca.* Triumphal Allegory *(reverse of pls. 39–40)*

42a. *Ferrarese School.* Madonna and Child, *c. 1480. Edinburgh, National Gallery of Scotland*

this time in a religious scene in another epochal example: the "Madonna and Child," circa 1480, in the National Gallery of Scotland (pl. 42a). Assigned to the Ferrarese School (perhaps Ercole Roberti), its conventional iconography is anything but conventional in conception. It combines instead prophetic suggestions of surrealism with trompe l'oeil artifice of the kind not encountered elsewhere until two centuries later in "letter racks" and *"quod libets"* (cf. pls. 175–78). Everything in the picture is in keeping with this initial paradox: the regal Queen of Heaven, with the Child on her knee and two angels in attendance, sits on a bench which is more like a massive arched aqueduct than a seat. She towers serenely above the highest peaks in the mountainous background and the folds of her snowy veil are tossed about like cloud wisps. But the strangest feature of all is that the picture appears as if painted not on the front but on the reverse of a stretched canvas. And at some time—the artist wishes us to believe—it had been hidden from view by a cloth covering drawn taut and attached to the border by a narrow band nailed at close intervals. Now at last, the covering has been torn away, leaving only the jagged fragments we see around it. It is truly startling to meet at so early a date the theme of the reversed canvas and the shreds of paper, which, to present knowledge, did not surface again until the seventeenth century.

42b. *Leonardo da Vinci,* Mona Lisa,
c. 1503–05. Paris, Musée du Louvre

The culmination of this portrait type with a figure set in front of a landscape vista is Leonardo da Vinci's "Mona Lisa" (pl. 42b). Vasari tells us that Leonardo "imparted to his figures not beauty only, but life and movement." He had the unique power to combine the highest poesy with a precisionism that astounded his contemporaries. Deterioration of the pigment has mitigated this effect, particularly in the flesh tones, and we must rely on Vasari's description to realize how lifelike it must have been.

> Whoever desires to see how far art can imitate nature may do so by observing this head wherein every subtlety and peculiarity have been faithfully reproduced. The eyes are bright and moist, and around them are those pale, red, and slightly livid circles seen in life, while the lashes and eyebrows are represented with the closest exactitude, with seperate hairs as they issue from the skin, every turn being followed and all the pores exhibited in the most natural manner. The nose with its beautiful and delicately red nostrils might easily be believed to be alive. The mouth, admirable in outline, is rose tinted in harmony with the carnation of the cheeks, which seem not painted, but of flesh and blood. He who looks earnestly at the pit of the throat must fancy he sees the beating of the pulse. It is a marvel of art.[7]

Leonardo conceived the object for the first time as "bathed in space." To achieve this, he evolved a method for representing light and shadow that became known as *sfumato*. But it is not only *sfumato* that makes the "Mona Lisa" a masterpiece of illusionism, for the lady was originally placed between two columns upraised on either side of the parapet behind her. Only remnants of these are still visible, for the picture has been cut down three inches on both sides.

Friedländer has expressed the opinion that the gradation of portraiture from profile to three-quarter and then to full face was a progression in the direction of greater artistry. The profile he felt to be merely "a fragmentary statement": "Here [in the profile] aloofness, aloneness; there [in the front view] intimacy."[8] But this can be true only in part, for the full-face rendering also omits some essential traits which only the profile view can show. Therefore, it too is "fragmentary."

To compensate for the effect of flatness inherent in profile portrayal, many illusionistic devices were employed. Most frequently used were the niche and the curtain, both, as we have seen, of ancient origin. Even the merest indication of either could bring about an immediate effect of depth. A fine early example is the "Portrait of a Man" of circa 1460, by a North Italian artist, where the model is depicted within a deep rectangular niche, his arm resting on a wide stone shelf covered with an overlapping oriental rug; to the right a window opens on a mountainous landscape (pl. 43). Receding planes and a niche were also used for the famous portrait of Giovanna Tornabuoni by Ghirlandaio (pl. 34). There is no outward opening in this instance, but in the niche behind the lady, a splendid jewel, emblematic of her loveliness and virtue, and rosary beads and a prayer book, emblematic of her piety, give the

43. *North Italian.* Portrait of a Man, *c. 1460. Washington, D.C., National Gallery of Art, Samuel H. Kress Collection*

44—45. Ercole Roberti. Giovanni II and Ginevra Bentivoglio, *c. 1485. Washington, D.C., National Gallery of Art, Samuel H. Kress Collection*

effect of depth. In two pendant portraits of Giovanni and Ginevra Bentivoglio, the noble pair flank a window, with sumptuous velvet portières drawn back just enough to afford a narrow vertical glimpse of a walled town (pls. 44—45).

In what is probably the most original version of the niche theme, the Spanish artist Pedro Berruguete painted in the 1470's a portrait of Federigo da Montefeltro and his son Guidobaldo literally "contained," or perhaps one should say "enshrined," in a low-ceilinged closet, a sort of diminutive oratory (pl. 46). The painting, now in the Galleria Nazionale delle Marche, Urbino, was once part of the Duke's famed illusionistic *studiolo* (see below). The tremendously dense composition with life-sized figures—the father sitting in a great high-backed chair, and the small son standing solemnly at his side—is compressed within the narrowest possible space; yet the illusionistic impact is such that we feel as if we could reach over and touch the figures, startling them out of their profoundly attentive concentration.

Two portraits of Giuliano de' Medici by Botticelli afford an unusual opportunity to assess the important contribution of illusionism to the art of the portrait. The two brilliant studies of an extraordinary model—one at the Bode Museum in Berlin and the other at the National Gallery in Washington

46. *Pedro Berruguete.* Federigo da Montefeltro and His Son Guidobaldo, *c. 1475. Urbino, Galleria Nazionale delle Marche*

47. *Botticelli.* Giuliano de' Medici. *Washington, D.C., National Gallery of Art, Samuel H. Kress Collection*

(pl. 47)—are identical in all essential respects, but for the plain background of the first and the recessive setting of the second. By some subtle alchemy, the illusionistic version far surpasses the other. The intriguing succession of receding planes, apparently sliding into one another like a nest of boxes, leads the eye from the bird on the foremost ledge to the mysteriously half-opened door with its final suggestion of escape into untrammeled space.

Something of the same mood, though more serene and far less adventurous, is encountered in another portrait by Botticelli: that of Smeralda Bandinelli, who appears within the casement window of a loggia, her hand still on the jamb, as if she had but this moment pushed open the shutter and revealed herself to view (pl. 48).

Botticelli favored the curtain as well as the niche. Both are recurrent in his work, although not always patently illusionistic. "St. Augustine in His Study," however, is undoubtedly a work of illusionism, and if it is small in scale, it is monumental in conception (pl. 49; frontispiece). The curtain purports to be an actual barrier, momentarily drawn back, between the room in which we stand and another, a space just as precisely delimited, within which St. Augustine sits. A true "space curtain" made visible.

48. *Botticelli.* Smeralda Bandinelli, *c. 1471*
London, Victoria and Albert Museum

49. *Botticelli.* St. Augustine in His Study, c. 1495.
Florence, Uffizi

50. *Francesco di Giorgio [?]. Intarsia Decoration from the* Studiolo *of the Ducal Palace, Gubbio, c. 1465. New York, The Metropolitan Museum of Art, Rogers Fund*

Botticelli is also known to have created cartoons for illusionistic schemes to be carried out in a highly unexpected medium, intarsia, which may be described as "ligneous mosaic," since it consists of fragments of various woods. In a sense, intarsia also relates to stained glass, since the bits and fragments are not of uniform shape and size, but are cut to conform with the designs. However, the color range is restricted; the woods were not tinted, but used in their natural states. It necessarily follows that when the purpose was illusionistic, the subject matter was limited. Yet this difficulty was brilliantly overcome.

The outstanding examples of this genre are the two famous rooms, completely wainscotted with intricate intarsia, which were created for the Duke Federigo da Montefeltro in his castles at Gubbio and Urbino. Of the two, the Gubbio *studiolo* (pl. 50), as the small apartment was called, is of greater interest for students of illusionism. In the *studiolo* at Urbino, the ornamentation also includes figures (after cartoons by Botticelli) as well as landscapes; but such elements, however lovely of themselves, can never be as successful illusionistically as the abstract shapes of objects to which, in the Gubbio example, the decoration is restricted. These are shown as if displayed on cupboard shelves, glimpsed through half-open latticed doors (pls. 50–51). They include musical instruments, scientific devices, books, papers, armillary spheres, and other objects whose function, now unfamiliar, has been established by researchers.[9] Always visually enchanting and of great rarity, they would have been prized by the enlightened Duke Federigo, to whom Piero della Francesca dedicated his treatise on geometry, and who presided over what was perhaps the most brilliant artistic and intellectual circle of the Renaissance.

In addition to the masterly solutions to the problems of perspective and foreshortening, another factor contributes to the success of the "deception" in this unlikely medium: the woods used range in color from the palest ivory to the darkest brown, and make the small room appear to be bathed in a warm amber glow, so that the eye glides effortlessly and not too critically over the delightful make-believe objects in this golden penumbra.

Unquestionably, the strongest impression is derived from the bold treatment of the jutting doors of the cabinets, and this element in particular may well represent the most aggressive use to date of a geometrical perspective, an unequivocal intrusion into the viewer's own plane at suprisingly close quarters.[10] It is also the main feature of the decoration of the Urbino *studiolo,* and not

51. *Intarsia Decoration in the* Studiolo *of the Ducal Palace, Urbino, c. 1465.*

surprisingly one finds it echoed in other works by outstanding practitioners of intarsia: Giuliano and Benedetto da Maiano; Fra Giovanni da Verona (pl. 52); Fra Vincenzo della Vacche (pl. 53); Guido da Saravallino; and the Lendinari.

52. *Fra Giovanni da Verona. Intarsia with Books and Objects. Verona, S. Maria in Organo*

53. *Fra Vincenzo della Vacche. Intarsia with Book and Instruments. Paris, Musée du Louvre*

54. *Nicolò Pizzolo*. St. Ambrose, *c. 1448–50. Formerly
Padua, Church of the Eremitani (destroyed World War II)*

The same sensational tridimensionality was striven for in a series of
paintings destroyed during World War II, the tondi by Nicolò Pizzolo in the
Chiesa degli Eremitani in Padua (pls. 54–56). The relationship to the intarsia
panels is unmistakable, but here of course wood does not replace pigment as
a "painting" medium. Instead, in the orthodox tradition of illusionism, it is
paint itself that counterfeits wood grain, and it does so with signal success.

55–56. *Nicolò Pizzolo*. St. Gregory *and* St. Augustine, *c. 1448–50. Formerly
Padua, Church of the Eremitani (destroyed World War II)*

57. *Fra Giovanni da Verona. Intarsia Decoration on Music Desk. Verona, S. Maria in Organo*

58. *German School, 15th century.* Open Book. *Lugano, Thyssen-Bornemisza Collection*

Such reversals of media of themselves were little more than entertaining incidentals. To the Latin mind, one of the merits of the painted tondi as well as of the intarsia panels was that they extolled the abstract beauty of geometrical forms. For Franco-Flemish artists, however, the illusionistic representation of textures—more particularly, of the grain in wood—held special appeal and interest for its own sake. One finds some of the intarsia themes translated into paint in the North: compare the Italian intarsia motif of a large open book represented on the shelf of a music desk (pl. 57) with its painted German counterpart (pl. 58), which probably served a kindred purpose originally, also as the shelf of a desk. In the same vein, panels painted with illusionistic shelves, niches, or cabinets with half-open doors were hinged to serve as actual doors (traces are still visible on some of the now-framed paintings). In time, all this counterfeit carpentry was reduced to the representation of a simple board of grained wood, the traditional background for countless trompe l'oeil subjects ever since.

It appears also to have been customary to use trompe l'oeil for the decoration of the verso of paintings, which indicates that although trompe l'oeil, at least in this capacity, did not rank highest of all, it was the kind of painting on which the eye rested habitually, since often the "shutters" were drawn open only on special occasions.

59. *Jan Van Eyck. The Ghent Altarpiece, Exterior, c. 1425–32. Ghent, St. Bavon*

60. *Jan Van Eyck. The Ghent Altarpiece, Interor, c. 1425–32. Ghent, St. Bavon*

Jan Van Eyck lavished as much beauty on the exterior as on the interior of his great polyptych, "The Adoration of the Lamb" (pls. 59–60). In every instance, the larger and bolder realism of the auxiliary trompe l'oeil subjects on the exterior acts as an effective foil for the impeccable and exquisite verisimilitude of the central scenes: the meticulously rendered jewels; the rich brocades with every thread of gold singly woven; the flowing locks where each hair can be counted in wonder.

Yet even this pales next to the strongly plastic figure of "Adam" (pl. 60, upper left), who indeed seems to embody the painter's quiet statement of protest against the artificiality of much that he was bound by contract to portray. Adam is the only major figure who is not fixed in a static position. Eve, although rendered with equal plasticity, remains relatively self-contained in her niche. By contrast, Adam appears to stride out of the narrow niche, and so vehement is the movement that his foreshortened foot, seen from below, trespasses the picture plane. In the 1450's, a Florentine painter, Andrea del Castagno, also depicted a series of figures as if the arched niches assigned them had proved too small—not only the tips of the feet, but even at times

79

an elbow, the pearl atop a diadem, overpass the limits of the frame (pl. 61). But Castagno's grandiose figures are equivocal, hovering half-way between reality and myth, whereas the poignant humanity of both "Adam" and "Eve" is dramatically brought out by contrast with the architectural setting of the stone arches with their carved grisaille ornamentation.

Van Eyck's most notable contribution to illusionism is found in the diptych of the Annunciation, in the Thyssen-Bornemisza Collection (pls. 62 –63), composed of two narrow panels with a dark, glossy ground (as if of black glass), each framed by a wide dark molding. Two monochrome figurines in full round, placed on octagonal pedestals, appear immediately beyond the frames. It is not a matter of their impinging upon the viewer's own plane by means of some tridimensional projection; here they have crossed the "space curtain" and come over in their entirety into our own sphere. They could not reenter the picture plane, even if they would. The only vestige of them retained in the painting is a vague reflection of their silhouettes, "as through a glass, darkly."

Trompe l'oeil representation of sculpture on the outer wings of polyptychs was to become a frequent practice in the art of Flanders and Holland. Notably, Hugo van der Goes used the same subject, the Annunciation, in twin panels of the Madonna and the Angel in a superb grisaille on the outer panels of the great Portinari triptych in Florence (pl. 64). Softer, cooler, more man-

(detail)

80

61. *Andrea del Castagno.* Cumean Sibyl, *c. 1450–55. Florence, S. Apollonia*

62–63. *Jan Van Eyck.* Annunciation. *Lugano, Thyssen-Bornemisza Collection*

64. *Hugo van der Goes.* Annunciation, 1476–78. *Exterior of the Portinari Altarpiece. Florence, Uffizi*

65. *Jan Van Eyck*. Giovanni Arnolfini and His Wife, *1434*

(detail)

nered than the Van Eyck examples, they also fall far short of the older master's unique blend of unaffected candor and royal grace. Nor do they incorporate the refined artifice of the reflecting mirror in back of the figures.

The theme of the mirror is significantly recurrent in the extant oeuvre of Jan Van Eyck, and it is also mentioned as having played an important part in some of his lost works. The most famous example, however, is probably the convex mirror that is the focal point in the double portrait, "Giovanni Arnolfini and His Wife" (pl. 65; color pl. 2). The French art historian Robert Gavelle, has advanced about it a theory of considerable interest:

> The aesthetic of illusionism—"mimesis," as it has been termed—is paramount in the oeuvre of Jan Van Eyck, as also in that of his followers, almost to the point of obsession. Ever since Archimedes, the mirror had seemed endowed with magical properties. It is not without good cause that the great chronicles of the medieval period were titled insistently: The Mirror of Nature, The Mirror of History, The Mirror of the Salvation of Man—their avowed purpose being to faithfully mirror the sum of all reality, spiritual as well as material. . . . The ancient Germanic folktale of Snow White told of the magic mirror that always answered truthfully. Van Eyck and his contemporaries were imbued with veneration of this symbol. Behind the Arnolfini pair, one sees at center a convex mirror on the wall and above it the inscription "Johannes de Eyck fuit hic," with the date 1434. The cryptic inscription has given rise to much speculation. If properly interpreted, it is indeed of the greatest importance. The rebus should be translated: "Jan Van Eyck was here:' the mirror," a formula that amounts to nothing less than his artistic creed. For the mirror was indeed the ideal of Flemish artists, who, much to the indignation of Michelangelo, chose to reflect reality as faithfully and as impartially as the looking glass itself, and who depicted pearls or teardrops with equal perfection and detachment.[11]

Accordingly, therefore, the mirror is essentially a second, sublimated signature Van Eyck's privy seal as an artist. This symbolism is to be distinguished from another explanation: that the mirror is material proof of the painter's role as legal witness to the Arnolfini marriage contract.[12] The Gavelle theory supplements this interpretation since the mirror does not seem to be essential to the "witness" theory, wherein a signed statement of presence would have sufficed. Awareness of the hypnotic presence of the mirror and of its role as an Eyckian artistic testament has been increasing steadily. An English art historian recently wrote that

66. *Quentin Massys.* Moneychanger and His Wife. *Paris, Musée du Louvre*

the convex looking glass upon the wall of the room distorts the
reality it reflects, but this distortion only draws attention to the
faithfulness of Van Eyck's art, the true mirror of the visible world.[13]

Many who followed in Van Eyck's footsteps not only emulated him in
his function as a dedicated recorder of reality, but insistently repeated the
very symbol he had used. The convex mirror occurs again and again in notable Flemish works: in the diptych, "Martin Nieuwenhoven and the Virgin,"
by Hans Memling (Musée de l'Hôpital de St. Jean, Bruges); in "St. Eligius
and the Lovers," by Petrus Christus (color pl. 3); and in the closely related
"Money Changer and His Wife," by Quentin Massys (pl. 66; color pl. 4).

Despite the fact that Christus was a pupil of Van Eyck, his mirror in

its plain circular frame is coarsely functional—a world away from the exquisite transcendental Eyckian conceit. In both instances the mirror speaks the truth, but each time a different truth. One may also compare these mirrors with a famous interpretation of the same theme almost a century later: the self-portrait of the young Parmigianino as reflected in a convex lens (color pl. 8). The hand of the painter is reaching out in the immediate foreground, bizarrely and hugely distorted, not merely like a dramatically three-dimensional giant's hand but even suggesting the intrusion of a denizen from the fourth dimension. This boyish, self-assured portrait may be one of the earliest and perhaps one of the most revealing indices of the assertion of the artistic ego, in sharp contrast to the medieval effacement and relative anonymity of Van Eyck's mirror. At either end of the spectrum, both versions are great illusionistic milestones.

67. *Parmigianino.* Self-Portrait in a Convex Mirror, *1524. Vienna, Kunsthistorisches Museum*

68. *Adriaen Isenbrandt (c. 1495–1551).* Madonna and Child. *Vienna, Akademie der bildenden Künste*

68. (detail)

North and South shared other illusionistic idioms. The legendary fly of Giotto, and of Crivelli after him (pls. 13–14), eventually wended its way northward. In a "Portrait of the Artist and His Wife" painted in 1496 by the Master of Frankfurt, the insect appears life-sized on the lady's coif of white lawn. It is not likely that this was intended as a pictorial pleasantry, since it has been established that even the decorative still-life elements in this solemn little painting possess symbolic significance: the bread and wine representing the Eucharist, and the fly symbolizing corruption. It was certainly with a like symbolic intent that a life-sized fly was included in the painting of the Madonna and Child by Adriaen Isenbrandt (pl. 68). The fly as an allegory of corruption is most frequently encountered in Northern lands with the so-called Vanitas subjects. Thus, it appears early and somewhat gruesomely on the top of a skull in a trompe l'oeil niche on the reverse of the portrait of Jane Loyse Tissier by Bartel Bruyn the Elder (pl. 69).

69. Bartel Bruyn the Elder. Vanitas, 1524 (reverse of portrait of Jane Loyse Tissier). Amsterdam, Rijksmuseum

87

70. *The Master of Mary of Burgundy. Page from a Book of Hours. Cracow, Czartoryski Library, Ms. 3025, fol. 151*

In a far happier mood, every insect of field, garden, and greenwood served as models for the Franco-Flemish miniaturists of the Ghent-Bruges School who adorned the famed books of hours so highly prized by noblemen and women of the later fifteenth and sixteenth centuries. In these magnificent volumes, the wide margins were almost invariably decorated illusionistically with themes derived from native flora and fauna. In a particularly subtle application of this style, one illustrator has fastened a few gracile wild flowers through feigned slits in the parchment. A similar blossom serves for the decoration of the capital letter, but the distinction is clearly established between this painted representation and the "real" flowers (pl. 70).

In contrast to this lightness of conception and touch, some fruit-laden cherry branches (pl. 71) are so vigorously plastic as to defeat their purpose. Instead of real fruit, they seem rather sculptural decorations superimposed on the page, suggestive of the reliefs in stucco on the walls of Gothic churches.

A beguiling use of the illusionistic floral motif was the scattering of short-stemmed blooms as if just plucked and strewn haphazardly on the page, and companioned by all the minute fauna of the garden: bees, moths, butterflies, and caterpillars. This device was particularly effective when the flower was the flat, multipetaled rose, or that other Gothic blossom par excellence, the ruffled, fringed, or picotee carnation. In Simon Bening's miniature, St. James, with the shell in his cap, dwells in the midst of a profusion of simple field flowers, each floweret casting forth on the page its own delicate but very precise shadow (pl. 72).

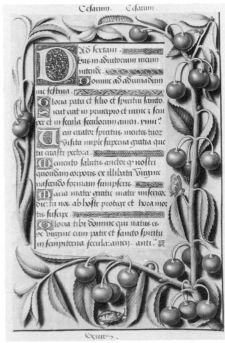

71. *Jean Bourdichon. Page from a Book of Hours. New York, Pierpont Morgan Library, Ms. 732, fol. 42*

72. *Simon Bening. St. James. Vienna, Österreichische Nationalbibliothek, Cod. 2706, fol. 230r*

89

73. St. Gregory the Great, *from the Book of Hours of Catherine de Clèves, c. 1440. New York, Pierpont Morgan Library, Ms. 917, fol. 240*

74. St. Ambrose, *from the Book of Hours of Catherine de Clèves, c. 1440. New York, Pierpont Morgan Library, Ms. 917, fol. 119*

75. St. Cecilia, *from the Book of Hours of Catherine de Clèves, c. 1440. New York, Pierpont Morgan Library, Ms. 917, fol. 308*

76. *The Master of Mary of Burgundy. Page from the Prayer Book of Engelbert of Nassau, c. 1485–90. Oxford, Bodleian Library, Ms. Douce 219, fols. 145v–46r.*

But the subject matter of illusionism in manuscript illumination was by no means restricted to biological naturalism. Even in the famed Book of Hours of Catherine de Clèves, where many of the decorative borders surrounding the masterly miniatures are still charmingly but somewhat belatedly Gothic (consisting chiefly of intricate arabesques interspersed with small stylized figures), there are a number of unusual features, startlingly bold and original. At once the simplest and the most effective of these is perhaps the miniature framed with gold and silver coins (pl. 73). The same artist was probably responsible also for the striking border composed of open mussels and a crab (pl. 74). In an unexpected and rather puzzling departure from realism, the inner tissues of the mollusks have been touched with gold dust. In the same mood, the border surrounding the image of Saint Cecilia (pl. 75) features four large feathers. Even though the feathers have been overlaid with falconry lures and the gold letters "CD," the trompe l'oeil effect is not disturbed.[14]

All small objects with low relief, such as coins or flat feathers, are ideal subjects for trompe l'oeil illustration. But at times the illustrators attempted far more ambitious themes, and against all odds, almost succeeded in accomplishing the impossible. In one instance, the artist divided the wide border into small compartments, each a deep square niche containing various vases and dishes, some with the monogram of Christ (pl. 76). According to all accepted rules, these subjects are much too large for the purpose, and although they are rendered with marvelous plasticity, the proximity of the page to the eye negates all efforts at illusionism. Nonetheless, one somehow cannot escape the impression that the objects depicted may be miniature versions of originals displayed in a compartmented jewel cabinet. (The glass goblets in particular suggest the famous Fabergé lapidary trompe l'oeil *objets de vertu*, with flowers carved of precious minerals standing in transparent containers; these appear to be glass vases filled with water, but are actually blocks of rock crystal, with each refracted stem of the blooms clearly visible.) If the treatment of such subjects in medieval illumination is not illusionism proper, it may at least be dubbed "suggestionism." In any case, these five-finger exercises were very earnestly preparing the way for the great outburst of technical virtuosity in still-life and trompe l'oeil painting of the next age.

76a. *Detail from the Prayer Book of Engelbert of Nassau*

91

77. *The Master of Mary of Burgundy. Page from the Prayer Book of Charles the Bold, c. 1480. Vienna, Österreich-ische Nationalbibliothek, Cod. 1.857, fol. 43*

One more especially dazzling example of Ghent-Bruges illumination is a flamboyant illumination by the Master of Mary of Burgundy (pl. 77), which stands in striking contrast to the lyric grace of his floral borders (pl. 70). This miniature is one of four pages added to the prayer book made for Charles the Bold, Duke of Burgundy. The central scene, the Nailing to the Cross, is not conventionally framed within a purely decorative border. Instead, we see it as if through the arched window of an oratory. On the broad sill, a pillow for the elbows, rosary beads of amber, and a prayer book all appear as if they had just been put aside by the worshipper. What we have here, therefore, is to all effects a stage setting, and although the scene cannot be illusionistic in actuality, it is definitely so in conception. The robust plasticity of the elements suggests that the tableau could easily be enlarged to life size. Clearly, the artists responsible for these delightful miniatures were illusionists of remarkable skill and versatility. Moreover, the divergence of style and concept between the illusionistically rendered borders and the comparatively two-dimensional, illuminated scenes suggests that more than one hand may have been at work on the miniature. The Master of Mary of Burgundy may well have entrusted the decoration of the surround to one of his best pupils. Indeed, it even seems possible that the workshops employed artists just for the illusionistic decoration of the borders, thus elevating illusionism to the rank of a skilled speciality.

77a. *Detail from plate 77*

4

Architectonic Illusionism

Renaissance to Baroque

The architectural setting used by Giotto had become an integral part of the painter's repertory by the fifteenth century, providing a new convincingness and sense of solidity to religious and historical scenes. At first, these settings were often little more than a suggestive tracery of gracile colonnades, balconies, and baldachins, charmingly decorative but only barely realistic, and by no means illusionistic. A typical example is the baptismal chapel at Castiglione d'Olona, decorated by Masolino in the 1420's (pl. 78). Anything more substantial than these airy structures would indeed weigh down on the slender figures. Yet even the ethereal Masolino surprises us with an unexpected display of volumetric vigor in the series of mock niches that appear to be scooped out of the underside of the low arch. The Fathers of the Church depicted within the niches seem not to be paintings, like the scenes on the walls, but instead full-round polychrome statuettes. The effect of depth is increased by such details as the jutting knee-hole desk in the second niche from the bottom. This use of a tall, narrow niche topped by a hemispheric arch is common to both painting and sculpture into the sixteenth century. But when found in painting, as for example in Sebastiano's "San Luigi di Tolosa," the niche is understood in its relation to sculpture and architecture, so that the effect is more dramatically illusionistic (pl. 79).

The architectural motifs in the paintings of Fra Angelico, although naturally reflecting contemporary styles, are still closely akin to those used by Giotto (cf. pls. 32 and 80) in that they are similarly small in relation to

78. *Masolino da Panicale. Frescoed Chapel in the Baptistery, c. 1435. Castiglione d'Olona*

79. *Sebastiano del Piombo.* San Luigi di Tolosa,
c. 1528–30. Venice, S. Bartolommeo

81. *Fra Angelico (1387–1455).* Annunciation.
Florence, Museo di San Marco (third cell)

80. *Fra Angelico (1387–1455).* Annunciation. *Florence, Museo di San Marco*

the figures. But, in his "Annunciation," the cloister vista is correctly proportioned, while in another lesser known painting on the same theme (in the third cell of the monastery at San Marco, pl. 81), Fra Angelico has created an even more harmonious environment, built on a subtle but firm interplay of recessed arches, a true perspectival fugue. This emphasis on architectural values in the oeuvre of the last of the Gothic artists of the South is significantly indicative of a continuing and pervasive interest.

A generation later, still in the same mood, the Dutch painter Albert van Oudwater placed the numerous personages of his "Resurrection of Lazarus" (Berlin) within a hemicycle of Romanesque arches, while in "Death and

82. *Hieronymus Bosch.* Death of the Miser, *c. 1490–1500. Washington, D.C., National Gallery of Art, Samuel H. Kress Collection*

the Miser" (pl. 82), Hieronymus Bosch used the narrow pointed medieval arch not only as the frame of the painting itself, but also as an entryway to the depth beyond the picture plane: the ogive in the foreground is the first of a series which forms the timberwork of the building where the scene takes place. It seems advisable to establish from the very start a clear distinction between architectural backgrounds brought forth with no other purpose than to form part of the composition of a painting—albeit enriching it with illusionistic suggestions—and the inclusion of similar elements to integrate the painted work within an existing architectural scheme. But it is often difficult to draw the line of demarcation between the two categories, since in the course of time many paintings have become separated from their original settings. This is the case, for instance, when wide low steps in the foreground of a painting seem to invite us to enter and join the actors. At times, a slight barrier, frankly more fictitious than real, such as the masonry border in Crivelli's "Annunciation" (pl. 83), is more of a subtle incentive than a true obstacle. Note there,

83. *Carlo Crivelli.* Annunciation, *1486. London, The National Gallery*

84. *Piero della Francesca.* Madonna and Child,
c. 1472–74. Milan, Pinacoteca di Brera

as a tempting touch, the trompe l'oeil fruit, seemingly ours for the reaching. Elsewhere, it may be a book or some other artifact carelessly left on the steps that fulfills the intermediary function between the imaginary world and ours. In the same vein, Botticelli draws back an imaginary curtain between his "Saint Augustine" and us (pl. 49).

To properly gauge the suggestive importance of architectural settings and their role as realistic foils for religious scenes, a very simple experiment is suggested. If one hides with a sheet of paper the upper half of Piero della Francesca's "Madonna and Child" (pl. 84), it immediately becomes clear not only that the scene loses much of its beauty and otherworldly serenity, but also that the actors in the lower half are suddenly deprived of much of their substance and visual credibility. But if the process is reversed, and the lower half of the picture covered instead, no comparable disturbance occurs. The great sounding shell, with its mysterious pendant egg, stands unperturbed. This is a superb and poetic example of what one might perhaps term "abstract" or "Euclidean" illusionism, for the term "architectural" does not seem to do full justice to its exalted character.

A little known but exceptionally early attempt at illusionism as an adjunct of architecture is found in a fourteenth-century work at the famed Alhambra in Granada. Painted on leather, the frieze of "The Moorish Kings" adorns the drum of a cupola in one of the halls. The figures appear to be looking down thoughtfully into the room, and one only regrets that the anonymous artist did not pursue the theme to its logical culmination and depict the semblance of a sky overhead. The first instance of this final conquest of illusionistic space was Mantegna's daring open cupola or oculus, painted in 1474 in the Camera degli Sposi ("Nuptial Chamber") of the ducal palace of the Gonzagas in Mantua (pl. 85). The famous apartment is embel-

85. *Andrea Mantegna. Painted Oculus in the Camera degli Sposi, c. 1473. Mantua, Palazzo Ducale*

lished with splendid illusionistic scenes on every wall (pl. 86), so that the distinction between picture plane and room has been done away with entirely for the first time. This epochal achievement has been justly described as

> the most far-reaching illusion of actuality attempted up to that time, . . . the side-wall frescoes and the ceiling being designed with a common, preestablished viewing point from which the illusion of actuality is complete, so that the observer finds himself in a painted world that simulates the world of nature to the last detail. In thus carrying to an extreme the concept of pictorial reality initiated in the earlier fifteenth century in Italy, Mantegna reveals the extent to which that world had become the dominant factor in the thought of the time.[1]

The outstanding feature of the decoration is indeed the oculus with its circular rim, or balcony, over which boldly foreshortened putti and spectators look down into the room. This conception is undoubtedly the precursor of all the Baroque extravaganzas on the theme of an open firmament. The decorative scheme of the walls also includes various trompe l'oeil devices now thought of as conventional, but which were then daring innovations: drawn curtains, imitation bas-reliefs, jutting accessories.

86. *Andrea Mantegna. Scenes from the Life of Lodovico Gonzaga, c. 1473. Mantua, Palazzo Ducale*

87. *Andrea Mantegna. Three Figures in a Grape Arbor. Detail from the* Transportation of the Body of St. Christopher, *1454–57. Formerly Padua, Ovetari Chapel, Church of the Eremitani*

The Gonzaga Nuptial Chamber, however, was not the first instance of Mantegna's concern with illusionistic effects. An especially charming example, done in the 1450's, when he was still working for Squarcione, is a detail of the decoration of the Church of the Eremitani (pl. 87), destroyed in World War II, to which his fellow student, Nicolò Pizzolo, had contributed a notable series of tondi (pls. 54–56). Unlike Pizzolo, Mantegna was not primarily concerned with textures or even with geometrical forms, although his three figures in a grape arbor easily transcend Pizzolo's best efforts. The most important element in the composition is clearly the illusionistic treatment of the figures, particularly that of the head of the youngest spectator against the window jamb.

103

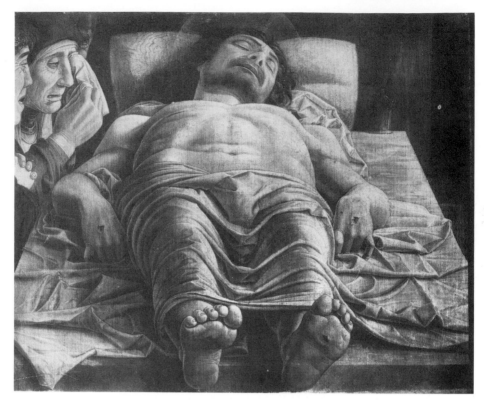

88. *Andrea Mantegna.* Dead Christ. *Milan, Pinacoteca di Brera*

Mantegna's interest in illusionism continued unabated to the end of his career—witness his extraordinarily foreshortened "Dead Christ" (pl. 88), a dazzling display of his mastery of the art and science of perspective as applied to the human form: "anatomical architecture," as it were. In a more directly architectural mode he had planned the decoration of the Palazzo Cornaro in Venice. It was to have consisted of a series of illusionistic friezes featuring episodes in the life of Scipio Africanus, a supposed ancestor of the Cornaro family. The classical figures were to appear in a grisaille frieze, as if carved in stone relief, against a background of red marble. But Mantegna died before he could complete the task, and the execution was entrusted to his brother-in-law, the Venetian Giovanni Bellini. Presumably, therefore, Bellini worked with Mantegna's cartoons, and the result bears the stamp of the master's grandeur (pl. 89).

89. *Giovanni Bellini.* An Episode from the Life of Publius Cornelius Scipio, *1507–08. Washington, D.C., National Gallery of Art, Samuel H. Kress Collection*

91. *Detail*

90. *Antonello da Messina.* St. Jerome in His Study, *c. 1474. London, The National Gallery*

In contrast to Mantegna, who was moved singlemindedly by "an impassioned emulation of the spirit and letter of Roman style,"[2] Antonello da Messina, by birth the southernmost of all Italian artists, paradoxically came closest of all, by choice and training, to the Northern European spirit. The Italian and Northern influences are commingled in his works nowhere more interestingly than in Antonello's "Saint Jerome in His Study" (pl. 90), where the figure of the Saint reading at his desk, rendered with minutious Northern realism, nevertheless plays a surprisingly minor role. The emphasis is definitely on the impressive architectural setting, and then on such delightful details as the stone step in the middle ground, upon which are painted two tame birds, a partridge and a peacock (pl. 91). This element is of particular importance in relation to illu-

105

92. *Antonello da Messina.* Salvator Mundi, *1465.*
London, The National Gallery

93. *Jan Van Eyck.* Leal Souvenir, *1432. London,*
The National Gallery

sionism when one recalls that Jacopo de' Barbari, who may have been a pupil, and was certainly an admirer of Antonello's, may have drawn inspiration for his most famous work (pl. 1), a milestone in the history of trompe l'oeil, from the animals in Antonello's "St. Jerome."

Antonello da Messina, like many of the Venetian painters with whom he associated during his stay in that city (among whom were the Bellinis and the Vivarinis), adopted the illusionistic device of the *cartellino,* a rectangular strip of parchment bearing a date and/or a signature, as seen in his famous portrait "Il Condottiere," or in his "Salvator Mundi" of 1465 (pl. 92). This was an elegant but less solemn equivalent of the monumental inscription that appeared as if incised on a tablet in such portraits as Van Eyck's "Leal Souvenir" (pl. 93). The *cartellino* was at first combined with the standard architectural feature of early Renaissance portraiture: the parapet, or sill-like bar, against which the subject of the portrait appears to be standing. Later on,

106

94. *Albrecht Altdorfer.* The Battle of Issus, *1528. Munich, Alte Pinakothek*

however, the *cartellino* followed a dual course: either it assumed ever-increasing plastic importance, culminating in Altdorfer's great tablet in the "Battle of Issus" (pl. 94), or else, at the other extreme, it became a "little card" apparently placed in a corner of the painting as a label, a means of identification. As such, it appears even in so important and serious a work as Zurburán's "St. Francis" (pl. 95).

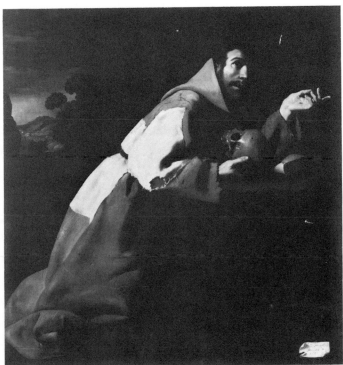

95. *Francesco de Zurburán.* St. Francis, *1637. London, The National Gallery*

96. *Pinturicchio.* Emperor Frederick III Crowning Aeneas Sylvius Piccolomini with the Poet's Crown, *1502 – 1503. Siena*

At this stage, one should perhaps pause to reflect that the progress of linear perspective and volumetric painting had already placed illusionism within the reach not only of the Mantegnas and the Antonellos, but of any properly trained, even if only moderately gifted, painter. The grammar of the art could now be learned, and correctness of visual expression was the least that was expected of a painter of any repute. Yet they were not expected to produce pictorial realism as we now understand the term. If "realism" signifies the duplication of reality as we meet with it in daily life, the great artists of the Renaissance were unrealistic. They did paint figures and objects in a manner that we find easily recognizable in accordance with a certain set of visual conventions. But this artistic reality had no existence outside the minds of its creators. This wonderful world, filled with figures moving about in settings of unparalleled magnificence and loveliness, bore no resemblance whatever to the world in which the artists lived. We now see the Renaissance in a golden aura of their conjuring. But if there was splendor then there was also squalor, and we may rest assured that even the sumptuous palaces of the Gonzagas, the Estes, and the Medicis fell far short of the inspired visions of their "decorators." The painted world of the fifteenth century was to the contemporary denizens of the real world very much what theater plays and film would be to later generations. The function of the artist was to effect communication between the two parallel worlds. In that sense, the ancient instinct that had regarded illusionism as magic had not proven far from the truth.

We have now grown psychologically immune to much that was undoubtedly intended as trompe l'oeil. Even the lowly picture frame, now purely utilitarian and meant solely to facilitate the handling of a painting, was initially an architectural element, scaled down to the size of the figures portrayed, and therefore very clearly an illusionistic device. The picture "frame," akin to a reliquary when it contained a Van Eyck panel, became a triumphal arch for Pinturicchio's great tableaux in the Piccolomini Library, Siena (pl. 96).

The integration of a painted scene into a given architectural setting affirms that the resultant illusionism was purposeful. One of the grandest and most nobly simple architectural illusionistic schemes of the Italian Renaissance is Leonardo da Vinci's "Last Supper." Although it has deteriorated badly and the fine details are irretrievably lost, the general outlines of the composition have survived. The artist has optically pierced the actual wall, replacing it with a painted extension that lengthens the room considerably. There, the group of Christ and his disciples appear to sit at an additional table set up in the refectory room of the monastery, as if on a dais, higher than the actual tables that were set for the monks.[3] At the rear, fictitious windows open on a cool blue sky and a typically Vincian mountainous vista. Thus, an otherwise commonplace room has been not merely enlarged but immeasurably ennobled.

More than three decades later, in Titian's "Presentation of the Virgin in the Temple" (pl. 97), we again find that the level of the actors is considerably higher than that of the viewers. In addition, there are at least two elements that are frankly trompe l'oeil, intended to establish an intermediary

97. *Titian.* Presentation of the Virgin in the Temple, *1534–38. Venice, Galleria dell' Accademia*

98. Michelangelo. The Sistine Ceiling, 1508–12 (detail). Vatican, Sistine Chapel

visual connection: the classic torso and the basket of eggs flanking the door at right, which is framed in an illusionistic masonry border. The door at left, on the contrary, brutally slashes the composition, making it evident that this second door must have been added at a later date. If the door had been there from the start, Titian would no doubt have found some genial way of handling the intrusion. The first door and the balance of the wainscotting are harmoniously integrated into the composition; the commonplace carpentry is transformed into an impressive pedestal, a glorified base or terrace, for the scene above. Titian could have avoided the problem of the door by beginning his picture at the level of the lintel and filling in the excess space with simulated wooden panelling or decorative motifs. That he chose to use the door in the composition strongly confirms his concern for the illusionistic integration of the painting into the given architecture of the room.

An interesting aside in Titian's career significantly relates to his development of illusionism. In 1563 he was chosen as a member of a panel (which also included Tintoretto and the architect Sansovino) convened by the Venetian Senate to decide on an illusionistic fraud. The Senate alleged that the workshop of the Zuccati had been producing, instead of mosaic tesserae, a faked, painted equivalent.[4] Sebastiano, the elder Zuccati, is believed to have given Titian his first drawing lessons, and his two sons, Francesco and Valerio, became famed mosaicists, authors of many of the mosaic decorations of San Marco. After inspecting the work in question, the panel reported that a fraud had indeed been perpetrated. But so indulgent was this age to the vagaries of illusionistic deceit that the verdict seems not to have interfered appreciably with the career of the Zuccati, for in 1579 they were executing the mosaic decoration of the cupola of San Marco instead of expiating their crime on the benches of some proud Venetian galley. It may be that Titian, out of gratitude to the father and attachment to the sons, interceded on behalf of his fellow "illusionists."

Sometimes the extant architecture did not accord with the purpose or style of the painter, who then had to proceed as well as he might. The greatest example of such a handicap successfully overcome is without doubt the Sistine Chapel (pl. 98). The original contract with Michelangelo had called for only a series of the twelve Apostles to be painted between the windows of the clerestory, and for the ceiling to be decoratively patterned—a reasonable scheme that could have been carried out with relative ease. But, urged on by his daemon, Michelangelo undertook not only to paint histories on the ceiling surface, but to attempt the impossible task of crowding a vehement host of superhuman figures within the narrow compass and angular projections at the springing of the vault. It is as though the entire canopy of heaven would hardly have sufficed for the tale Michelangelo had to tell.

The result, all know. The simulated stone heaves like a sea, in a complex maelstrom of shifting planes. Not one inch of the surface appears level; even the sense of direction has become confused, and one wonders if one has not been transported into a mysterious fourth dimension. This is illusionism raised to the metaphysical plane, yet Michelangelo did not disdain to include as a framework for his titanic composition a host of trompe l'oeil elements: pedestals, tablets, pilasters, and the great circular medallions as if of bronze.

The next step was taken by Giulio Romano, an assistant of Raphael, whose Sala dei Giganti ("Hall of the Giants," pl. 99) at the Palazzo del Te, in Mantua, suggests nothing so much as a sixteenth-century equivalent to a Cecil B. De Mille set. Giulio was justified in creating these extraordinary illusionistic effects by the highest possible authority. According to Vasari, the young Leonardo da Vinci (in his one known attempt at outright pictorial trompe l'oeil, barring perhaps theatrical projects for Lodovico Sforza)[5] had also attempted to strike terror in the spectator's hearts. The result must have been the trompe l'oeil to end all trompe l'oeil.

There is a story that a peasant at Ser Piero's [Leonardo's father's] country place brought a homemade shield, a piece of a fig tree he had cut down, and asked that Ser Piero have it painted for him in Florence. As the man was a very able huntsman and a great favorite with his master, the latter willingly promised to have it done.

He took the wood therefore to Leonardo, not telling him for whom it was, and asked only that he paint something on it. Leonardo took the shield in hand, but since he found it crooked, coarse, and badly made, he straightened it before the fire and sent it to a turner, who returned it smooth and delicately rounded. Leonardo covered it with gypsum [gesso] and prepared it to his liking. He then considered what to put on it and thought of the head of a Medusa and the terror it would strike in the hearts of those who beheld it. He therefore assembled in a room that no one entered but himself a number of lizards, hedgehogs, newts, serpents, dragonflies, locusts, bats, glowworms, and every sort of strange animal he could lay his hand on. He fashioned a fearsome monster, hideous and appalling, breathing poison and flames and surrounded by fire, issuing from a rift in a rock. He labored while the room filled with a mortal stench of which Leonardo was quite unaware in his interest in his work. When it was done, long after both his father and the huntsman had stopped inquiring for it, Leonardo went to his father and told him he might send for the shield when he liked. Ser Piero went himself to fetch it. When he

knocked, Leonardo asked him to wait a little. He darkened the
room and placed the shield where a dim light would strike it, and
then asked his father in. Ser Piero drew back, startled, and turned
to rush out, but Leonardo stopped him, saying, "The shield will
serve its purpose." The work seemed more than wonderful to Ser
Piero, so he bought another shield, which was decorated with a
heart transfixed by an arrow, and this he gave to the peasant,
who cherished it all his life. Leonardo's shield he secretly sold to
a merchant for a hundred ducats. It subsequently fell into the
hands of the Duke of Milan, who paid three hundred ducats for it.[6]

Leonardo's shield must indeed have been comparable to the shield of
Achilles. Its mysterious disappearance—with no record of anyone actually
having seen the marvel or knowing of its eventual fate—is all the stranger in
that the shield is said to have become part of the collection of a great nobleman
and a famous patron of the arts. However, "*si non è vero, è ben trovato*,"
and the story at least indicates the high esteem in which illusionism was held.

In the Palazzo del Te, Giulio Romano, in addition to the ponderous
Hall of the Giants, also painted the "Hall of Psyche." There, under a cloud-
filled cupola, amorous mythological figures gambol in a garden apparently
cut off from the room only by a light garlanded trellis. In another chamber
at the Palazzo del Te, two of Giulio's collaborators, Rinaldo Mantovano and
Benedetto Pagni, created the bizarre but strikingly illusionistic decoration in

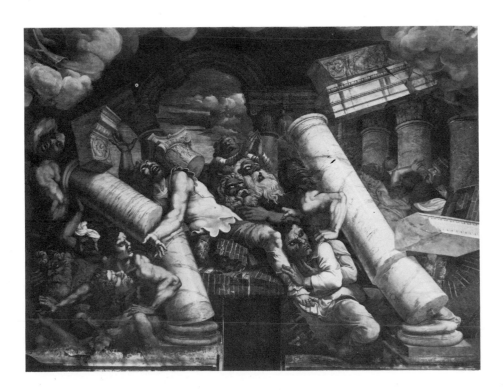

99. *Giulio Romano*, Fall of
the Giants, *1527–30. Mantua,
Palazzo del Te, Sala dei Giganti*

100. *Rinaldo Mantovano and Benedetto Pagni. Decoration in the Sala dei Cavalli, c. 1525. Mantua, Palazzo del Te*

the "Hall of the Horses" (pl. 100). The subject was certainly suitable, since the Palazzo del Te seems to have served the dukes of Mantua primarily as a glorified stable. But the life-sized animals are precariously and most improbably perched high around the room on an exceedingly narrow ledge, where they alternate with colossal simulated statuary in great niches. The unusual scheme is nothing less than an excursion into the land of the Houyhnhnms fully two centuries in advance of Gulliver.

Giulio Romano also contributed to the decoration of the Villa Farnesina in Rome, where the "Hall of Columns" (pl. 101) is nobly architectural, with lofty columns painted in the foreground and a loggia beyond. There are details, however, such as the camouflaging of an ordinary fireplace with a trapezoidal flue, that now appear strained and bombastic. And the numerous variations on the theme of colonnades, such as that carried out by the Pesenti brothers at the Palazzo del Giardino (Mantua, Sabbioneta), were destined to be worked to death for the next century or so.

114

101. *Baldassare Peruzzi et al.
Hall of Columns, c. 1516. Rome,
Villa della Farnesina*

102. *Andrea Palladio (executed
by Vincenzo Scamozzi). Stage
perspective, 1579–1581. Vincenza, Teatro Olimpico*

But if painters invaded the territory of architecture in this guise, architects did not scruple to reciprocate. Palladio's last great work, the Teatro Olimpico in Vicenza, finished after his death by Vincenzo Scamozzi, includes an illusionistic stage perspective with a receding view of a street (pl. 102). The complex architectural frontage, with a majestic arched gateway at center, appears to lead to yet another archway in the distance between rows of town houses; similar vistas seem to stretch out at right and left. But only the facade has substance; all else is painted.

Religious art, too, was susceptible to the allure of illusionism. Far re-

115

103. *Ambrogio Borgognone*. Monk at a Window. *Certosa di Pavia*

moved from the sophistication and elegance of Giulio Romano and Palladio, is the fresco Ambrogio Borgognone painted for the Charterhouse of Pavia around 1490—an illusionistic representation of a white-robed monk apparently glancing down into a courtyard from one of the monastery's ogival windows (pl. 103). The element of entertainment cannot be discounted here, and the deceptive effigy no doubt played a dual role as a welcome relief to the austerity of monastic life as well as a "tourist attraction."

Illusionistic exterior decoration such as Borgognone's was practiced not only in the South, where the climate favored its preservation, but even in the inclement North. No lesser an artist than Hans Holbein was commissioned to decorate the entire exterior of a building in Basel known as the "House of the Dance." By the beginning of the present century, the decorations had fallen into such decay that they could not be preserved, and they are now known to us only by a model (pl. 104). Holbein lavished a wealth of inventiveness and ingenuity on this gargantuan exercise in trompe l'oeil, although he must have known that the exposed murals certainly could not long survive the rigors of the Swiss climate. The plain, tiled roof atop the imaginary palazzo appears ludicrous in the model, but one should recall that it would not actually have been visible from street level because of the recess of the slanting roof, and furthermore that the entire house was hemmed in closely by other buildings. Still, what a wonderful experience to have rounded the street corner

116

104. *Hans Holbein the Younger. Model for the House of the Dance, Basel, Historisches Museum*

and come upon all this phantasmagoric architecture—and what a homage paid to the prestige of the Italian Renaissance by the good city of Basel that it should have so fervently wished to capture at least its reflection through the white magic of illusionism.

It is possible that the task may have been assigned to Holbein as a result of the early interest he is reputed to have taken in executing feats of trompe l'oeil. According to this tale, so characteristic of the popular lore of illusionism, Holbein as a young student played a prank on his master by depicting his own legs as they would have appeared had the truant apprentice been standing hard at work on a scaffolding, assiduously completing his appointed task in a fresco decoration. The artist's serious interest in problems of optics is evidenced by the puzzling anamorphic skull in the foreground of his painting "The French Ambassadors" (see pp. 152–53 and pl. 141).[7]

There is another realm of illusionism which is more difficult to study, and which can often be only imagined from written descriptions: the decorative triumphal arches that were frequently set up for state occasions—Imperial receptions, royal weddings, entries of ambassadors, and the like. As with the "House of the Dance," the greatest artists were called upon for the design and execution of these ephemeral productions. It is probable that they were highly illusionistic, not only in the representation of stonework but in the inclusion of other elements as well. One thinks with bitter regret of Leonardo's

117

105a–d. *Frederik Sustris and Alessandro Scalzi. Stair-well Decoration with Scenes from the* Commedia dell'
Arte, *1575–79. Landshut, Trausnitz Castle*

105b.

work of this type for the ducal court of Milan, of the first Caravaggio's reputed
ornaments of the same genre, done in Rome in his early years, and of the triumphal arches he is known to have designed to celebrate the return of Emperor
Charles V from his expedition to Sicily. (Even the great set of tapestries
woven to memorialize the event, now in the Alcazar of Seville, includes one
illusionistic element: a border of simulated marble.) Had such work been preserved, we would no doubt have full scale pendants to Piero della Francesca's
imaginary "triumphs" of Urbino (pls. 41–42), which must have been based
at least to some extent on actual "floats" used in a ducal pageant.

In many instances, the themes may have been suggested by the patrons'
personal interests. Frederik (or Federigo) Sustris, a Dutch-born but Italian-
trained painter, worked on the decoration of the catafalque of Michelangelo,
was later in the employ of the Duke of Lorraine, and eventually made his
way of the Bavarian court. There he was entrusted with the task of decorat-
ing an antiquated medieval stairway at Trausnitz Castle in Landshut, north of

105c.

105d.

Munich. In collaboration with Alessandro Scalzi, he adorned the stairwell with murals depicting farcial episodes from the Italian Commedia dell'Arte (pls. 105a–d). In this exeedingly lively and lusty conception, a troop of buffoons issuing from feigned doors at the side scale the stairs in wild haste, one personage still atop his donkey. Much of the veracity of the scene is due not only to the extraordinary sense of movement but also, paradoxically, to the stylized theatricality of the renderings, the disproportion of the figures, and the histrionic vehemence of their gestures. These are not naturalistic human semblances but caricatures with each actor wearing the mask of his role, as on the classical stage or in the theater of the Orient.

In the Sustris decoration the relationship between the spectator and the painting was one of proximity. But another current in sixteenth-century art was conceived from the opposite point of view, with the emphasis placed increasingly on an effect of depth and distance, and what might be called "celestial" rather than earthly aspects. This could be taken in a literal sense,

119

106. *Correggio.* The Vision of St. John on Patmos, *1520–21. Parma, S. Giovanni Evangelista*

as when a sky vista enlarges a room, or it could be a vision of the empyrean. The theme of a cloud-filled cupola was taken up by Correggio in the decoration of the Church of St. John the Evangelist in Parma (pl. 106). Correggio, who appears here as successor to Mantegna, achieved a special coloristic luminosity which is very effective, but the individual components of his design seem unsatisfactory. It became popularly known as "the nest of frogs," because of what was judged the unfelicitous foreshortening of the figures, seemingly crushed by the weight of the atmosphere.

Niccolò dell' Abate, a pupil of Correggio, emulated both his master and Mantegna in an intriguing work known as "The Musical Family" (pl. 107). The subject is a group of musicians gathered in an octagonal opening from which they apparently look down on visitors to the room. The single defect of this otherwise pleasing work is the crowding of the figures, so that the sense of light and vastness, so keenly felt in Mantegna's cupola, is totally lacking. Dell'Abate may have been more successful on other occasions, but much of his reputedly illusionistic work has been lost, both in his native Italy and in France where he worked with Primaticcio.

Venice was the city of pageantry par·excellence, painted as well as actual, and pageantry and illusionism seemed to go hand in hand. It is not surprising, therefore, that a Venetian painter (by adoption), Paolo Caliari, known as Veronese, should also be one of the great practitioners of architectural illusionism. His giant "Wedding at Cana" (pl. 108) takes place within

107. *Niccolò dell'Abate.* The Musical Family, *c. 1540. Modena, Galleria Estense*

108. *Veronese.* Wedding at Cana, *1562–63. Paris, Musée du Louvre*

109–12. *Veronese. Decorations at the Villa Barbaro, c. 1560. Maser*

110.

111.

112.

what is perhaps the most architecturally impressive (although historically improbable) setting ever devised for the illustration of an episode of the Gospels. In the illusionistic decoration of the Villa Maser, however, Veronese put his mastery of architectural perspective and visual simulation to far more justified use (pls. 109–12). The trompe l'oeil elements there include not only what might be called the decorative frame of a door—niches with pretended polychrome statuary, moldings, carvings, masks, camaïeu medallions—but also the human figure: a young man, cap in hand, is asking admittance at a half-opened door; between the two panels of another, a small girl hovers in timid hesitation. A remarkable detail is the broom depicted in one corner, as if left there by a careless charwoman. Other humorous touches similarly relieve the general opulence of the decoration in the main reception hall: the parrot and the dog on the balcony, and the wizened old servant (probably the nurse) next to the comely young mistress. Every detail, every spark of color assumes extraordinary relief against the dazzling whiteness of the architectural setting.

123

113. *Veronese.* Triumph of Venice, *c. 1583. Venice, Palazzo Ducale*

114. *Guercino.* Aurora, *1621.*
Rome, Villa Ludovisi

A verdigris tonality replaces this in Veronese's "Triumph of Venice" in the Great Council Hall of the Doges Palace (pl. 113). Most notable there, however, is the triumph of delusion: one views the scene at a forty-five degree angle when entering the room, yet it appears to be towering overhead. This particular perspective had been innovated by Titian thirty-five years earlier in a series of ceiling medallions for Santa Maria della Salute, though not with the pomp and dramatic effect of the dogal ceiling. A sensible solution to an optical problem, practicable for the painter and acceptable to the viewer, it was to remain basically unaltered to the present day. Its chief characteristic is the vertical reversal of vision in relation to the painted scene. Note, for instance, that the dog, apparently in the immediate foreground, is actually painted at the farther end of the long oval, while the angels at the very apex of the composition are in fact painted at the end nearer to the viewer. Paradoxically, neither the tremendously weighty architecture, nor the ponderous horses with heavily armored riders, nor the massive figures in the apothesis detract from or contradict the plausibility of the effect. The huge assemblage, the first of the *grandes machines,* appears to soar effortlessly in the empyrean. It is magnificently self-assured, but also self-contained and bearing no essential relationship to its locale; it could theoretically be removed and replaced with another scene (provided the perspective is observed), precisely as one slide can be replaced with another in a projector.

In a later work of the kind, Guercino's "Aurora" in the Villa Ludovisi (1621; pl. 114), the mythological scene is not depicted within a rigid geomet-

125

rical frame. Rather, it appears to take place in the open sky overhead: the room in which the spectator stands is presumed to be roofless, and there is nothing to prevent him from figuratively ascending into the pictured Elyseum. The highest matter-of-fact tribute to the effectiveness of the illusion occurs time and again when viewers, judging solely from photographic reproductions, assume that while all else is painted, the great pilasters and cornices are actual structures—and this even though one of the four great supports is shown without its entablature and with some wild vines rooted in the ruined corner.

The luminous "Aurora" should have heralded the dawn of a new golden age of neoclassical illusionism. But in this age of the Counter-Reformation, illusionistic ceiling decoration was also pressed into the service of the Christian faith, particularly by the Jesuit order. Their sumptuous churches remain inseparably connected to the illusionistic ceilings of the Baroque and Rococco era, although the first classic example of the genre, Pietro da Cortona's "Triumph of Divine Providence," adorns the ceiling not of a church but of the main salon of the Palazzo Barberini (pl. 115).

Pietro da Cortona was an architect as well as a painter, and one suspects that in this pictorial masterwork he has given far freer rein to architectonic fantasy than if he had been building an equivalent structure (although the edifice is architecturally feasible). Illusionistically, he has combined the forty-five degree perspective with the "roofless" device of Guercino. However, while the primary view point is focused on the figure of Providence in the central panel, the four accessory groups at each side can be viewed best as the spectator moves around the periphery of the room. This aggregate of five different viewpoints significantly complexifies Veronese's single focal point in the "Triumph of Venice."

At the center of the great vault of the Church of the Gesù in Rome, Giovanni Battista Gaulli, called Baciccio, depicted another symbolical triumph—the "Triumph of the Name of Jesus" (pl. 116). At the center of the composition, a host of cherubim and seraphim throng about the sunlike sacred monogram. Here the spectator is not asked to participate but merely to be receptive: it is heaven itself that has broken the natural bounds and burst forth upon the earth. But a conception that could have been Dantesque is weakened by the theatricality of the bloated clouds that turgidly overlap the architecture.

The undoubted masterpiece of Jesuit illusionism was created by an artist who was also a member of the Jesuit order, Padre Andrea Pozzo. This is the famous "Apotheosis of St. Ignatius" in the Church of St. Ignatius in Rome (pl. 2), both a tribute to the founder of the Jesuits and a glorification of the achievements of the order. Padre Pozzo has superimposed upon the already imposing extant architecture a fantastical architecture of his own

115. *Pietro da Cortona.* Triumph
of Divine Providence, *1633–1639.*
Rome, Palazzo Barberini

116. *Giovanni Battista Gaulli
(Baciccio).* Triumph of the Name
of Jesus, *1676–79. Rome, Il Gesù*

127

117. *Giovanni Battista Tiepolo.*
Institution of the Rosary, *1737–
39. Venice, S. Maria dei Gesuati*

which towers to vertiginous heights, concluding with the same kind of entablature that Guercino used. Above this level, symbolic of man's highest achievements, are the limitless reaches of the firmament, that is, divine goodness and wisdom. Every element of the composition, architectonic or figural, converges towards the summit of a pyramid, at whose apex the Saviour sits enthroned on cloud banks. There is no possibility of "head-on" collision, as would certainly occur in the Cortona ceiling, because here all figures and elements are soaring towards the same goal. Had Padre Pozzo stopped right there, and indicated the divine presence abstractly—solely as a dazzling brightness, perhaps—the illusionism would then have been unimpeachable, and the perspective completely peripheral: it would not have been necessary to view the scene from any particular point. But with the inclusion of the figure of Christ, it became imperative to indicate a viewing point by a circle on the floor below, so as not to see Christ upside down. Even with the best of intentions, this prepara-

128

tion automatically precludes perfect illusion. Nevertheless, one must recognize here the supreme triumph of *quadratura.* No one before or since has carried architectonic illusionism as far, or rather as high as did the Jesuit artist.

Innumerable illusionistic ceilings were produced throughout the sixteenth, seventeenth, and eighteenth centuries, all variations on the three models set by Mantegna, Veronese, and Guercino. Even as late as 1738, so great and original an artist as Tiepolo felt no qualm about following faithfully the basic composition of Veronese's "Triumph of Venice" for his "Institution of the Rosary" in the Church of the Gesuati in Venice (pl. 117). The wide difference of style and mood need hardly be pointed out, but the pyramidal composition slanting upward at a forty-five degree angle remains the same, with the figure of the Virgin replacing the personification of Venice. In what was undoubtedly a maquette (it measures barely six feet) for a ceiling in the Royal Palace in Madrid, "The World Pays Homage to Spain" (pl. 118), Tiepolo has combined peripheral perspective for objects and figures in a broad illusionistic quadrangle with diagonal and centripetal elements again suggesting a pyramid of which the apex, here uncrowded and airy, is at center of room. The figure of Spain, enthroned at center and flanked by two classicistic statues, recalls that of Venice in Veronese's picture. Tiepolo also echoes Veronese in his murals, where he is fond of using snowy shafts of tall columns that recall the loggia of the Villa Maser (pl. 109); at times he incorporates even more personal Veronesque elements, such as the toy dog on the second step of the dais

118. *Giovanni Battista Tiepolo.* The World Pays Homage to Spain, *1762–66. Oil Sketch for a Ceiling in the Madrid Royal Palace. Washington, D.C., National Gallery of Art, Samuel H. Kress Collection*

in his "Banquet of Anthony and Cleopatra" (pl. 119) which is surely a descendant of that portrayed by Veronese.

The splendid *quadratura* that upholds all this—except for the actual window and door openings, all is trompe l'oeil—was the work of Tiepolo's collaborators, competent artists such as Gerolamo Mengozzi-Colonna. Yet the credit should not be shared, for technical skill alone does not suffice when the master's genial spirit is lacking. This may be seen clearly in works where Tiepolo himself played no part: for example, "The Triumph of Alexander," at the Palazzo Pitti in Florence, painted by Mengozzi-Colonna and another artist of second rank, Agostino Mitelli. It is an uninspired conception where grandiosity is but a poor substitute for Tiepolo's Elysian visions.

The precisionistic discipline of these architectural decorations is far removed from the poetry of the scenes contained within them—Tiepolo's great mythological pageants, where heroes and demigods appear draped not in sumptuous cloth but in swathes of sunset splendor. Nevertheless, Tiepolo's intention was also illusionistic; and not only illusionism of the whole but of trompe l'oeil in the details. Note at the right of the "Sacrifice of Iphigenia" (pl. 120) the hand on the column; and at left, the group of a hind and cherub which, borne on a luminous cloud, appears against all reason to be proceeding from our world into that of the painted tableau. We are not intellectually deceived for a moment by this or any other part of the representation. Yet who is to say that Tiepolo did not achieve his purpose? For we are made aware of a glorious enlargement of the surrounding space; a sense of triumph is all pervasive—the golden notes of trumpets seem to resound and linger—and we instinctively draw a deeper breath, as if through the majestic colonnade not only a flood of light but a purer, keener air had rushed into the chamber. Thus could this great visual poet transmute "deception" into a higher truth.

To rival such effects, if only on the decorative plane, became the goal of many highly competent if uninspired artists such as Lanfranco, Buonamico, Saraceni, the Bibbienas (the last named, a dynasty of fashionable decorators, spanning several generations). Through their activities during the second half of the seventeenth and the first half of the eighteenth centuries, architectural illusionism in the grand Italian manner was disseminated throughout Europe and emulated by native artists who, unavoidably, translated the style into their own characteristic idioms. In Spain, for instance, where East and West do meet, Italianate influence brought about the creation of a unique kind of grisaille decoration that is unmistakably Iberian, and is even echoed in the churches of Mexico and South America. Ornamentation of this type was executed by Valdes Leal and his son Lucas in the Sacristy of the Church of the Hospital

119. *Giovanni Battista Tiepolo*. The Banquet of Anthony and Cleopatra. *Painted Architectural Decoration by G. Mengozzi-Colonna, 1747–50. Venice, Palazzo Labia*

120. *detail*

120. *Giovanni Battista Tiepolo.* Sacrifice of Iphigenia. *Architectural Decoration by G. Mengozzi-Colonna, 1757. Vicenza, Villa Valmarana*

of the Venerable Fathers of Seville. It was also used in the Cathedral of Malaga, where complex illusionistic "frames" surround two large altar paintings and seemingly cast shadows on the wall. the painted facade of the church of Santa Cruz la Real in Granada is another instance of Spanish illusionism of that period. Yet, in all of these, in spite of the familiar subject matter (cupola, balustrade, feigned windows opening on a pale ice-blue sky, looped baldachins, and graceful urns), the intricate decoration evokes nothing so much as the Moorish carvings of the Alcazar and the Alhambra, with their stalactiform pendentives and crystalline tracery in the same silvery color scheme.

Another characteristic instance of national adaptation is met with in Portugal, where architectural illusionism was carried out in a most unlikely medium, one which can be considered the Portuguese equivalent of Italian mosaics: the renowned painted ceramic tiles called *azulejos,* in which blue tones predominate. Striking effects were created in this camaïeu color scheme as, for example, in the simulated statues of two halberdiers on a stair landing in the restored seventeenth-century Palazzo Azurara in Lisbon (pl. 121).

121. *Decoration of a Staircase Landing in the Palazzo Azurara, Lisbon, 17th century (executed with* azulejos*)*

122. *French School, early 17th century. Decorative Panel at the Château de Beauregard (Blésois)*

There was obviously no intention to feign live figures; instead, the impression desired (and successfully achieved) is of statues placed well in front of the ornately "carved" balustrade. In actuality, all is only tiled wainscotting on one flat plane. The plumed helmets of the men-at-arms, as well as the peaks of their weapons, have been carefully outlined and stand out with convincing plasticity against the plain white wall above the tall parapet. The artist appears only to have overlooked the inclusion of shadows, but the peculiar coolness of the color scheme and evenness of lighting mitigates this omission; one is hardly aware of the oversight when first viewing the scene. And it is a tribute to the illusionistic effect that one should spontaneously think of it as such.

In France, the southernmost of Northern lands, a middle course was also adopted to meet the special requirements of French taste and French tradition. The rule seems to have been that decoration might be as splendid as possible, yet it had to remain decoration and never overstep these assigned limits. The result is that the ornamentation is frequently compartmented in recessed or flat panels, and with subject matter consisting of minor motives—flowers, in vases or garlands, fruits, heraldic devices, and small landscapes or miniature scenes, such as those found at the Castles of Cadillac and of Tournoël, dating from the end of the sixteenth century.[8] The most interesting early example of illusionistic mural decoration in France is the remarkable series of panels at the Château de Beauregard, in the Blésois, which has been assigned to the first quarter of the seventeenth century (pl. 122). In both style and subject matter, however, the panels hark back to the Renaissance—a dating that was once seriously considered—and are surprisingly reminiscent of the intarsia work of that period. The approach is cool, graphic, one might almost say abstract; above all, it is fragmentary, an attitude necessarily inimical to the unbroken, all-enveloping flow of architectural illusionism which tends to abolish barriers, or at least enlarge space, while compartmented decoration (like some Pompeian works in this respect) on the contrary, appears to raise additional limitations. Even when a decorative scheme was planned as a single entity, this characteristic remains. The grisaille decoration of the Grande Galerie at the Château de Tanlay, circa 1650, consists of a juxtaposition of feigned sculptural elements, such as statues in niches, medallions in relief within recessed panels, etc., which are totally independent and bound together in an harmonious whole solely by the monochrome color scheme. This is even more evident in the decoration of the chamber of the Maréchale de la Meil-

123. *Simon Vouet (attrib.). Decoration in the Chambre de la Maréchale de la Meilleraye (the so-called Cabinet de Sully), 1637. Paris, Bibliothèque de l'Arsenal*

134

124. *Simon Vouet (attrib,) Decoration in the Chambre du Maréchale de la Meilleraye (the so-called Cabinet de Scully), 1637. Paris, Bibliothèque de l'Arsenal*

leraye—the so-called Cabinet de Sully (pls. 123–24)—where the tridimensional effect is brought about only by the compartmentalization and illusionism, if it can be said to be present at all, is reduced to the barest minimum.

There were of course exceptions. Simon Vouet and Charles Lebrun are known to have carried out some major imaginative ensembles, unfortunately lost: Vouet at the Château de Richelieu (demolished) and Lebrun in the famous "Escalier des Ambassadeurs" (1652; destroyed). But on the whole, what was desired apparently was not the evocation of an imaginary world troublingly close to the real one, but merely some handsome settings, decently unobstrusive, for royal pomp or private pursuits. Grisaille themes were the great favorites, often combined with camaïeus of bronze, marble, and semisprecious lapidary substances such as lapis lazuli, coral, malachite and the like; mother-of-pearl incrustations and gold chasing were also frequently included in illusionistic ornamentation. Many excellent painters specialized in this field, notably Louis Testelin and Nicholas Loyr.[9] Monumentality was not excluded: the main hall at the manor of Charentonneau on the Marne River was reputedly decorated with oversized statues of Greek deities interspersed with "tolerably good" landscapes.[10] In every instance, however, one senses that the real thing would have been preferred. The truest note was struck in a naive but perceptive definition of the merits of illusionism (and/or trompe l'oeil) by Joseph Pernéty in 1757:

135

125. *Antonio Verrio.* The Heaven Room, *before 1696. Northents, Burghley House*

The pleasure caused by imitation stems from the reproduction
and multiplication of the objects portrayed. We should therefore
look upon the arts of imitation as a heavenly favor, a kind of
consolation which divine wisdom has deemed necessary to human
existence.[11]

Italian artists were not equipped by taste or training to satisfy the Gal-
lic bent toward this "reproduction and multiplication of objects." Not surprisingly, therefore, the many Italian artist-decorators who left their native land
in search of lucrative commissions only passed through France, sojourning instead in the German principalities or the British Isles, where they found far
richer pastures. Antonio Verrio, who first worked in Toulouse, was called to
England by King Charles II. There he worked at Chatsworth and at Burghley
House, the residence of Lord Exeter, where he created the famous "Heaven
Room" (pl. 125). Verrio's grandiose conceptions go beyond the grandest stage
sets. They might be defined as stage sets in reverse, for Verrio does not beck-

126. *Antonio Verrio. Frescoes on the East Wall of the King's Staircase, Hampton Court*

on the viewers into his painted world; instead, he attempts to project his host of oversized mythological beings into the actual world. The effect is not always entirely pleasant; the gigantic Greek colonnade does not enlarge but engulfs the seigneurial drawing room, and the crowded Elysium above appears to press down uncomfortably on the beholders. At Hampton Court, though, Verrio, still working on the same grandiose scale, confined his figures somewhat more within their own space, so that the effect, although still pompous in the extreme, is not quite as overwhelming (pl. 126).[12]

A truly distinguished artist, Sebastiano Ricci, arrived in England in 1718 at the urging of his nephew, Marco Ricci. He was to stay until 1728, and during this time his chief works were a chapel for the Duke of Portland and the ceiling for Chelsea Hospital. Ricci was undoubtedly the most accomplished and graceful among practitioners of illusionism in England. His painterly sophistication and his innate talent for architectural illusionism is evident

137

even in such smaller works as "The Last Supper" (pl. 127). The choice of a native artist, Sir James Thornhill, for the decoration of the cupola of St. Paul rankled the proud Italian, fully conscious of his superior powers, and led to his decision to leave the country.

Thornhill, father-in-law of Hogarth, continued to enjoy uninterrupted royal favor and patronage. In his murals at the Royal Naval College in Greenwich, he expressed his gratitude and patriotic enthusiasm in the panorama entitled "The Golden Age of George I," where Mercury, god of Commerce and Industry, raises a giant curtain over an impressive display of the wealth and power of England (pl. 128). There, too, the actors are restricted to the painted space under the tremendous arch—and as the contemporary figures are garbed in contemporary costume, the scene carries with it a certain plausibility and courtly solemnity and grace. Nevertheless, if the painted curtain appears to have been just raised, we remain aware of the "space curtain," which, we recall, it is the very purpose and ideal of illusionism to do away with. Neither the stately poses at Greenwich nor the gesticulations at Burghley House achieve that desired end.

127. *Sebastiano Ricci (1659–1734).* The Last Supper. *Washington, D.C. National Gallery of Art. Samuel H. Kress Collection*

128. *Sir James Thornhill.* The Golden Age of George I. *Greenwich, Royal Naval College, Upper Hall*

129. *Louis Laguerre the Elder. Decoration in the Saloon at Blenheim Castle, c. 1720 (detail)*

William Kent's decoration of the King's Staircase at Kensington Palace, with the Mantegna-like ceiling, was inspired by Le Brun's "Escalier des Ambassadeurs" and therefore possesses dual interest: on its own merits, and as a reflection of the painter's lost scheme. The style and technique of the famed artistic dictator of the court of the Sun King was brought to England by one of his pupils, Louis Laguerre the Elder, godson of Louis XIV, who had worked with Verrio at St. Bartholomew's, Hampton Court, and Blenheim Palace. At Hampton Court, Laguerre was also entrusted with the restoration of Mantegna's "Triumph of Caesar." At Blenheim, one of the best fragments includes a dignified, bewigged figure above the artist's signature—and may well be his self-portrait (pl. 129).

Louis Laguerre's "Allegory of the Life of the Duchess of Somerset" at Petworth House, Sussex (pl. 130) was ranked the artist's best work by George Vertue, the famed contemporary critic. It is hardly convincing illusionism—none of these mythological *grandes machines* truly was—but the accessory decorative scheme does achieve the essential illusionistic purpose: the double row of columns, with Borrominesque capitals and intricately decorated shafts, and the complex grisaille dado combine to create a sense of weighty tridimensional magnificence. That the actual architectural elements—the baluster and the panelled doors—fall far short of the painted opulence, passes completely unnoticed.

Laguerre's son John (known as "Honest Jack" Laguerre) was also an artist of note. The young man pursued both a literary and a theatrical career.

129a. *John Laguerre (attrib.). Decoration from a House at 44 Grosvenor Square, London. London, Victoria and Albert Museum*

He is best known today for his witty caricatures, his theatrical decors, and engravings on theatrical subjects. John Laguerre also collaborated with Verrio on the ceilings at Windsor. Some recently discovered illusionistic murals found in a London house at 44 Grosvenor Square, have been safely transferred to the Victoria and Albert Museum (pl. 129a)—a happier fate than that accorded to a similar group of illusionistic decorations found at 75 Dean Street in 1919 which were damaged beyond repair while in transit to the Chicago Institute of Arts.

130. *Louis Laguerre the Elder.* Allegory of the Life of the Duchess of Somerset, *c. 1715. Petworth House, Sussex*

141

131. *Donato Bramante. Painted Illusionistic Apse, 1480's. Milan, S. Maria presso S. Satiro*

The theme of both the lost Dean murals and the preserved Grosvenor murals was the familiar formula of a loggia and balcony with onlookers, surrounding a stairwell. It is presumed that in both instances the traditional open cupola formed part of the original composition.[13] To this John Laguerre added yet another tried device, the drawn curtain. All this is properly effective, but beyond the illusionism, his figures have a winning charm and naturalness. It may be that his theatrical propensities stood him in good stead, helping him to avoid stilted and awkward posturing.

Both Laguerres, father and son, made use in their settings of Borrominesque capitals: Louis at Petworth, and Jack in the Grosvenor murals. This was a characteristic practice of the age: but if painters felt free to borrow from architects, architects in turn did not hesitate to reciprocate in kind. As a result, it has been said particularly of Borromini's style that "it is the achievement of one aim of Baroque art: the blending of painting with sculpture, of sculpture with architecture, so that one cannot tell where one leaves off and another begins, and the whole ensemble assumes a unity that could not have been achieved in any other way.[14] But this achievement had only been gradually attained, for the intermingling of the three arts had begun considerably earlier. One recalls Masaccio's indebtedness to Brunelleschi for the architectural background of his epochal "Holy Trinity" (pl. 35) painted in 1427. More than seventy-five years later, Bramante erected the famous feigned apse for the sacristy of Santa Maria presso San Satiro in Milan (pls. 131–33)—a make-believe

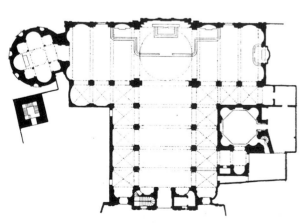

133. *Ground plan of S. Maria presso S. Satiro Showing Actual Depth of Apse*

132. *Donato Bramante. Detail of pl. 131.*

134. *Francesco Borromini. Passageway in the Courtyard of the Library, c. 1635. Rome, Palazzo Spada*

135. *Gianlorenzo Bernini. Scala Regia, 1663–66. Vatican Palace*

decoration of stucco and terracotta, a mere four feet deep, which simulates in perspective a vast arched choir with coffered vaulted ceiling.

Bramante's influence extended through the sixteenth and seventeenth centuries, as can be seen in Palladio's illusionistic perspective for the Teatro Olimpico (pl. 102). Yet the impact of Bramante's work seems slight compared to Borromini's structural illusionism which competed in earnest with pictorial illusionism. In the Palazzo Spada (pl. 134), the imaginative architect created the semblance of a vast portico, apparently stretching out in the far distance toward a monumental statue. In actuality, both the width and the length of the corridor are quite modest, and the focal figure is the size of a small child. Borromini created an artificial perspective by shortening the columns as they receded so as to optically extend the short corridor. (The conception was indeed in keeping with the mood of the mansion, where one important hall, the Sala del Pompeo, is handsomely adorned with illusionistic colonnades on the lower level, and balconies above upheld by caryatids and peopled with men-at-arms and other figures.) Borromini again made use of the same optical devices in the central bay of the Oratorio dei Filippini, next to the Chiesa Nuova, in Rome.

144

Whereas Borromini limited himself to abstract geometrical elements,

Bernini went considerably further. He was the master magician par excellence, and even as he had conjured bright fountains to relieve the aridity of Rome, he made use of every possible artifice as it suited his versatile purpose: "adorning buildings with different coloured marbles, as though he wished to do a kind of painting in sculpture, adding bronze and gold, false curtains in stucco. . . ."[15] He turned to illusionism for the solution of a knotty problem: how to endow with suitable dignity and grandeur a staircase in the Vatican Palace that was intended for the formal reception of ambassadors but which had to be built within a relatively short space. Bernini's solution, like that of Borromini, was to create an artificial perspective by narrowing the barrel vault and entablature and shortening the columns as they receded. The result was the famed "Scala Regia" (pl. 135).

In the same mood, but in a more modest idiom, the choir grille of the chapel of the Benedictine monastery at Einsiedeln, designed by Vincenz Nussbaumer, 1675–1685, echoes the imaginativeness of architectural illusionism: what is actually a flat outline of forged ironwork suggests the receding depth of an arched gateway (pl. 136). Even at this late date, as in the more monumental Roman examples, what has been attempted is to place illusionism in the service of the Baroque ideal.

136. *Vincenz Nussbaumer. Choir Grill, 1675–85. Switzerland, Einsiedeln Monastery*

139. *Hans Holbein the Younger.* Madonna of the Burgomaster Meyer, *1526–1530.*
Darmstadt, Collection of the House of Hesse

5

The Proliferation of the Object

Renaissance to Baroque

In the man-centered world of the great humanists of the Italian Renaissance, pictorial illusionism had been assigned the task of providing the universal man with a setting worthy of him—not one which simulated reality but one which created an idealized pseudoreality. This remained basically true even as late as the second period of the Counter-Reformation, when artists of the Baroque era depicted for the edification of the faithful illusionistic visions of celestial rather than earthly character (pls. 2, 115–16).

In the North, however, matters stood quite differently. In spite of the interchange of influences, it was obvious from the start that Franco-Flemish. artists were strongly inclined to objective observation of things as they are rather than as they should be. Illuminations featuring coins, feathers, shells, or wild flowers apparently tucked into slits of the parchment page as if in the album of a botanist (pls. 70–76) are early instances of objects lovingly studied and depicted solely for their own sakes.

Realism of this kind did not by any means leave Italian artists and their public indifferent—not even during the transition period when the Gothic mood still held its own in the North against the inroads of the new classical revival. Northern European painters may have appeared a bit *retardataire* to their Italian colleagues. But one recalls that when Albrecht Dürer visited Venice much wonder was aroused by the marvellously skillful way in which he painted long wavy tresses. At first, Giovanni Bellini, the German artist's friend and admirer, was convinced that Dürer must have achieved this effect by means of special brushes. These, Bellini supposed, must be "rather spread out and divided, else such regularity of curvature and spacing cannot be attained." Dürer then proved by actual demonstration that the sole equipment needed was standard brushes such as Bellini himself used. The wonder was the extraordinary surety of hand that enabled Dürer to draw each filament individually, with the perfect symmetry and grace Bellini had thought impossible by normal means.[1]

In later days, painterly minutiae of this kind would be scorned by Michelangelo as trivia and encumberments—somewhat unjustly, for the practice was based on much more solid ground than a vain wish to make a show of superlative craftsmanship. What it revealed, though as yet unconsciously, was the primary vocation of the Northern European artist as scientist and naturalist rather than as philosopher or rhetorician. This, of course, in the most generalized sense, for the North certainly was not deprived of these latter. Nevertheless, tendencies were already evident that would eventually bring about a new order of pictorial supremacy. By the second half of the sixteenth century, while the artists of the South were painting the glory and bliss of the Christian paradise, their Northern counterparts were busily engaged in looking through the other end of the spyglass, focusing their attention on the precise and the minute.

To understand how this came about, one must remember that while the Renaissance in Italy was truly a revival of ancient cultural traditions after a long dormant interval, elsewhere the event was a new birth rather than a mere rebirth. Slowly and gropingly at first, and then with sudden brilliance and power, the artists of the North sought their own way. But the interest of the greatest Germanic artists went far beyond realism into undoubted illusionism, as is evidenced in an anecdote told by Christoph Scheurl in 1508:

> And finally what shall I say about Albrecht Dürer, whom everyone recognizes as the foremost painter of this century? When he visited Italy once more, not long ago, he was greeted as the second Apelles by the painters of Venice and Bologna. . . . Not only Zeuxis in ancient times, as reported by Pliny, created such deceptions, luring birds with painted grapes—or Parrhasios in turn tricking Zeuxis with a painted curtain—but our own Albrecht was able to deceive a dog in the same manner. It happened when he painted his self-portrait from a mirror and set it out in the sun to dry. His little dog happened along, and began to fawn upon the portrait, believing it in truth to be his master. I can testify to this, because the marks are still to be seen on the painting. And how many times have maids [in this household] attempted to remove spiderwebs which were in fact not real but painted?[2]

137. *Albrecht Dürer.* Nosegay, *1503. Drawing, Vienna, Albertina*

138. *Albrecht Dürer.* The Christ Child as Salvator Mundi, *1493. Vienna, Albertina*

If the illusionism of the portrait was unintended, there can be no doubt that the cobwebs were indeed meant to deceive: one does not paint cobwebs to beautify one's surroundings! Other instances in Dürer's oeuvre that, if not intentional trompe l'oeil, come very close to it, are his famed watercolor studies of insects, pieces of sod, and perhaps above all the exquisite nosegay of violets apparently cast on a blank page (pl. 137).[3] Another enchanting example is the Child Jesus fondling a golden ball within a rectangular niche that suggests some rough stone texture (pl. 138). Had any of these been carried out in the oil medium, they would undoubtedly have crossed the tenuous borderline separating them from illusionism.

It is significant that, although oil painting may not have been invented in the North, it was certainly improved and developed there. Whether this was cause or effect remains a moot point to this day: did the artists actually seek out a medium flexible enough to carry out the effects they wished to achieve, or did they begin to strive for such effects only after they had chanced upon a medium that made them possible?

149

Geographical considerations also influenced the special character of Northern art. In an age of limited communications, the two worlds of North and South were antipodal in almost every respect—dwellings, habiliments, even nourishment—and therefore were fated to be so culturally and artistically as well. We have seen how decorative illusionism in the South took the form of grandiose schemes, suited to the edifices they adorned and to the temperaments of their creators: the most prestigious commission for an Italian artist was in the monumental medium of fresco painting. Even before Michelangelo's titanic deployment of figures and painted architecture in the Sistine Chapel, Ghirlandaio, one recalls, had expressed the wish to paint the entire periphery of the city walls of Florence. In the North, on the contrary, both the demand from patrons and the preference on the part of artists was for work of a smaller scale. This can be looked upon as a logical continuation of the tradition of illuminated manuscripts for which Franco-Flemish painters had long been even more renowned than the Italians. While the Latin artist was conditioned to a monumental conception of art by extant architectural and sculptural vestiges of classical antiquity, his Northern counterpart lacked this intense visual experience. The result was a "nearsightedness," if one may so call it, that would in time make possible the accomplishments of the twin genres of still life and trompe l'oeil.

Nevertheless, the art of the North was fully able to incorporate architectonic elements, even in the fifteenth century. One thinks, for example, of the columnar hemicycle that serves as a background in Oudwater's "Resurrection of Lazarus"; of Memling's "The Two St. Johns" within their Gothic niches; of Holbein's "Madonna of the Burgomaster Meyer" with its great fluted shells and voluted capitals in the rear, and in front the frankly illusionistic detail of the crumpled carpet (pl. 139). But all this still seems minor in comparison with the sum of architectonic illusionism in Latin lands. It was only when the artists of the North focused their talents on the rendering of the object for its own sake that they began to make their own unique contribution. *

This was not fully achieved until the seventeenth century. Up to that moment, illusionistic accomplishments in the North remained sporadic and still marked with Italianate influence. When Jean Fouquet, for instance, used the traditional device of the curtain in his portrait of King Charles VII of France (pl. 140), was it derived from Italian models or created spontaneously by the French master? We encounter the motif of the *cartellino* in the famed still life / trompe l'oeil by Jacopo de' Barbari (it is claimed as the modern prototype for both genres) depicting a dead partridge with a mailed

150

*See p. 146.

140. *Jean Fouquet,* King Charles VII of France, *c. 1445. Paris, Musée du Louvre*

141. *Hans Holbein the Younger.*
The French Ambassadors, *1533.*
London, The National Gallery

glove and arbalest shaft which probably represents a combined allegory of
the hunt and of war (pl. 1). The German painter Altdorfer produced an interesting variation on the theme of the Venetian *cartellino* in his "Battle of
Issus" (pl. 94). There the modest slip of paper or crumpled card has been
transformed into a monumental tablet suspended above a vast panorama.

There is hardly one of Holbein's great portraits that does not include
as mere accessories the stuff of a half dozen superlative trompe l'oeil subjects.
This is especially true of the double portrait of "The French Ambassadors"
(pl. 141) representing no less than three tiered trompe l'oeil compositions at
the center of the painting. The first is set on the upper shelf of the sideboard

152

142. *Detail of pl. 141*

covered by an oriental carpet with a projecting fold, and consists of a globe and various scientific instruments; below this, the bottom shelf displays musical instruments and books (pl. 142); and lastly, on the floor in the foreground is an oddly elongated object which is actually a distorted skull, to be restored to normal perspective by means of prisms or mirrors on the facing wall. The first group clearly symbolizes worldly knowledge; the second, the fine arts; and the third, religion, as it is a subtle *memento mori* confronting two great personages of this world (one of them a churchman), perhaps placed there in this puzzling guise at their own suggestion. The skull is in fact a display of anamorphosis rather than an actual trompe l'oeil, and indicates the interest taken by the elite of the age in the subject of optics. The painting is illusionism of the highest order, and thus it may come to be labelled some day, when the attempt is made to place it in the most effective setting and perspective.

By the time of Holbein—that is, the mid-sixteenth century—the repertory of illusionism had already been established. There is hardly a subject encountered in later art whose prototype cannot be found prior to 1600. From this latter date on, the crucial difference will be the shift of emphasis: minimization, and finally, complete elimination of the human figure and proliferation of the object. This process has been described as an "advance" that turned into an incontrollable "invasion."[4] Its causes and effects have been best defined by a historian of still life with special reference to illusionism:

> The new vogue of illusionism paralleled a peculiar intellectual curiosity, which centered in strange and rare things. During the late Renaissance the first steps were taken toward the establishment of the modern museum. The first stage was the curio cabinet, in which were included natural history, works of art, and all kinds of odd things that appealed to the collectors—most of whom were princes, merchants, or influential scholars. From the late sixteenth to the early eighteenth century, curio cabinets were established all over Europe. They supplied an answer to a widespread, passionate interest in the unknown, one barely satisfied by the natural sciences, then in their infancy, and one that was largely responsible for the upsurge of astrology, alchemy, and magic-esoteric doctrines that flourished during the Baroque period. All these branches of occultism agreed in attributing a mysterious life to dead matter. Not only was an object considered to be what it represents to the scientific mind, but, under favorable circumstances, it could have supernatural properties like those attributed by primitive man to his fetish. This is the background of the belief in amulets, which during this period was raised to the level of a highly

153

complex, pseudoscientific theory. The so-called "doctrine of signatures" was likewise an essential part of this system of thought—a doctrine according to which a natural object through an accidental similarity to a diseased human organ could become the bearer of a magic healing power. Some of the gallery interiors of the seventeenth century show in the homes of famous collectors, grotesquely shaped stones and shells, stuffed exotic birds and fishes, horns of foreign animals and other rarities, spread out among fine paintings, antique sculptures, and masterpieces of the minor arts.

Among its varied showpieces a well-furnished curio cabinet also contained mechanical instruments, particularly optical instruments, which more often than not were like toys. They included automata and peep shows, or even combinations of both. Peep shows enjoyed a great popularity during the Baroque, for *they epitomized illusionism, which was the common trait of the painters of the period.*[5]

Since trompe l'oeil painting of that period often uses the same subjects as still life proper, it becomes essential to discriminate carefully between the two genres. The criteria for this distinction have already been indicated in the introductory chapter but should be reexamined briefly.

The treatment of the background is probably the most important means of differentiation. If precisionistic technique alone were the only standard, we would have to accept as illusionistic the myriad productions of so many excellent practitioners of still-life painting active during the seventeenth cen-

154

143. *Pieter Claesz.* Still Life, *1627. The Hague, Mauritshuis*

144. *Sebastian Bonnecroy.* Vanitas. *Strassburg, Musée des Beaux-Arts*

144a. *William Claesz. Heda.* Still Life, *1627. Dordrecht, Collection J. M. Rodelee*

tury in France and in the Netherlands, the justly famed *petits maîtres*. This was an age of artistic mass production, albeit of an extraordinarily high quality, geared to satisfy market demand. It was also the time when luminous backgrounds, against which forms stood out fully revealed with joyous candor, gave way to the mystery of shadows in which figures and objects would be guessed at, almost on an emotional basis, instead of being clearly and logically apprehended (pl. 143). This sense of drama is inimical to the spirit of trompe l'oeil, where the background should eschew the "spotlight" effect; on the contrary, it should be as neutral, as unobstrusive, and self-effacing as possible. This can be accomplished either by bringing the fictional background so close that it almost merges with the spectator's own plane—as when a parapet with a *cartellino* occupies the foreground of a painting (pl. 92)—or else, if an effect of greater depth is desired, by limiting the fictional setting with sharply defined borders, as of a niche or a cupboard (pl. 33). The subject depicted should be self-contained, that is, the viewer cannot be asked to assume, or imagine, the existence of elements not actually depicted. Thus, although a tabletop display may be acceptable under certain circumstances, or at least stand on the borderline between the two genres (pl. 158)—and the same applies to the shelf type (pl. 156)—the table *corner* and the shelf *corner* obviously must be rejected (pls. 144, 144a).

155

145. *Hans Memling (1430 / 35–1494).* Chalice of St. John the Evangelist *(reverse of* St. Veronica*). Washington, D. C., National Gallery of Art, Samuel H. Kress Collection*

146. *Hans Memling.* Still Life *(reverse of* Portrait of a Donor*). Lugano, Thyssen-Bornemisza Collection*

In addition to these limitations, objects depicted in a trompe l'oeil painting should be presented with every appearance of stability. This excludes not only actual movement, but even the minor melodrama of uncertain equilibrium (for instance, tumbling piles of books, flowing liquid, ascending smoke, etc.). Any factor at odds with plausibility is a visual dissonance, felt rather than reasoned, that alerts the eye and nullifies even the best efforts toward illusionism. Trompe l'oeil, therefore, is not merely a certain kind of still-life painting; it should in fact "out-still" the stillest of still lifes. Ideally, it should be poised, immovable, with no turbulence and no excess of any kind. In accordance with these severe tenets, the trompe l'oeil artist must renounce all conscious displays of individualism, to the extent that the objects portrayed must *seem* to have been brought together as the result of pure hazard (regardless of whatever symbolical interpretation he may assign to the final result). This artistic abnegation was its own reward, since the practitioners were thus able to avoid overabundance and ostentatiousness.

147. *Flemish School, 16th century.* Books and Washbasin in a Niche.
Rotterdam, Museum Boymans-van Beuningen

The niches and shelves that in medieval and Renaissance paintings held so few objects (though those few, as in the Ghirlandaio portrait [pl. 34] are laden with rare beauty and significance) were to be put to a very different use by Franco-Flemish and Netherlandish illusionists of the next age. Memling still retained a nobly lyrical simplicity: in his "Chalice of St. John the Evangelist" (pl. 145); or in the deep, shadowed rectangular niche with a lily plant on an oriental carpet on the reverse of his "Portrait of a Donor" (pl. 146). But another illusionistic niche, possibly after Dieric Bouts (pl. 147), is already considerably more cluttered, far less serene. This tendency is again

157

148: *Master of the Aix Annunciation.* The Prophet Jeremiah. *Brussels, Musées Royaux des Beaux-Arts*

exemplified in the disarray of books and artifacts in the lunette above the tall niche by the Master of the Aix Annunciation (pl. 148; note also that the figure of the Prophet Jeremiah is standing on an illusionistic pentagonal pedestal, suggesting that the representation is in fact of polychrome statuary rather than a living being—so that the entire work, not merely the architectural setting, is conceived illusionistically).

By the second half of the sixteenth century, an anonymous painter of the Flemish school, having dismissed all religious connotations, presents the telltale medley on some penurious scholar's shelves in a frankly anecdotal vein (pl. 149). A new subtlety would later be brought to this theme by the use of the "cabinet" or "cupboard" shown intriguingly ajar so that the contents, a conglomeration of bibelots and trivia, are only partially revealed. The genre was brought to its height of formal beauty and illusionistic effectiveness by two painters bearing the same family name, though believed unrelated:

159

149. *Flemish School, 16th century.* The Closet. *Amsterdam, Rijksmuseum*

Cornelis Norbertus Gysbrechts of Antwerp and Copenhagen, and Franciscus Gysbrechts of Leyden (pls. 150–51), both active in the latter half of the seventeenth century. Cornelis Gysbrechts is probably the archetypal painter of trompe l'oeil, with an oeuvre of at least half a hundred works (pls. 152–57), in contrast to Franciscus Gysbrechts, whose style is almost identical to that of the older artist, but with only six extant pictures to his credit.[6] Many of Cornelis Gysbrechts' works are to be found in Denmark, where the artist was court painter to two successive monarchs, Frederick II and Christian V. The range of his subject matter is more varied and complex than that of any other practitioner of trompe l'oeil up to that time. He may not have created the vocabulary of trompe l'oeil single-handedly, but he gave it unprecedented amplitude and originality. Gysbrechts was not the first to make use of a wooden background for still-life subjects (pls. 156–57), but because of his intense interest in illusionism, the choice of this particular background may have been prompted by the realization that a wooden background for illusionistic subjects provided substance and solidity without increasing the apparent depth (as was the case with niches and shelves); the shift in focus is thus made all the easier. After Gysbrechts, wood became, and has remained ever since, the special preserve of illusionists.

In the representation of musical instruments, too, Gysbrechts was a popularizer rather than an innovator (pl. 157)—he may have been familiar with intarsia panels or, closer to him, the works of the Italian painter Evaristus Baschenis, or even the trompe l'oeil painted for the organ of the Oude Kerke in Amsterdam by Cornelisz Brize. Similarly, it has been noted that all of Cornelis Gysbrechts' letter racks (e.g., pl. 152) are predated by the famous single example painted by the Fleming Wallerant Vaillant (color pl. 12), provided that the date that appears as such a prominent feature in the Vaillant work is indeed the date of execution (see pp. 178–79). Nevertheless, it was Gysbrechts who brought this genre, and many others, to a pinnacle. He is also justly renowned for his matchless illusionistic simulations of cabinets with doors ajar. But his masterpiece in this field is probably the extraordinary double-sized "jewel cabinet" with the *closed* glass door. This is in fact an actual wooden door, painted on both sides of the panel: on one side, we see the interior of a cabinet through the imaginary glass panes; on the other, we see merely the panes themselves, and the backs of the letters, the quill pen, and the pocket knife that has apparently been stuck into the framing.

Gysbrechts is notable for his unique interpretation of the ancient theme of the Vanitas (pl. 156), an allegorical still life whose objects symbolize the

150. *Franciscus Gysbrechts (active c. 1674).* Cupboard. *Collection I. Tetley-Jones, Esq.*

151. *Franciscus Gysbrechts.* Cupboard. *Brussels, Collection Robert Finck*

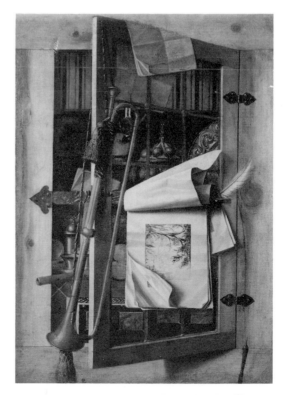

152. *Cornelis Gysbrechts.* Letter Rack. *Ghent, Musée des Beaux-Arts*

ephemeral nature of worldly pleasures and the inevitability of death. Gysbrechts renounced the familiar use of the niche, or rather he did use it, but once removed: the Vanitas attributes are still placed within a niche, but the niche and its contents appear as if painted on a dilapidated canvas partly detached from its stretcher, one frayed corner hanging down. There is a new refinement, an additional "turn of the screw": while we see the three-dimensional objects in an illusionistic setting in depth, we are made aware nevertheless that they are portrayed on the patently flat surface of a canvas. The composition, therefore, is a trompe l'oeil of a trompe l'oeil. The painting of the skull in the niche is surrounded by numerous symbolic props (candlestick,

162   153. *Cornelis Gysbrechts.* Easel. *Copenhagen, Statens Museum for Kunst*

154. *Cornelis Gysbrechts.* Turned-Over Canvas. *Copenhagen, Statens Museum for Kunst*

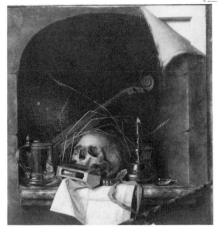

156. *Cornelis Gysbrechts.* Vanitas
Boston, Museum of Fine Arts

157. *Cornelis Gysbrechts.* Vanitas with the Painter's Attributes. *Valenciennes, Musée des Beaux-Arts*

155. *Cornelis Gysbrechts.* Vide Poche. *Brussels, Collection Robert Finck*

shell, horn, hourglass, documents, books, etc.). Our attention is distracted at every step, and we are very far indeed from the stark confrontation of Bartel Bruyn (pl. 69).

In some of Gysbrechts' Vanitas pictures the allegory is even more veiled, the skull being replaced by such objects as a nautilus shell or a violin (pl. 157). In another (Musée de Carcassonne), the composition corresponds basically to

163

that of the other Vanitas, but the only suggestion that remains of worldly transience is the implication furnished by the torn and frayed canvas.[7] The characteristics of Gysbrechts' Vanitas theme were echoed by H. Le Motte, a contemporary Huguenot painter who had taken refuge in Holland (pl. 158).

It has also been suggested that the reason for painting the Vanitas against a wooden background was to enable the pictures to blend into an actual background of the same material, such as a wall, closet, door, or the recess of a cabinet.[8] Such a location would of course result in the optimum illusionistic effect. This theory is strengthened by the fact that Gysbrechts eventually took the ultimate step in that direction, dispensing entirely with the painted background and depicting only the imaginary objects. Thus, he appears to have been the innovator, or at least one of the earliest practitioners of the *chantourné* (cutout or silhouetted) trompe l'oeil. His achievements here range all the way from the great "easel" grouping (pl. 153) to the starkly simple "Turned-Over Canvas" (pl. 154), oddly prophetic of indigenous American interpretations of the same theme over two hundred years later. The most whimsical example of Gysbrechts' *chantourné* style may well be the multitiered, or pocketed, catchall (*vide poche*; pl. 155). This even includes a mirror, for greater convincingness—a forgivable lapse of orthodoxy in an artist who more than any other has demonstrated his eminent powers to achieve superlative illusionism without the aid of such questionable crutches.

Naive popular interpretations of the *chantourné* trompe l'oeil are found under the form of life-sized figures, human and animal, supported by means of braces and used as room decorations. This appears to have been largely a Dutch specialty, although a great number of these illusionistic "dolls" were brought to England during the reign of George I. A noted amateur of the decorative arts of the seventeenth century, the late Charles de Beistegui, believed that the cutout figures had originally been intended as fire screens. Accordingly, he placed a life-sized *poupée* at the corner of an enormous fireplace in the main hall of his château at Groussay, which had been restored and entirely furnished in the seventeenth-century style of Louis XIII (pl. 159).

Whether or not the *chantourné* figures served exactly this purpose, the conceit continued well into the eighteenth century. A specimen of that later age holds special Anglo-American interest: the figure of a Grenadier, shown in pl. 309, is reputed to have been painted by the talented and ill-fated young Major André, of Revolutionary War fame. By an interesting coincidence, *chantourné* trompe l'oeil was revived by American photorealists (see p. 359 and pl. 439.

164

In seventeenth-century Europe nothing surpassed the popularity of the realistic alimentary displays, for which the Dutch School in particular is re-

158: *H. Le Motte.* Vanitas.
Dijon, Musée des Beaux-Arts

159. *Illusionistic* Chantourné *Fire Screen.* *Château de Groussay*

160. *Alvise Vivarini (c. 1446–c. 1503).* Madonna and Child. *Venice, Chiesa del Redentore*

nowned. This was an age when those who had sufficient means enjoyed to the full not only the satisfactions of appetite, but also liked nothing better than to be reminded pictorially of those pleasures. Although ideally suited for still life, food displays were not always appropriate for trompe l'oeil. More substantial viands should logically be displayed on the traditional "groaning board," not as isolated elements. Desserts, on the contrary, combine brilliance of coloring and delicacy of form with a suggestion of permanency: nuts, candies, cakes, and other dainties are entirely plausible when shown in shelves or cabinets, the formal receptacles of trompe l'oeil. In addition to practical considerations of this order, fruit in particular belonged to the repertory of illusionism by right of ancient tradition. Not only did this subject hark back to classical antiquity (pls. 25–26), it also played an important role in Christian painting, where various fruits were frequently set on a wooden or stone shelf in front of the Madonna and Child, sometimes as symbols of the Passion (pl. 160). In time, other undeniably illusionistic elements were added: the rim of a plate or cup jutting over a ledge, or the handle of a knife apparently protruding into the viewer's own plane, as in the painting by Joos van Cleve (pl. 161).

In Caravaggio's "Basket of Fruit" (pl. 162) all religious connotations have been left behind, and the illusionistic purpose is foremost. The basket

161. *Joos van Cleve.* Madonna and Child, *c. 1525. Private Collection*

162. *Caravaggio.* Basket of Fruit, *c. 1595–1600. Milan, Pinacoteca Ambrosiana*

is outlined against a plain, light ground, and appears to stand high on a shelf of which we see only the thin edge. The intense chiaroscuro effects normally associated with Caravaggio are as yet undeveloped in this early work—to the benefit of trompe l'oeil.

Conversely, in the *bodegones* of the great masters in seventeenth-century Spain, it is precisely the exaggeration of chiaroscuro—a harsh, almost cruel, juxtaposition of highlights and shadows, endowing these works with an unexpected feeling of serene aloofness—that differentiates them irrevocably from true still life. The magnificently delineated forms, chosen in accordance with a mysterious unearthly logic in the masterpiece by Juan Sanchez Cotan (pl. 163), or those by Francisco de Zurburán (pl. 164), at once fail and transcend the purpose of still life. In spite of their plasticity, they are somehow dematerialized, mere shells and appearances for the burning mystic spirit that inhabits them. This is not yet surrealism, but one might call it perhaps "supernaturalism," or even "sublimated still life."[9]

This was after all the age of the Counter-Reformation and of profound mysticism, a tremendous and troublous age of transition and soul-searching. Juan Sanchez Cotan, a Carthusian friar and author of a treatise on perspective and another on music, also painted the hypnotic, nightmarish series of frescoes in the Charterhouse of Granada, depicting the persecution of members of the order by Henry VIII of England, and embodying a number of optical delusions. (In the refectory of this same Charterhouse, the artist rendered his masterpiece, the life-sized illusionistic "Christ Crucified.") Floris van Schooten

163. *Juan Sanchez Cotan (1561–1637).* Quince, Cabbage, Melon and Cucumber. *Collection of the Fine Arts Society of San Diego, Gift of Anne R. and Amy Putnam*

164. *Francisco de Zurburán.* Still Life, *c. 1633. St. Louis, City Art Museum*

165. *Floris van Schooten.* The Dessert Table, *1617. Gudbammar Hova, Sweden, Collection Mme. Dagmar Carlsson*

conceived his "The Dessert Table" (pl. 165) in the same spirit, for the exquisite fruits set on an altarlike table appear almost as sacrificial offerings we are asked to renounce rather than to enjoy. The same kind of metaphysical mood, though less poignant—a gentle implacability truly Jansenist in spirit— is encountered in the works of Lubin Baugin and Sebastian Stosskopf. Both

169

166. *Lubin Baugin (1610–1663).* Flask with Wine Glass and Wafers. *Paris, Musée de Louvre*

the "Flask with Wine Glass and Wafers" (pl. 166) and the "Basket of Glasses and Pâté" (pl. 11) share the same characteristics—the lucidity and inexorability of Euclidian theorems—yet seem to resound with crystalline echoes of passionate sonority. A similar reticence and discretion of statement also mark the works of the other French artists of that period who comprise the group known as "les peintres de la réalité" (Louise Moillon [pl. 167], Jacques Linard [pl. 168], Francois Garnier, René Nourrisson, etc.). Yet while all these artists could prove subtle allegorists as well (the subject of Linard's painting is "The Five Senses"), they never quite take the plunge into darker waters. Stosskopf is perhaps the sole exception. Some of his paintings of drinking glasses are less serene than the example shown here (pl. 11), for they depict broken, glittering fragments, so trenchant and threatening as to set the teeth on edge. Admittedly, although it may be excused by the purported symbolism (purity and fragility), there is a touch of morbidity there, and a hallmark of the age it truly is, though seldom so poetically expressed.

170

167. *Louise Moillon (1609–1696).* Still Life. *Grenoble, Musée de Peinture*

Earlier ages, whatever else their differences, had united in the worship of beauty, but this ideal has now been replaced by an irresistible interest in every evidence of vetusty and decrepitude. It is no more the flawless flower of fruit that charms, but that which has felt the first touch of decay, the gnawing of the worm. This melancholy mood is not lacking even in Caravaggio's otherwise limpidly lyrical "Basket of Fruit," where the leaves show spots

171

168. *Jacques Linard.* The Five Senses. *Strassburg, Musée des Beaux-Arts*

169. *Philippe de Champaigne.* Portrait of Omer Talon, *1649. Washington, D. C., National Gallery of Art, Samuel H. Kress Collection*

of rust. It is clearly asserted in Philippe de Champaigne's formal portrait of "Omer Talon" (pl. 169). The red robe of the powerful minister trails over but does not hide the ravages of time—the holes and cracks in the great stone slabs. There can be no doubt that the Franco-Flemish painter was aware of the weight of his slightest pictorial statement, for he was a deeply thoughtful artist and his association in particular with Port-Royal, the Jansenist stronghold in France, had marked him ineradicably. And even though as a moralist he would certainly have been repelled by the idea of deception, Champaigne was nevertheless influenced by the prevalent current of illusionism: his portrait of Arnauld d'Andilly presents the subject within a windowlike stone embrasure, his hand and billowed sleeve projecting forth on the narrow ledge (pl. 170).

170. *Philippe de Champaigne (1602–1674).* Portrait of Arnauld d'Andilly. *Paris, Musée du Louvre*

An unusually interesting Vanitas was painted by an artist of Champaigne's circle after a lost work by Philippe de Champaigne himself (pl. 171). A grinning skull at the center of a small table is outlined against an unrelievedly dark background and flanked by a well-rendered hourglass and a small round glass vase with a single tulip. The tulip symbolizes fleeting worldly vanity: tulipomania was then sweeping Europe, and vanity and waste were eminently combined in the extravagant prices paid for a single bulb—as much as the value of a rich estate. The hourglass refers to the passage of time and the skull to mortality—a *memento mori*. The top of the skull and all ridges have been polished to a high luster; as a result, it has assumed a sort of gruesome brightness and gaiety. There is a sense of drama there, lucid and unmuddled. Regarding technique, the still life shows strong Caravaggesque influence and demonstrates the effectiveness of a dark ground against which forms stand out with lapidary precision and vigor. Not infrequently, a painting that hovers between still life and trompe l'oeil may be justifiably placed in the second category precisely because such a background has been used.

The origin of this illusionistic Vanitas against a dark ground goes back to the fifteenth century, to the reverse of Roger van der Weyden's Braque Triptych, which is believed to be the earliest of all easel paintings on this theme (pl. 172). On a more mundane plane, however, game scenes began to furnish a counterweight to mystical allegories. The great animalier, Melchior de Hondecoeter, took up the theme initiated by Jacopo de' Barbari (pl. 1)

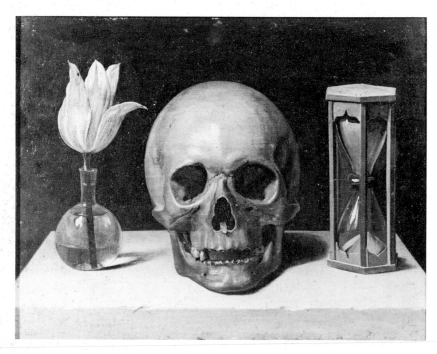

171. *French School, 17th century.* Vanitas. *Le Mans, Musée des Beaux-Arts*

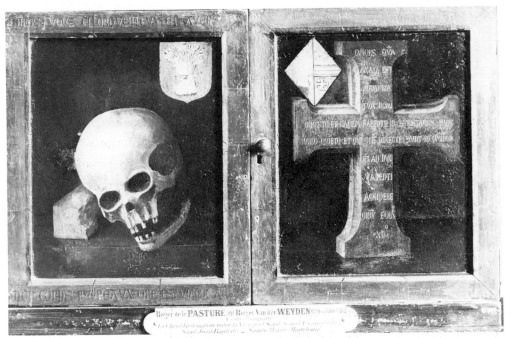

172. *Roger van der Weyden.* Skull and Cross. *Exterior Wings of the Braque Triptych, c. 1452. Paris, Musée du Louvre*

but adapted it to his own flamboyant temperament: he chose to depict a gorgeously ruffled cock against a boldly grained wooden panel (pl. 173). It proved to be the first of an endless series of variations on the theme for the next two centuries. But few knew how to relieve the monotony of the theme and add a welcome touch of fantasy as did Jost Sustermans in his study of two wild fowls (pl. 174), where the arabesque of the hooks provides an element of graceful design that is too often missing in the innumerable "hunting pieces" spawned by more pedestrian practitioners.

173. *Melchior de Hondecoeter (1636–1695).* The Dead Cock. *Brussels, Musées Royaux des Beaux-Arts*

174. *Jost Sustermans (1597–1681).* Wild Duck. *Florence, Palazzo Davanzati*

At the same time, the wood-grained background began to serve another purpose: as setting for the *quod libet* ("what you will") or "letter-rack" subjects. In the first instance, the artist disposed against this background a medley of objects of any and all descriptions, purely in accordance with his own fancy and aesthetic interests. Since trompe l'oeil requires that they be shown in actual size, these objects necessarily had to be small and consisted primarily of bibelots and slight artifacts. Description would be superfluous, and the illustrations may be left to speak for themselves (pls. 175–76). The letter rack in the strictest sense was precisely what the name indicates and depicted assorted oddments of manuscript and printed paper, slipped behind narrow bands of ribbon, on a flat background described in contemporary inventories as "wooden" or "of deal planks well planed" (pls. 153, 177–78). The two types frequently overlap: the *quod libet* is seldom devoid of paper trivia of some kind, and the letter rack, in turn, generally includes a few items logically associated with correspondence (quill, pen knife, sealing wax, scissors, ink horn, sandbox, a pair of spectacles) as well as unrelated items (a comb, some coins, and other small artifacts, the function of which sometimes eludes us). The essential requirement was that these should be of sufficiently low relief to avoid a drastic change of focus. The artist differenciated clearly between the stringent laws of trompe l'oeil and the more lenient ones ruling still life.

Both *quod libet* and letter-rack subjects were natural developments of the older Vanitas or *memento mori*. At first, as we have seen, the meaning of the allegory was tempered by the removal of the skull, and the admonition thereby became merely a warning against abuse of the pleasures of this world, or against intellectual pride in human achievement. The domed cranium, which had been the main element of the composition, was replaced by a globe, a lute, or the like, fair equivalents in terms of form which also carried symbolic meaning. But without the austere reminder of the brevity of human life, these auxiliary elements carried little weight. It was easy to disregard the allegory entirely and to accept the objects at face value; eventually, to replace them altogether with others, as fancy dictated. Choices that now appear to us haphazard or cryptic were no doubt perfectly clear to contemporaries. The grouping of particular objects, carefully and meaningfully chosen to reflect facets of a personality (whether the artist's own or that of his sitter), or to suggest, to symbolize, certain beliefs and attitudes, turns *quod libet* or letter-rack subjects into literal portraits, professions of faith, or political protests. Although we miss many of the allusions, we can be certain that nothing was left to chance in those pictorial acrostics.

The examples illustrated here express widely different personalities. In Edward Collier's *quod libet,* the well-thumbed copy of *Apollo Anglicanus*

175. *Edwart Collier.* Quod Libet, *1695.*
Collection Ronald A. Lee, Esq.

176. *Edward Collier.* Quod Libet, *1701. London, Victoria and*
Albert Museum

177. *Cornelisz Brize (1622–c. 1670).* Documents.
Collection John Hay Whitney

("The English Apollo") reveals the tastes and interests of its owner (pl. 175). Cornelis Gysbrechts (pl. 156) retains one essential feature of the Vanitas: the hourglass. The curtain is impressive illusionistically, effective compositionally, and intriguing psychologically. Its function is secrecy: the correspondence, presumably of importance, can be withdrawn from prying eyes. The ribbands are unfrayed and tacked at regular intervals, forming the neatest possible grid, its arrangement the work of an efficient secretary.

The date 1658 prominently featured in Wallerant Vaillant's letter rack: (pl. 178) may not refer to the date of execution of the painting but rather to

178. *Wallerant Vaillant.* Letter Rack. *Berlin, Staatliche Museen*

179. *Flemish School, 17th century.* Holy Family. *Collection Mr. & Mrs. Oscar Salzer*

178

that year in Vaillant's life, with the objects furnishing a kind of allegorical visualization of it. The letter at the center is addressed to the artist himself, "peintre au château"—and it is known that Vaillant remained in France from 1652 to 1662—but the envelope in the upper right corner is inscribed "A Monsieur mon frère, Monsieur le Prince Jean Maurice de Nassau. . . ." The formula "Monsieur mon frère" would have been used only by a royal personage. It is certainly not accidental that this missive should occupy the place of honor, at upper right. It may be that the letters displayed have been gathered because they played an important role in the painter's life, involving perhaps commissions, recommendations, and the like. The two letters turned over and placed at left—the side of the heart—may have been of an intimate nature.

A third use of the illusionistic wooden background in the late seventeenth century stands midway between the *quod libet* and the letter rack. This is the trompe l'oeil representation of a painting or an engraving, shown as if attached to the grained board by pins or wax seals. A fine and robust example is "The Holy Family" by an anonymous Flemish artist (pl. 179). Inevitably, this brings to mind the Ferrarese Madonna we have already encountered (pl. 42a), but in the later work the canvas has been removed from the stretcher. The representation of the Holy Family is not particularly striking by itself, yet it acquires unexpected charm from the illusionistic presentation. Similarly, in a trompe l'oeil by Edwart Collier of an engraved portrait of Erasmus, the buff tones of the wide wooden border around the engraving and the bright notes of the red wax seals bring the glamour of color to an originally monochrome creation (pl. 180). In a more complex grouping by Jan

180. *Edwart Collier.* Portrait of Erasmus, *1693. Pasadena, Collection Dr. James H. Robertson*

179

Mienze Molenaer, no less than six miniature paintings are set off against a tawny ground (pl. 181).

In contrast to the above, which are all unquestionably trompe l'oeil of the strictest discipline, David Tenier's illusionistic rendering of his own engraving after his painting "The Smoker' (pl. 182) must be disqualified. The technique is impressionistic rather than precisionistic, so that brushstrokes are visible. Further, the maulstick crosses the picture diagonally but is not seen in its entirety. Both ends are outside the picture, and moreover, only a small part of a second illustration is seen in the lower right corner. Either of these elements is sufficient to cancel the illusion, even though the hybrid creation includes several devices which are patently trompe l'oeil: the nail with its shadow, the pin, the sheet of paper with turned-over corner, and most of all, the fly.

The same infractions disbar as trompe l'oeil the beautiful "inorganic" still life, "The Painter's Studio," by the Spanish painter Marcos Correa (pl. 183). Other examples by this same artist, however, are unimpeachably illu-

181. *Jan Mienze Molenaer (aft. 1605–1668)*. Oil, Paintings, *London, Courtesy of the Brian Koetser Gallery*

182. *David Teniers the Younger (1610–1690).* The Smoker. *Paris, Private Collection*

183. *Marcos Correa.* The Painter's Studio. *Private Collection*

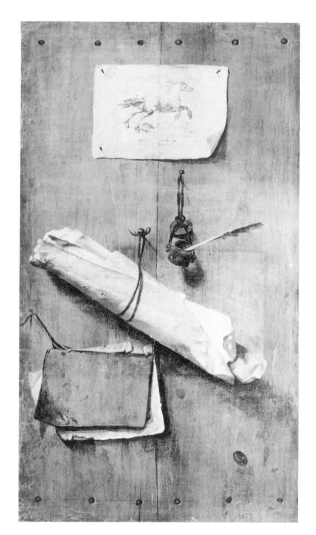

184. *Marcos Correa.* Trompe l'Oeil. *New York, Courtesy of the Hispanic Society of America*

185. *Marcos Correa.* Trompe l'Oeil. *New York, Courtesy of the Hispanic Society of America*

sionistic (pls. 184—85). Correa's two paintings share one characteristic: they chronicle the personal aspect of an artist's life by depicting the casual objects of his studio. The letter-rack type is of its very nature more literary—or scholarly and historical. Nevertheless, both functions could also be combined: a painting by another Spanish artist, Juanfranco Morales, betrays by its choice of subject its creator's preoccupation with spiritual life, poetry, and possibly astrology (pl. 186). The austere elegance of this grouping contrasts with the miscellany which an artist of the Flemish School chose to depict (pl. 187). Compositionally, however, the two works are closely related to each other. They have in common a basic feature, the shelf at the bottom, with both ends abruptly cut off, and both therefore should be assigned to still life rather than trompe l'oeil. Yet one is strongly tempted to make an exception in favor of Morales on two counts: the darker background neutralizes the slight incongruity of the cut-off shelf—the only trespass in this case, which is admirably "self-contained" in all other respects, according to the strictest canons of trompe l'oeil (see p. 19). If it does qualify, it is by the narrowest possible margin, although one should recall that works of this kind were created as integral parts of a decorative scheme and with a special perspective: above doors, windows, as inserts in panelled wainscotting.

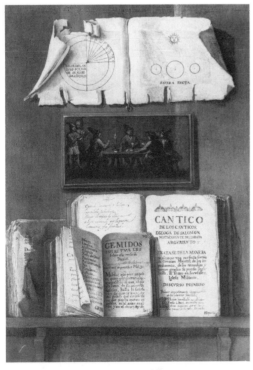

186. *Juanfranco Morales.* Books on a Shelf. *Edinburgh, National Gallery of Scotland, Collection Major David Gordon*

187. *Flemish School, 17th century.* Still Life with Palette. *Collection Mrs. Charlotte Frank*

183

The "Goldfinch" by Carel Fabritius (a pupil of Rembrandt) was originally painted on the door of a cupboard, perhaps as a memorial to a particular
household songster (pl. 188). The famous illusionistic "Violin" (pl. 189) at
Chatsworth, seat of the Dukes of Devonshire, was also painted on the actual
door, which, a few years ago, was unhinged and brought to America for a
visit.[9a] Many illusionistic paintings of this kind, however, have not remained in
their original locations but have been raised for various reasons—such as the
destruction of old buildings—to the supposedly higher dignity of easel works.
The most unfortunate result is that they are no longer seen in the setting for
which they were painted. (This problem will be discussed again with regard
to the *devants de cheminée* of the eighteenth century; see p. 222).

From the start, intarsias had often been replaced in Northern lands by
their pictorial equivalents. Ingvar Bergstrom has pointed out the unmistakable
relationship between the designs of Gubbio and Urbino (pls. 50–51) and

188. *Carel Fabritius.* The Goldfinch, *1654. The Hague, Marits-
huis*

184

185

189. *J. van der Vaart (1647–1721), attrib.* Painted Violin. *Chatsworth, The Devonshire Collection, Courtesy of the Trustees of the Chatsworth Settlement*

190. *Gerard Dou (1613–1675)*. Still Life with Hourglass. *Hartford, Courtesy of the Wadsworth Atheneum*

191. *Gerard Dou.* Still Life, *c. 1660. Dresden, Gemäldegalerie Alte Meister*

Gerard Dou's small illusionistic gem, "Still Life with Hourglass" (pl. 190).[10] One might add to this perceptive comment that a niche, if not actually indicated, is at least implied here along the right edge. Because of his pronounced leaning towards illusionism, Gerard Dou was particularly fond of both the niche and the curtain devices and, on occasion, combined them effectively. In his "Still Life" in Dresden (pl. 191)—undoubtedly a Vanitas with candle, Nuremberg egg watch, and (double symbolism) the large hourglass in the background—the curtain is drawn to the right of the great stone niche, where the painter's signature appears as if carved in the masonry. In the "Self-Portrait" (pl. 192), a whimsical trompe l'oeil of a trompe l'oeil, a curtain is similarly drawn to the right to reveal the trompe l'oeil of the artist's self-portrait, as if set within a niche and less than life-sized. One must remember that curtains were actually hung in front of valued pictures in meticulous Dutch households to protect them from dust and to minimize the fading of pigments. This tradition may have been very ancient: not only does one recall the curtain of Parrhasios, but some of the curtains depicted in Italian Renaissance art—such as that found in Raphael's "Sistine Madonna"—may reflect utilitarian originals and can be seen as illusionistic props.

186

192. *Gerard Dou.* Self-Portrait, *c. 1645. Amsterdam, Rijksmuseum*

Other Dutch artists, such as Nicolaas Maes and G. Houckgeest, made use of the curtain device even more ambiguously. In their works, unlike the Dou self-portrait, one is uncertain whether the trompe l'oeil is of a painting with its protective curtain drawn back to allow it to be viewed, or whether the purpose of the drapery is to separate our space from another space. This second, purely pictorial space, existing only in the painter's imagination, can be the next room (as in Maes' "Interior with Listening Servant," Christie's,

London) or even, as in Houckgeest's "Interior of the Old Church at Delft" (pl. 193), a plunging vista into a large building which the viewer apparently surveys from a gallery.

In Dou's "Self-Portrait," the shadow cast by the head, the jutting book, and the strongly plastic *cartellino* are additional trompe l'oeil features; the artist was never sparing in this respect, as evidenced in another famous work, the delightful genre scene at Buckingham Palace of "Woman Selling Grapes" (pl. 194). The subject matter there is considerably more complex than the title implies. The woman is selling grapes out of a niched stall, with a customer and three more figures in the background, while the wealth of details adds up to a veritable primer of the repertory of trompe l'oeil. Dou's "Old Woman at a Window" (pl. 195), on the contrary, consists only of this single figure and three accessories: a blooming plant in a large clay pot, a great varnished jug, and a bird cage at the upper right. What is most notable, however, in relation to both these illusionist works, is that while they are by no means small, they are not quite monumental enough to achieve the desired effect. The purpose in both these instances was the representation of actual living figures, and nothing stood in the way of this realization, but the reduced scale. While it seems permissible to err somewhat on the side of magnifica-

193. *G. Houckgeest (1580/90–1644).* Interior of the Oude Kerk at Delft. *Amsterdam, Rijksmuseum*

188

194. *Gerard Dou.* Woman Selling Grapes, *1672. London, Buckingham Palace*

195. *Gerard Dou.* Old Woman at a Window, *c. 1660–65. Vienna, Kunsthistorisches Museum*

189

tion in illusionistic depiction—a slight increase of scale not only is accepted without protest by the eye, but at times seems to be helpful to the deception—the contrary is by no means true. Even minimal reduction proves oddly disturbing, and the adverse effect is out of all proportion to the optical deviation. The problem does not arise, however, with Dou's "Self-Portrait" where he has depicted not himself, but his own painting of himself, which could plausibly be any size at all.

Samuel van Hoogstraten rendered Dutch interiors in a hauntingly surrealistic manner which bordered on illusionism, as exemplified in his "View Down a Corridor" (pl. 196). He also demonstrated his keen interest in illu-

190

196. *Samuel van Hoogstraten (1627–78).* View down a Corridor. *Dyrham Park, A Property of the National Trust*

197. *Samuel van Hoogstraten. Interior of a Peep Show, c. 1660. London, The National Gallery*

sionism even more conclusively by adapting similar themes to what may perhaps now seem a lowly use: the so-called peep shows (pl. 197), which in his case were actually displays of anamorphosis related to the Holbein skull (pl. 141). The broom in a corner, suggestive of Veronese, and the melancholy long-eared hound are recurrent props in these compositions, though not al-

197a. *Alessandro Magnasco (1667–1749).* Peep Show in an Inn. *Formerly New York, Duveen Brothers, Inc.*

191

198 *Samuel van Hoogstraten.* Man at a Window; *1653. Vienna, Kunsthistorisches Museum*

ways included. But Hoogstraten's chief illusionistic feat is without doubt the famous head of a man looking out of an oddly mullioned window within a massive stone frame (pl. 198). This forceful and mysterious rendering perhaps comes as close to absolute literal deception as is possible on the insurmountably difficult theme of the human semblance.

Rembrandt is known to have painted a life-sized portrait of his maid specifically for the purpose of placing it in an open window "and in this manner deceiving all passersby."[11] Now lost, the painting can be considered a secular pendant to the fifteenth-century "Monk at a Window" by Borgognone (pl. 103). The undoubted trompe l'oeil by the great Dutch master was seen, admired, described, and finally acquired in the course of a visit to Holland by Roger de Piles, indeed the man to appreciate it. De Piles, a painter and engraver in his own right, as well as a commentator and teacher of art, expressed the universal opinion of his contemporaries when he said that "the ultimate goal of painting is not so much to beguile the mind as to deceive the eye." Of the Rembrandt trompe l'oeil, now his cherished possession, de Piles only commented, to our everlasting regret, that it was "most beautifully and strongly painted."[12]

One cannot forget that Rembrandt and his pupils "sculpted" with impasto—not so much to express the texture, as the very "soul" of metal (*vide* the so-called portrait of Rembrandt's elder brother in a golden helmet and breastplate, pl. 199). On a less exalted level, attempts were made to achieve not merely pictorial but literal illusionism by means of practices which would

199. *Rembrandt School. "Portrait of Rembrandt's Brother." Berlin, Staatliche Museen*

193

200. *Bartolommeo Bettera (1634–1700)*. Still Life with Musical Instruments. *San Francisco, California Palace of the Legion of Honor*

strike the disciplinarian as meretricious—as when a cloth was pressed into fresh paint to obtain the tactile effect of a weave (a "trick" practiced for instance by Bartolommeo Bettera, pls. 200–201).

One visual record exists of Rembrandt's interest in illusionism: the etching entitled "Jan Sylvius, Preacher," where the minister expounds the Bible and, as if transported with zeal, reaches out of the oval frame towards

201. *Bartolommeo Bettera*. Still Life with Attributes of the Arts. *New York, Collection Victor Spark*

us, dramatically casting his own shadow and that of the sacred book beyond the picture plane into our own (pl. 202).

A favorite device of seventeenth century portraiture was the architectonic cartouche supposedly framing the subject proper, beyond which one element appeared to protrude into the viewer's own world. This was essentially an adaptation of the very ancient tradition of showing the subject as if entirely outside the frame (e.g., pl. 3). In continuation of this, Jan Gossaert van Mabuse had depicted a child model as obviously standing forward of the supposed frame (see color pl. 7).[12a] The so-called "Portrait of a Jeweller" by W. van Valckert depicts an earnest young man thrusting forth what may well have been a betrothal ring, while "The Toasting Fiddler" of Gerald van Honthorst leans forward over the broad ledge of a casement or loggia, jovially tendering a filled beaker. (Both paintings are in the Rijksmuseum, Amsterdam.) But the richly voluted cartouche was the special contribution of the Baroque. Although it is still nobly simple in Murillo's "Self-Portrait" (see color pl. 13), the complex *cartellino* at bottom subtly reverses, as in a mirror image, the curves of the oval frame above.

Joost van Attevelt also chose for his forthright characterization of a Dutch burgher ("Portrait of a Man," pl. 203) a windowlike oval aperture, on the sill of which the model rests his left arm, holding a great broad-brimmed hat that juts out towards us.

In other instances, however, as is apparent in the works of Daniel

202. *Rembrandt.* Jan Sylvius, Preacher, *Etching*

203. *Joost van Attevelt (1621–1692).* Portrait of a Man. *Utrecht, Centraal Museum*

204. *Daniel Seghers (1590–1661).* Portrait of a Man.
Antwerp, Musée des Beaux-Arts

205. *Daniel Seghers.* Portrait of St. Ignatius.
Antwerp, Musée des Beaux-Arts

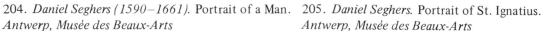

Seghers (pls. 204–5) and of Jan Davidsz. de Heem—the cartouche is hardly visible, being smothered under an abundance of blooms. Although the primary function of these was to provide an effect of depth, and the flowers did stand out with extraordinary relief, the illusionism generally extended also to the portraits framed within: in the "St. Ignatius" by Seghers, the book held by the saint trespasses the space curtain (pl. 205), while in de Heem's portrait of the young William of Orange (Palais de Saint Pierre, Lyon), one front paw of the naturalistic lion in the foreground realistically overhangs the ledge on which the symbolic beast appears to be resting.

The most complex use of the architectonic cartouche in portraiture was probably made by Adriaen Hanneman in his "Portrait of Constantin Huygens and His Five Children" in the Mauritshuis at The Hague (pl. 206), where the portrait of the father is set at center in an oval medallion surrounded by six similar frames containing the portraits of his five children, with the sixth, at bottom, reserved for an inscription apparently carved on a convex oval shield. In turn, the entire pleiad is placed within a large oval frame, with every interstice filled with simulated statuary—all but the portraits in illusionistic grisaille simulating stonework.

196

In earlier periods, full-scale imitation of architectural settings and of statuary had been prized chiefly for the illusory grandeur it brought to decorative schemes. Now the emphasis shifted to the texture of stone for its own inherent beauty; no more the pomp of Italian *quadratura* but the more intimate and frankly sensuous appeal of what might be termed "tactile deception": the grisaille of stonework, the creamy glow of marble enlivened by a dazzling variety of precious textures. Malachite, lapis lazuli, bronze, ormolu, coral, and pearls are supplemented with flowers, fruits, game (all of these latter elements, as one authority has remarked, belonging rather to the repertory of still life than of trompe l'oeil).[13] There were purists, however, such as Jacob de Wit, who specialized in purported "marble" and "stucco" bas-reliefs, with bands

206. *Adriaen Hanneman (1601–1671).* Constantin Huygens and His Five Children. *The Hague, Mauritshuis*

197

207. *Dutch School, 17th century (Monogrammist L. R.).* Nativity. *Los Angeles, Collection Mr. and Mrs. Oscar Salzer*

of playing children in the manner of antiquity or of the Italian Renaissance. Another practitioner of this subtle form of art was the Flemish painter known only as the Monogrammist L. R., whose delicate interpretation on the theme of the Nativity (pl. 207) perhaps does not copy an actual sculpture of his own or that of another artist, but instead may be a spontaneous illusionistic creation.

A similar association of imaginativeness and technical brilliance is met with in the decoration of houses and gardens, particularly in France. The eighteenth-century art chronicler d'Argenville and the historian of Paris, Hurtaut, record curious trompe l'oeil decoration at the royal seat of Marly, executed at the King's instigation.[14] It appears that one alley in the gardens of Marly was so heavily shaded that the plants would not grow satisfactorily, and the gardeners, try as they might, could not succeed in establishing the leafy hedge necessary to balance the horticultural plan and to ensure privacy. To remedy this, the King commanded that leaves be cut out of tin and affixed in a natural manner to a trellis. The task of painting the leaves, however, was not assigned to a craftsman but to no lesser man than the excellent still-life and landscape painter, Fontenay, assisted by the painter Chavanne, another artist of the first rank. Nor was it the first royal commission of this kind Fontenay had undertaken: before this, he had been ordered on several occasions to decorate illusionistically the borders of artificial ponds with painted flowers, presumably water plants.

Nevertheless, it would be a complete misunderstanding of the spirit of the age to believe that artists of definite merit and taste carried out work solely under compulsion. On the contrary, the Abbé de Monville, the biographer of Pierre Mignard, records that in his youth the painter had decorated a wall of the house where he was then living with an illusionistic fresco showing what the chronicler calls "a perspective." One presumes this to have been a garden vista, since it included the figure of a cat stalking a turtle that was creeping under some low plants. And, in the best tradition of trompe l'oeil lore (which there is no good reason to disbelieve), we are told that on several occasions dogs were deceived into dashing against the wall in pursuit of the cat into the imaginary garden—much to their distress, as bloody stains testified.[15]

From the sixteenth century, the development of the natural sciences, the increase of oceanic navigation, and the resulting era of colonization and flourishing commerce with the Orient all contributed to the inclusion of exotic fauna and flora as popular subject matter for trompe l'oeil as well as still-life painting. This new vogue of exoticism was grafted with ease onto a robust native scion: the pan-European tradition of Gothic illumination, of

199

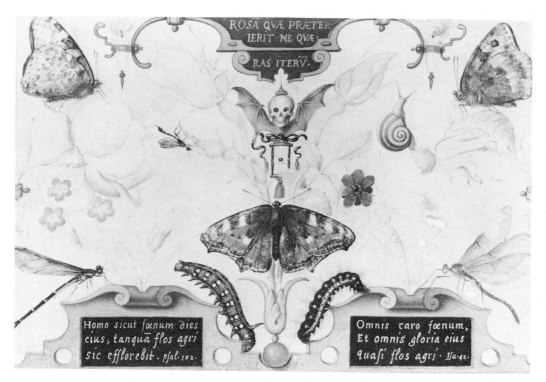

208. *Georg Hoefnagel. Diptych with Flowers and Insects, 1591 (left half). Lille, Musée des Beaux-Arts*

which the last exponent, in a broad sense, was the Flemish miniaturist, Georg Hoefnagel, active in the second half of the sixteenth century (pls. 208–9). Hoefnagel was as much a scientist as an artist, precursor as well as ancestor, and the founder of the admirable school of "scientific naturalism." This early

209. *Georg Hoefnagel. Diptych with Flowers and Insects, 1591 (right half). Lille, Musée des Beaux-Arts*

210. *Jacques de Gheyn II*. Vase of Flowers, *1612.*
The Hague, Gemeentemuseum

211. *Ambrosius Boschaert the Elder (act. 1588–*
1640). Vase of Flowers in a Niche. *The Hague,*
Mauritshuis

development of botanical/zoological naturalism at a time when familiarity
had not yet dulled the edge of wonder was to lead in time to one of the
most delightful developments of illusionistic painting: the flower piece (pls.
210–12). The three examples illustrated feature the basic composition of a
vase on a shelf within an illusionistic niche—directly descended from Memling's lily-plant in a faience pot (pl. 146). The most skillful exponents of this
theme were Jacques de Gheyn (pl. 210) and Ambrosius Boschaert the Elder
(pl. 211), and the most poetic and imaginative, Roelandt Savery (pl. 212).
Their variations on the theme, although repetitious, were never monotonous.
Savery in particular enlivens his compositions with an extraordinary variety
of small "personages": frogs, lizards, songbirds, moths, scarabs, butterflies,
sea shells, all faultlessly rendered and seemingly supernatural rather than
natural, a delicate, fantastic elfin mythology. Yet none of these details de-
tracts from the illusionistic purpose; the one exception occurs in Savery's undoubted masterpiece, the tall flower-vase with the crown-imperial blossom,
where the small white parrot is much too dramatic to be acceptable on the

201

plane of trompe l'oeil. In works by pupils and followers, Balthasar van der Ast, for instance, the line is not clearly drawn between trompe l'oeil and illusionistic flower piece, frequently because the niche is omitted or else is not shown in its entirety (as in the beautiful flower piece by Christoffel van den Berghe [pl. 213]).

An interesting backwater of illusionism was formed when many of the devices of the art were used in the illustrations of treatises on the natural sciences. Shared devotion to the wonders of nature inevitably drew together the savants and their illustrators to mutual benefit. In the works of George Flegel, Hans Hoffmann, Maria Sybilla Merian, and Anthonie van Borssom, utmost precisionism combines with poetic illusionism (pls. 214–17). Significantly, the designs created for frontispiece illustrations often echoed the themes of architectural illusionism. The title was framed within an arch and one favorite motif was that of a classical portico or arch in ruins, with tufts of straggling grass in the crannies—recalling Guercino's "Aurora" (pl. 114).

Regrettably, illusionistic work of this very fertile age is frequently

212. *Roelandt Savery*. Vase of Flowers, *1624. Utrecht, Centraal Museum*

213. *Cristoffel van den Berghe*. Bouquet of Flowers. *Philadelphia, The John G. Johnson Collection*

214. *Georg Flegel.* Still Life with Blue Titmouse, *1629.*
Formerly Berlin, Kupferstichkabinett

215. *Hans Hoffmann.* Rabbit, *1587. Berlin,*
Kupferstichkabinett

216. *Maria Sibylla Merian (1647–1717).* Studies
from Nature. *New York, The Metropolitan Mu-*
seum of Art, Fletcher Fund, 1939

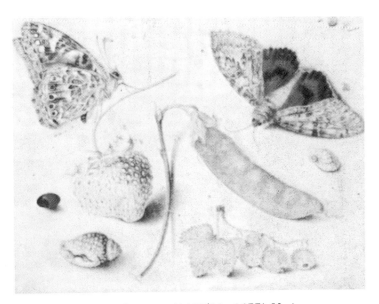

217. *Anthonie van Borssom (1629/30–1677).* Varia.
Berlin, Kupferstichkabinett

203

anonymous, or at best merely monogrammed. The explanation for this phenomenon may be due partly to the fact that a signature does invalidate the effect of a trompe l'oeil. In such instances where the artist was reluctant to affix his name on the front, an indication of the identity of the painter may have been furnished on the reverse, only to be lost in the course of time. A French artist almost, but not quite, circumvented the difficulty by means of the single initial "G," which appears as if delicately incised at the bottom of the illusionistic border in his beautiful trompe l'oeil of a cage with various implements (perhaps of falconry, pl. 218). Yet, while this initial might have been meaningful to contemporaries, we cannot now identify the artist. In other examples, the anonymity may have been voluntary and fully conscious: the author of a very handsome but stern *memento mori* prominently featuring a penitential scourge (pl. 219) may have refrained out of religious scruple, as the ultimate abnegation, from signing a work of which he could be so justly proud.

218. *French School, 17th century (Monogrammist G).* Still Life with Cage and Horn. *Hartford, Courtesy of the Wadsworth Atheneum*

219. *French School.* Memento Mori, *c. 1700. Los Angeles, Collection Mr. and Mrs. Oscar Salzer*

As a rule, however, we can believe that anonymous illusionists were generally victims of their feelings of esthetic delicacy. One such would be Domenick Remps, known now only from a eulogistic passage in Pater Orlandi's *Abecedario Pittorico* of 1733, which yet makes clear that this artist was certainly one of the most dedicated practitioners of trompe l'oeil of his time.

> The delight of this elegant painter was in simulating wooden panels, in the middle of which he painted landscapes, views, letters, playing cards or printed sheets, glasses, boxes, drawings, combs, knives, inkwells, feathers, annals, and other things resembling the real so closely that the eye was deceived and the mind beguiled into believing to be natural what was painted.[16]

Frescoes in the Bedroom from Boscoreale [p. 41]

PLATE 1

Jan Van Eyck. *Giovanni Arnolfini and His Wife*, detail [pp. 81–83]

PLATE 2

PLATE 3   Petrus Christus. *St. Eligius and the Lovers* [pp. 84–85]

Quentin Massys. *The Moneychanger and His Wife* [p. 84]

PLATE 4

PLATE 5

Masaccio (1401–1428). *Trinity Fresco* [p. 59]

Fra Filippo Lippi. *Madonna and Child with Two Angels* [p. 61]   PLATE 6

PLATE 7   Jan Gossaerts van Mabuse (1478–1553). *Portrait of a Little Girl* [p. 195]

Parmigianino. *Self-Portrait in a Convex Mirror* [p. 85]   PLATE 8

Titian. *Filippo Archinto* [pp. 355–56]

PLATE 9

Veronese. Decoration at the Villa Barbero [p. 123]

PLATE 10

Flemish School, 17th century. *Holy Family* [p. 179]

PLATE 11

Wallerant Vaillant. *Letter Rack* [pp. 178–79]   PLATE 12

Bartolome Esteban Murillo (c. 1617–1682). *Self-Portrait* [p. 195]

PLATE 13

Gabriel Germain Joncherie. *La Chaufferette aux Oeufs* [p. 251]

PLATE 14

George Washington Marks. *Young Girl at the Door* [p. 283]

PLATE 15

William Aiken Walker. *Blue-Winged Teal Drakes* [p. 277]

PLATE 16

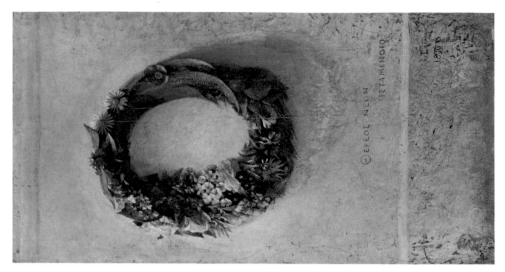

John La Farge. *Love Token* [p. 289]

P. Thiaucourt. *Le Pain* [p. 255]

De Scott Evans. *The Parrot* [p. 288]   PLATE 19

PLATE 20   John Haberle. *Japanese Doll* [p. 302 ff]

John Peto. *Office Board for John F. Peto* [p. 301]

PLATE 21

PLATE 22   Trade Cards [pp. 325–29]

Donald Evans. *Mangiare 1944* [p. 363]

PLATE 23

220. *Antonio Forbera.* Easel, *1686. Avignon, Musée Calvet*

6

The Mind Beguiled

The Eighteenth Century

If the seventeenth century was the golden age of illusionism as well as of still life—lusty, fecund, and fantastically imaginative—the next century can lay claim to having refined and purified that gold. The age of reason was also the age of taste; it did not make dramatic innovations but instead analysed and tempered. The repertory of trompe l'oeil remained very much the same as that enumerated by Pater Orlandi, but there was a new motivation. No longer was there the ingenuous wish for "duplication of objects" or even the more complex desire for escape into an imaginary world. Rather, the men and women of the eighteenth century esteemed nothing so much as a display of intelligence, and they derived vicarious satisfaction from the illusionistic painter's display of mastery over reality.

A typical reaction was that of Charles de Brosses, President of the Parliament of Dijon, when he visited Avignon in 1739 on his way to Italy. One of the most knowledgeable and versatile personalities of that brilliant age—a legist, philologist, geographer, historian, and archaeologist[1] de Brosses was transported with admiration upon viewing a *chantourné* trompe l'oeil by the Italian artist, Antonio Forbera (pl. 220):

> Upon entering, I saw an object which so took my fancy that it deserves considerable space in my narrative. At the end of the room there was an easel upon which had been set a painting, not quite finished, depicting the Empire of Flora, after the original by Poussin. The painter's palette and his brushes had been left

207

next to the picture. Above this, on a piece of paper, the drawing of the same painting, done in sanguine; next to it, a landscape engraved by Le Clerc. Below the easel, a small painting had been thrown, turned over to the unpainted side of the canvas, and slipped behind the stretcher frame, an engraving of a landscape by Perelle. I saw all of this at a distance first and then close by without noting anything out of the ordinary; but upon attempting to pick up the drawing, I was astounded to find that all I have described was in fact one single painting, done entirely with oil colors. The plate mark of the metal plates on the paper of the two engravings; the difference in the textures of the papers; the threads of the turned-over canvas; the holes and the wood of the easel—all this was so wonderful that I could not help exclaiming. . . . The painting is unframed, not rectangular, but shaped so as to follow the outlines that would be those of the group of objects in reality; this device further deceives the eye.[2]

The Forbera painting is clearly a variation on the great "Easel" of Cornelis Gysbrechts, painted fifty-three years earlier (pl. 153). But if the appeal of this type of illusionism proved timeless, one senses nevertheless that the impression produced in de Brosses' time differed basically from what it would have been for a contemporary of Forbera. *Deceiving the eye* remained the means; *beguiling the mind* was the effect. The subject of the deception, therefore, mattered little. There was no more need to depict objects of great worth and rarity. Henceforth the veriest scraps and oddments were deemed models.

This applied particularly to the representation of paper in any and all forms: printed or manuscript, parchment or pulp, etchings, sketches, blueprints, broadsides, all that Pater Orlandi had named, and much else that he had left out. "Papyromania" may be a useful term to define this obsession for the illusionistic representation of paper. But such representations were known to be within the ken of any reasonably competent painter, so that the popularity of the subject could not have stemmed solely from a misplaced appreciation of the skill required for these renderings. One must look deeper for the true reason. Paper was not yet the commonplace staple it is today. This may have played a role, but more important, paper—an above all, *printed* paper—symbolized the new communion of minds, the dissemination of knowledge, the hoped-for emancipation. The age of reason, paradoxically, was also the age of revolutions: the printed page was the swift universal messenger charged with the task of dispersing the incendiary doctrines of the rights of man and the supremacy of natural law.

In addition to this implied significance, there may be a subtle symbol-

221. *Gabriel Gresly.* La Gourmandise, *1752. Barnsley, Courtesy of the Trustees of the Cooper Art Gallery*

222. *Gabriel Gresly.* Le Rieur. *Besançon, Musée des Beaux-Arts*

ic message in a trompe l'oeil entitled "La Gourmandise" by Gabriel (often miscalled Gaspard) Gresly (pl. 221). The central feature represents the artist's own etching of a glutton, while the writer's quill slipped in back of the engraving and the sealing wax may suggest that the etching is a letter in pictorial form. The pamphlet dangling below (inscribed *Dieu soit beny,* " Blessed be God") appears to excite the derision of the young glutton. His scorn is ironically accentuated by the fragment of a playing card from which the pamphlet is suspended. In another work by Gresly (pl. 222), the composition of "La Gourmandise" is almost duplicated, but the pamphlet at bottom is omitted and a fly has been added. The quill, however, is again a significant feature. These typical compositions by Gresly may interestingly be compared with that by Edwart Collier on the same theme of a print seemingly attached to a wooden board (pl. 180).

223. *J. Deutsch.* Tray *(Niderviller ware), 1774. London, Victoria and Albert Museum*

Whatever the motivation, the wide sweep of "papyromania" extended even to utilitarian decoration, particularly of pottery and porcelain. A tray of Niderviller ware is characteristic in this respect (pl. 223). The tray itself mimics a wooden background, and at center appears a print with the usual crumpled edges and folded corners. This simulated print is signed in the margin "J. Deutsch" and dated 1774. It is therefore too early to have been the work of the noted lithographer, François Joseph Deutsch, born in Niderviller in 1784; but it was perhaps executed by an obscure forebearer who obviously contributed designs to the factory of Niderviller established in that Alsatian town in the latter part of the eighteenth century.

Eighteenth-century pictures of the *quod libet,* letter-rack, or *vide poche* type, like those of the previous age, are still equivalent to cryptic portraits of now anonymous personalities. As a general rule, the emphasis is on the masculine. One of the few exceptions is a delicate version by Gresly that is transparently feminine (pl. 224). Against the usual wooden board, the artist has depicted an open pouch, its several compartments holding needle, pin cushion, and other minute tools of a seamstress; to the side, a pair of scissors is suspended by a ribbon. The pouch is lace edged and richly embroidered with a floral design and a crowned monogram. One senses the dainty and discrete presence of the woman whose tastes and occupations are so clearly expressed there: she was fond of the color blue (repeated in the ribbon and the monogram), and while of high birth, she was mindful of modest household duties and preferred the simple pleasures of the country to court life—a print pinned in the background depicts a bucolic landscape.

210

224. *Gabriel Gresly.* Vide-Poche. *Private Collection*

225. *French School, 18th century.* Quod Libet Letter Rack. *Rennes, Musée des Beaux-Arts*

An anonymous French combination of letter rack and *quod libet* (pl. 225) goes somewhat further: it not only expresses a feminine personality but may well have been the work of a woman artist. The authors of letter-rack paintings had one advantage over those of other trompe l'oeil subjects: they were able to include a signature in a completely plausible and unobtrusive manner under the form of a letter bearing name and address. The letter in this painting may thus carry the name of the artist "Mademoiselle de Robien," with the address of an aristocratic family residence, "Hôtel de Robien, Rennes." The objects depicted combine feminine artifacts—needle case, pin cushion, embroidery scissors, necklace of beads—with evidence of artistic activity—palette and brushes, compass, magnifying glass. The noble amateur from Brittany cannot have been very young, for a pair of spectacles is also included. An inkling of the date of execution might be found in the "New Almanac of Bissextile Years" at left.

211

Far more disquieting undertones are found in the trompe l'oeil depicting a torn royal edict and signed with a graffito on the wooden background: "de la croix 1773" (pl. 226). It is hardly possible that an ordinance levying a tax on the inhabitants of Fontainebleau and displayed prominently for public viewing was lacerated accidentally, or that it was solely the aesthetic appeal of the fragments that inspired the artist to record them for posterity. Political protest is evident; if not the artist's own, then an objective record of contemporary events.

Social changes were similarly reflected in the architectural illusionism of the period. "Deceptions" in the grand manner—the grandiose concepts of the Renaissance and the opulent Baroque extravaganzas—were replaced in the Rococo palaces by subjects more in keeping with the gracious informality and asymmetry of the new style. While this decoration still made use of architectural elements—columns, porticoes, "temples of love"—it was with extreme lightness and discretion, a suggestion rather than a statement. More frequently, the illusionistic ornaments merely added a bright and airy touch without unduly overwhelming the actual architectural scheme: occasional swathes of drapery, gracefully dropping from the cornice (Queluz Palace, near Lisbon); the ever popular motifs of vases of flowers and of pet animals on the low border that seemingly separated a room from an imaginary garden beyond which bright birds flitted across opal-tinted skies.

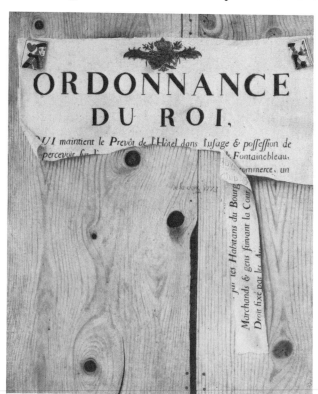

226. *"De la Croix."* Ordonnance du Roi, *1773. Collection Charles J. Robertson, Esq.*

212

227. *Giuseppe and Domenico Valeriani.*
Painted Decoration of the Ballroom at the
Villa Stupinigi, 1731. Turin

Precisely such a theme had been used early in the century by an artist
whose career bridged the two ages and who might have been expected to
cling to the ancient tradition. The tale is told by a contemporary chronicler
of the famous portraitist Nicolas de Largillierre's two known illusionistic
flights of fancy. The first came as a result of a dare. While visiting the estate
of a wealthy patron, Largillierre was asked by a fellow houseguest what he
might suggest to improve what was considered by consensus to be a dreary
and unpleasant prospect: a barren wall at the end of a long orangerie. "I can,
whenever I choose, cause you all to see through that wall," was Largillierre's
answer. At once, the necessary implements were called for, and the artist was
asked to perform the feat there and then. Within a mere eight days, he obliged
with a vast sky, a lush garden vista complete with baluster, and in the foreground the familiar presences of the household parrot and cat, and whenever
he renewed his visit, he added one more agreeable trait.[3] Marvellous though
the achievement was, it was in a sense a repeat performance, for a room in
Largillierre's own house in Paris had been similarly enlarged and embellished,
and so convincingly that the painter's own dog is said to have bloodied his
nose by trying to rout a turtle half-hidden at the base of the shrubbery.

Whenever, on the contrary, the emphasis was placed solely on architectural elements to the complete exclusion of natural aspects, whimsicality
of approach defeated the purpose, as in the Villa Stupinigi, in Turin (pl. 227),
where the billowy mock architecture frothes up as light as whipped meringue
or spun sugar.

228. *Italian School, 18th century.* Musicians. *Padua, Palazzo Capodilista*

Wherever the human figure was included, the approach was no longer mythological or historical but instead wittily theatrical. At the Palazzo Capodilista (pl. 228), the pastoral world smiles and beckons amongst lingering echoes of lutes and mandolins, against a dazzlingly white facade that would be overwhelmingly grandiose but for its faeric unreality. Similarly, at the Villa Lechi (pl. 229), the towering pompousness of the setting is belied by the nonchalant grace of the two figures descending the lordly staircase. Even as late as 1748, the ancient farcical characters of the Commedia dell' Arte

214

229. *Giacomo Lecchi and Carlo Carloni. Decoration at the Villa Lecchi, Brescia*

230. *J. Lederera. Commedia dell'Arte scene, 1748. Krumlow Castle, Bohemia*

were still in favor and were depicted on the walls of Krumlow Castle (pl. 230), with appreciable emasculation so as not to offend the delicate taste. In the Orangerie at Lazienki Palace in Warsaw, the interest has shifted to the spectators, who are represented as watching the performance in a deep, logelike lunette: they gaze down upon the stage with such rapt attention that we believe not only in their own actuality but in that of the shadowy play on the stage below.

The culmination of this graceful art is found in the decoration of the apartments of Frederick the Great at the Castle of Charlottenburg (pl. 231).

231. *Antoine Pesne (1683–1757). Murals in the Apartment of Frederick the Great. Charlottenburg Castle*

232. Martin Engelbrecht. Peep Show, c. 1720. New York, Courtesy of the Cooper-Hewitt Museum of Decorative Arts and Design, Smithsonian Institution

The room is wonderfully enlarged not through weighty architectonic devices but through skillful grading and spacing of figures. The uncrowded groupings—ladies in wide, floating, panniered gowns and their dapper cavaliers—seem barely out of our reach beyond the sheerest of space curtains. Elsewhere the figures appear to be wandering away into the luminous distance, where, with the slightest conscious effort, we might overtake them. The goal of the painter-decorator—in this instance, Antoine Pesne—was no more to magnify but to abolish entirely the architectural limitations of a given room, so that the room became a stage. Although translated to a level of supreme elegance in Pesne's conception, decoration of this type was kindred in mood to the popular peep shows of the period, such as those by Martin Engelbrecht (pl. 232).

The perennial theme of the loggia or balcony was used in the decoration of a stairwell of the Hôtel de Luynes (now in the Musée Carnavalet, Paris) by a father-and-son team of Italian artists, the Brunettis (pl. 233 reproduces a painting by the American artist, Walter Gay, after the Brunetti decoration). Here the gracious denizens of this courtly world are not only unmistakably French but uniquely contemporary, unencumbered by either majesty or haughtiness. The Brunettis also created illusionistic decorations for the Marquise de Pompadour at Bellevue, for the Palais Soubise, and for a number of *hôtels* in Paris. Later, the younger Brunetti carried out the neoclassical decoration of the chapel added in 1764 to the ancient church of Sainte-Marguerite in the Faubourg-Saint-Antoine (pl. 234), probably the most important single example of grisaille decoration in existence.[4]

216

233. *Walter Gay, after the Brunettis' Decoration for the Hôtel de Luynes (Musée Carnavalet). New York, Collection Victor Spark*

234. *Paolo Brunetti. Decoration in the Chapel of the Souls in Purgatory, 1764. Paris, Eglise Sainte-Marguerite.*

217

235. *Music Pavillion of Madame,
Countess of Provence. Oculus,
1784. Montreuil*

By the second half of the eighteenth century, the Rousseau-inspired *culte de la nature* had brought into vogue as subject for illusionistic decorations idyllic landscapes, or garden vistas, framed in architectural settings of the neoclassical revival. A masterpiece of this type is the recently restored music pavillion of Madame, the Countess of Provence, sister-in-law of Louis XVI and later Queen of France in her own right (albeit in exile, when her husband became Louis XVIII). The illusionistic decor of the pavillion starts with the peristyle at the entrance, where actual statues are placed within niches of simulated marble (long hidden by overpainting). The first inner room is the circular "temple of Flora" with its classical colonnade and oculus decorated with bas-reliefs, all feigned (pl. 235–36). But the charm of the room depends essentially on the enchanting garden vistas that open between the tall white columns. For Madame, these held special personal appeal: the artist had depicted there a variety of her favorite flowers (she was a dedicated floriculturist) as they grew and bloomed in the park outside: Spanish carnations, snowballs, hollyhocks, hyacinths, honeysuckle, phlox, and bellflowers all against a verdured setting of tall trees. The final poetic touch is supplied by the misty play of cascading waterfalls. Four doors opening into the surrounding rooms are hardly visible; the very faint rectangular outlines can barely be made out in the illustration.[5]

Major illusionistic schemes of this kind were usually restricted to royal seats, or at least to seignorial residences. In private dwellings, even of the affluent, decoration as a rule consisted of easel works. But even this practice now largely fell out of favor and rooms were more often decorated with graceful panelling in soft pastel tones. Brightness and lightness was the keynote, and to achieve this effect, an abundance of mirrors and light sconces was incorporated within the wainscotting, so that little space remained for painted decoration of any kind. This new fashion resulted in a dearth of commissions: it is a matter of record that Dirk van der Aa was forced to decorate coach panels in lieu of tasks more worthy of his talent. Within new dwellings, almost the only place left for the painter's brush was the removable panel placed in the hearth during the summer when a fire was not kept burning, to hide the dark opening—the *devant de cheminée*.

219

236. *Music Pavillion of Madame, Countess of Provence. Colonnade, 1784. Montreuil*

237. *French School, mid-17th century.*
Devant de Cheminée. *Bourg-en-Bresse,
Musée de l'Ain*

238. Devant de Cheminée. *Venice,
Palazzo Labbia*

Like Largillierre's barren wall, this was thought to be an "unpleasant prospect," and it had long been the custom to ask artists to remedy the situation.[6] Not all hearth paintings, however, particularly the earlier examples, were illusionistic. At first, they consisted merely of graphic designs or of the obvious conceit of a vase filled with flowers, such as a fastidious housewife might set down to fill the empty cavity. The illusionistic *devant de cheminée* goes back to the seventeenth century: an inventory of the apartment of Molière in 1673 describes a *"devant de porte et un de cheminée"* with green and blue taffeta valences, ornamented with fringes. Eventually, it became clear that the most natural and pleasing subject would consist of a realistic representation of whatever objects might naturally be placed in the empty hearth. This might be a tumbling pile of books, as in the early example at the Musée de l'Ain in Bourg-en-Bresse (pl. 237), or a grouping of Oriental porcelains, generally white and blue, shown against a rich red ground, as in the *devant de cheminée* installed at the Palazzo Labbia (pl. 238). A design by Daniel

Marot for an hearth screen shows a related arrangement of potiches and vases (pl. 239) and a painting in the Stedelijk Museum in Amsterdam depicts a dwarf orange plant in a white and blue porcelain tub. There must have been inumerable variations on this particularly pleasing theme. Trompe l'oeil paintings of Chinese porcelains are known to have adorned the royal castle of Maisons-Lafitte as well as the château of the Marquis de Chalmazel at Saint-Marcel-de-Félines en Forez.[7]

A delightfully fantastic departure from this handsome but basically conventional type of decoration is the *devant de cheminée* by Vigoreux Duplésir (pl. 240) depicting a lively chinoiserie as if on a miniature stage. The

239. *Daniel Marot. Engraved Design for a* Devant de Cheminée, *late 17th century*

240. *Vigoreux Duplésir.* Devant de Cheminée, 1700.

221

composition also incorporates the familiar illusionistic device of the curtain and the representation of a feigned bas-relief made to appear as if part of the actual chimney wall.

Whether illusionistic or conventional, the *devant de cheminée* of the seventeenth century led to an important variation in perspectival representation and lighting. The *devant de cheminée* represents the sole exception to the otherwise capital rule of illusionism: even lighting.[8] Because the niche to be pictured had to duplicate the actual deep square niche, the artist had perforce to represent the objects as strongly lighted in the foreground, where the light from windows or candles would strike them, and as in an indistinct penumbra in the background, where they virtually disappeared from view. The arduous task was to unite the precisionism of trompe l'oeil in the foreground with the chiaroscuro of still life in the background. Since the *devants de cheminée* that have survived are of superlative quality, many have been isolated, framed as easel paintings, and considered as independent works of art. Their identification as hearth screens can be discovered only by observing the special factors of lighting and perspective that indicate their original function.

The eighteenth century brought to an undreamed-of level of excellence what had been merely a kind of superior household furniture. The most famous of all *devants de cheminée* is certainly Jean-Baptiste Chardin's "White Tablecloth" (pl. 241), a low table painted as if actually within the rectangular opening. Since the tablecloth drapes to the floor, nothing is seen below

241. *Jean-Baptiste Chardin.* The White Tablecloth. Devant de Cheminée, *1737.*
Courtesy of the Art Institute of Chicago

242. *French School, 18th century.*
Devant de Cheminée. *Paris, Collection M. Emmanuel Motta*

it. There are a number of hearth screens by other artists painted with kindred subjects but without the cloth, so that it is possible to see under the table. In such instances, we generally find a pet installed below, as in pl. 242, where a cat is asleep beneath the table, which has evidently been pushed under the hearth mantle for its special protection from damp and updraft.

The portrayal of a household animal within the recess was the most natural choice, since the empty hearth provided a ready kennel. But it also raised the question of observance of the law of illusionism regarding the inclusion of animal life. The cat, being asleep, is motionless and therefore no problem. But the famous painter and animalier, Jean-Baptiste Oudry, in his *devant de cheminée* "Dog with a Porcelain Bowl" (pl. 243), faced a more difficult challenge: he has shown the great hound standing as if it had only this very moment sprung to attention, its eye bright and alert but every

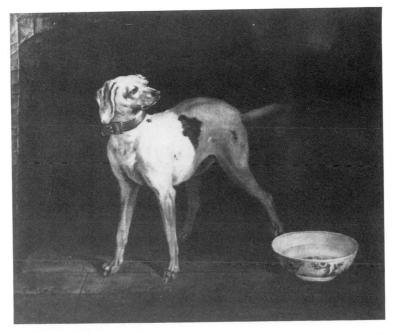

243. *Jean-Baptiste Oudry (1686–1755).* Dog with a Porcelain Bowl.
Paris, Musée du Louvre

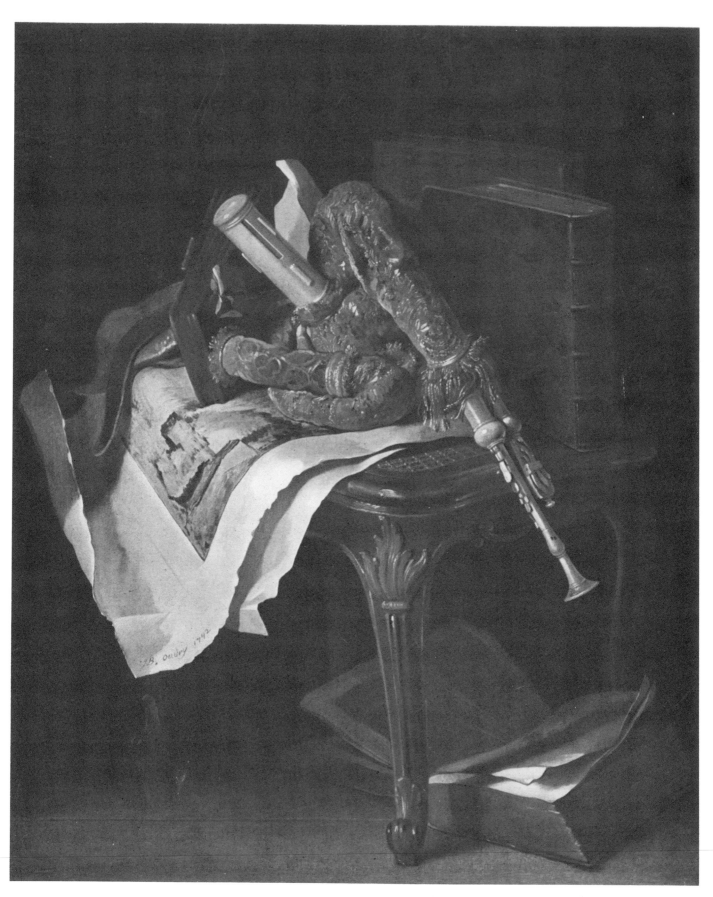

244. *Jean-Baptiste Oudry.* Le Tabouret de Laque, *1742. Paris, Collection Cailleux*

fiber of its body held in trancelike immobility. Note also how the totally dark background creates a mood that is both abstract—almost stylized—and yet intensely dramatic, the strong shadow across the animal's back contributing to this effect. There are two known versions of this famous subject done by Oudry: the first, exposed at the Salon in 1751 and the replica at the Louvre (pl. 243), where one may still clearly see the *chantourné* outline of the canvas, as it was fitted to a specially shaped stretcher conforming to the chimney frame. There, also, the tiling within the fireplace is visible. One wonders if the first painting might not have been an actual portrait of a favorite hound and the second, an adaptation to the function of *devant de cheminée.*

Another favorite theme for *devant de cheminée* was the representation of a low stool bearing musical instruments. In Oudry's "Le Tabouret de Laque" (pl. 244), it is a richly caparisoned musette. Another variation on the same theme (pl. 245), this time by Roland de la Porte, Oudry's best pupil, includes a similar stool and musette as well as a water bowl of Oriental porcelain strongly reminiscent of the one depicted by Oudry next to his standing hound. In the de la Porte interpretation, the dog is not depicted, but the water bowl suggests its presence. But, if the pupil emulated his master's subjects, it was not because he was unable to achieve illusionistic fame on his own. He met with special success for his rendering of a feigned bronze crucifix, now lost, which was exposed at the Salon of 1761. This work was praised even by the artist's inveterate enemy, Diderot. De la Porte is known to have repeated the subject on the same velvet ground but of a different color. Another lost work was his trompe l'oeil of a marble bust of Vespasian, an oval bas-relief placed in a gilded frame, apparently attached to a wooden background, with a playing card depicted as if slipped between the medallion and the frame. An anonymous article in a contemporary gazette reported that many viewers had not realized that this card was also a simulation. To you and to me, reader, as the Brontës

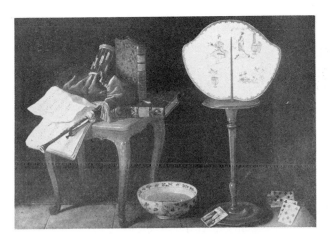

245. *Roland de la Porte.* A Screen Decorated with Chinoiserie. Devant de Cheminée, *c. 1750*

225

246. *Louis Tessier.* White Porcelain Bucket. Devant de Cheminée, *1756. Paris, Musée des Arts Décoratifs*

might apostrophize, this may seem difficult of credence. Yet they came unprepared, for many were viewing illusionistic paintings for the first time; until then, only visitors to the seats of royal patrons had been privileged to see such things.

Engraved reproductions of this genre were not common primarily because they would not carry the full effect of the illusionism. This visual naiveté, therefore, is not surprising. How many—or rather, how few—would ever have seen the masterly *devant de cheminée* with a large white and blue porcelain bucket at center (pl. 246) painted by Louis Tessier for the office of the Marquis de Marigny, brother of Madame de Pompadour? But it would of course have been scrutinized by its owner, and the artist wittily took advantage of this to present his own petition for royal commission to the all-powerful Minister under the form of one of the letters apparently casually tossed away in the elegant paper basket.[9] The letter, upright at the rear center of the basket, begins "A Monsieur le Marquis." As Tessier executed no less than four *devants de cheminée* commissioned by the Marquis de Marigny "pour le service du Roy," the petition was evidently successful.

226

247. *Jean Baptiste Oudry.* Orange Plant.
Devant de Cheminée. *Paris, Private Collection*

The Tessier work is evidence that the vogue for Oriental porcelain had by no means abated. Oudry himself painted for another *devant de cheminée* (pl. 247), an orange plant bearing both flower and fruit, in a porcelain tub set into the rich ormolu mount then customary for these precious objects. Roland de la Porte, however, did not disdain to paint a flowering plant in a simple pot of terra-cotta, made as precious as porcelain by the matchless skill of the rendering. The proportion, perspective, and lighting of this fine picture suggests that it, too, may originally have been a *devant de cheminée*, perhaps, as was often the case, trimmed down for framing.

But the range of Oudry as illusionist was by no means confined to the *devant de cheminée*, however much he excelled in that specialty. He was also renowned for his imitations of bas-reliefs and some of his masterly still lifes of game were presented against the traditional background (pls. 248–49).

248. *Jean-Baptiste Oudry.* Hunting Still Life, *1764.*
Grenoble, Musée des Beaux-Arts

249. *Jean-Baptiste Oudry.* Still Life, *1740. Algiers,*
Musée National des Beaux-Arts d'Alger

250. *Jean-Baptiste Oudry.* Devant de Cheminée. *Montpellier, Musée Fabre*

Nor, in addition to sumptuous pheasants, grouse, or the lordly hare, did he disdain to depict illusionistically the minor denizens of the air and the bestiary of field and garden. The most touching and beguiling of his works may be the two very early (1712) pendants originally at the Château d'Aiguillon and now at the Préfecture d'Agen. The subject is small dead birds—sparrow, goldfinch, and titmouse—companioned by butterflies, a bumblebee, a wasp, a lady bug, a live mouse, cherries, and gooseberries, a repertory that evokes that of the medieval illuminators rather than of a court painter of the Sun King, the regent Philippe d'Orléans, and Louis the Well-Beloved. For this was in no way the ingenuousness of youth: thirty-eight years later, Oudry again reverted to the same subject of a pathetic little trophy of song birds affixed to a wall.

251. *Gabriel Moulineuf (1749–1817). Trompe l'Oeil Door. Private Collection*

228

It was Oudry, too, who endowed with new appeal an ancient theme—the large open book propped against a pile of smaller books (pl. 250). A green ribbon marker further brightens the expanse of white paper. While this was in a sense a reversal to the depiction of great volumes during the Renaissance (pl. 186), Oudry's picture, displaying the now rare illuminated volume, suggests the special pride of the bibliophile.

An illusionistic scheme by Gabriel Moulineuf is worthy of special attention (pl. 251). It represents the logical extension of the *devant de cheminée* panel device to the blocking or masking of other undesired but larger openings. The objects—which include a cello, music stool and desk in the foreground, as well as a table covered with an oriental carpet—are depicted in actual size and appear as if placed within a curtain-draped stone archway leading into the open. This composition was certainly created to cover a specific area, most likely a door, given its large dimensions (2.26 x 1.50 m.).

The sophistication of the age was not receptive to the basically naive appeal of *chantourné* trompe l'oeil, even though there were talented artists to carry on the tradition, such as the pair of anonymous illusionists who depicted a "Painter's Table" and an "Open Desk," both objects displaying an array of appropriate paraphernalia (pls. 252–53). In contrast to *chantourné*,

229

252. *French School, 18th century.* Painter's Table. Chantourné. *Paris, Private Collection*

253. *Dutch School, 18th century.* Open Desk. Chantourné. *Paris, Private Collection*

the vogue for the eloquent illusionistic elements in portraiture suffered no setback. The great English painter William Hogarth, in a unique interpretation of the antiquated "cartouche" formula, presents his self-portrait not only unframed but merely as one of several components of a trompe l'oeil composition—palette at left, books piled as support for the oval canvas, and the faithful pug as immovable sentinel at right (pl. 254)—although with the all-important difference that in the Hogarth picture the effect of depth is achieved not by the placement of the portrayed painting within a concavity that recedes into the background, but rather, by its detachment from the pictorial background and a slight but definite projection towards us.

In A. Pujos' engraving of Buffon (pl. 255), the portrait is quite conventional, although the complex frame is unusually structural. But a touch of tridimensionality—the projecting ring at the top of the frame with the pronounced cast shadow—raises the conception out of the ordinary. The function of this object is puzzling (was it perhaps a lamp holder?), yet both the illusionistic impact and the symbolic message of the device—placed like a crown or "halo" above the head of the famed naturalist—are inescapable.

230

254. *William Hogarth.* The Painter and His
Pug, *1745. London, Tate Gallery*

255. *A. Pujos.* Portrait of Buffon. *Engraving*

256. *Jean-Baptiste Chardin (1699–1779).* The Game of Cards. *Paris, Private Collection*

      Chardin's interest in architectonic illusionism is evidenced by the settings he used in a number of his paintings: "The Game of Cards" in its circular masonry niche (pl. 256) as well as "Blowing Bubbles" (pl. 257), a variation on the parapet type of portrait. Chardin also made effective use of a deep oval niche for his "Attributs de la Musique" (pl. 258).

257. *Jean-Baptiste Chardin.* Blowing Bubbles, *c. 1731–33. Washington, D.C., The National Gallery of Art*

Musical instruments remained favorite models for almost all artists of the age. We have renderings by Oudry of the cello and violin (pls. 259–60)—and we have already encountered his bagpipes (pl. 244), as well as the version by de la Porte (pl. 245). Nevertheless, these beautiful shapes were not used in trompe l'oeil nearly as much as one might expect. Jeaurat de Bertry, for instance, did not always cross the threshold from still life into illusionism with his handsome groupings featuring a flute, violin, or drum (pls. 261–62). How-

258. *Jean-Baptiste Chardin.* Les Attributs de la Musique, *1765. Paris, Musée du Louvre*

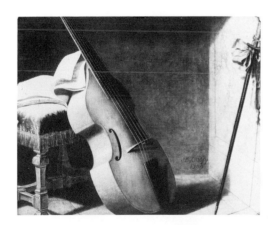

259. *Jean-Baptiste Oudry.* Cello. *Paris, Musée du Louvre*

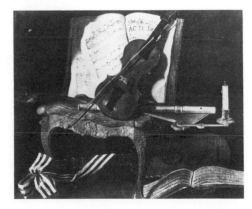

260. *Jean-Baptiste Oudry.* Still Life with Violin. Devant de Cheminée. *Paris, Musée du Louvre*

233

ever, both a violin and a great horn play important roles in what was possibly an illusionistic *devant de cheminée* by the same artist. "Les Attributs des Arts" (pl. 263), where the shadow on the painter's box seems to have been cast by the mantelpiece above.

261. *Nicolas-Henry Jeaurat de Bertry (1728–aft. 1796).* Drum and Sword. *Fontainebleau, Musée National du Château*

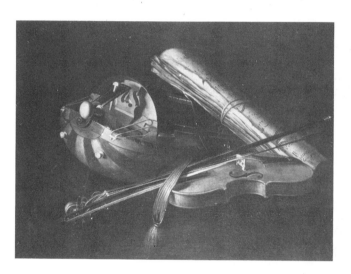

262. *Nicolas-Henry Jeaurat de Bertry.* Musical Instruments. *Paris, Musée Carnavelet*

234

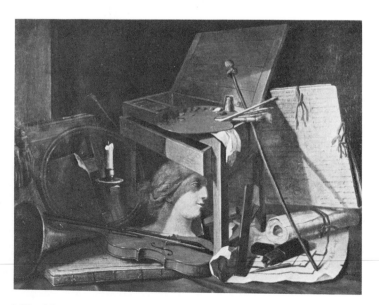

263. *Nicolas-Henry Jeaurat de Bertry.* Les Attributs des Arts. *Private Collection*

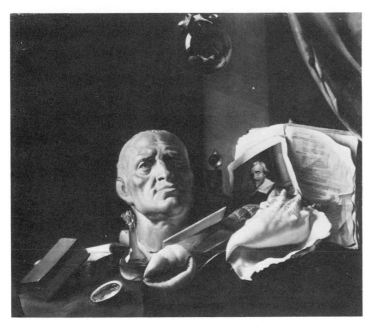

264. *Caesar Boetius van Ever-dingen (1606–1678).* Vanitas Still Life. *City Art Museum of St. Louis*

Representation of statuary was also included in the still lifes of the period, but the treatment, however realistic and even precisionistic, generally falls short in one respect or another of the requirements of orthodox trompe l'oeil. On the whole, they are nothing more than variations on themes that had already been worked threadbare in the previous century (e.g., by Caesar Boetius van Everdingen, pls. 264–65). Once in a while, however, an artist ventured beyond this to introduce one frankly illusionistic element in the

265. *Caesar Boetius van Ever-dingen.* Still Life with Bust. *Collection Mrs. A. Staring Wilden-borch, Castle Vorden, Netherlands*

235

composition, as did Pierre Subleyras in "Les Attributs des Arts," where the painter's brushes are depicted as jutting boldly forward (pl. 266). Most painters, though, chose rather to apply their illusionistic talents to the representation of bas-reliefs which were inherently far better suited to trompe l'oeil than statuary in the round (pl. 276).

The choice of bas-relief subjects was by no means an innovation. As has been shown, they had been familiar from the Renaissance onwards. But the term by which we now designate them—grisaille—is a relatively modern development. Although French lexicographers have traced it as far back as 1625, it was used at first purely as a technical qualification and not as a substantive: "peinture *en* grisaille," i.e., painting in grisaille, similar to "painting in oil," or "painting in distemper."

The more generic term, "camaïeu," appears to have come into use considerably later, in 1727. Originally a synonym for cameo, it now assumed a new function: it was made applicable to trompe l'oeil paintings of bas-reliefs in various materials—bronze, terra-cotta, onyx, marble, or any other substance (not excluding wood)—provided that the picture was executed in a monochrome scheme of the appropriate color (pl. 267). A camaïeu of a terra-cotta relief, for instance, would reproduce the natural reddish tones of the clay. (However, if the representation of feigned dust was included, introducing some grayish tones, purists might be justified in looking upon the painting as polychrome rather than camaïeu.) It would not be incorrect, therefore,

236

266. *Pierre Subleyras (1699–1749).* Still Life (Les Attributs des Arts). *Toulouse, Musée des Augustins*

267. *French School, 18th century.* Rome. *New York, The Cooper-Hewitt Museum of Decorative Arts and Design, Smithsonian Institution*

to describe a trompe l'oeil of a stone bas-relief (e.g., pls. 10, 319) as a gray camaïeu, but it is certainly more specific and convenient to make use of the term "grisaille" (first found in English usage in 1848).

What remains invariable in either camaïeu or grisaille is that the painted representation of sculpted form is implied. Although license has been taken in modern times, drawings or prints in a monochrome color scheme do not properly belong under either heading, camaïeu or grisaille. The definition also excludes certain trompe l'oeil paintings where the color gray predominates but which do not represent sculpture—for instance illusionistic representations of etchings or drawings shown under broken glass (pl. 268). Although the

268. *French School. 18th century.* The Deception. *Houston, Collection Peter and Lesley Schlumberger*

237

color scheme is predominantly gray, the pictures nevertheless are not grisailles, nor are they designs or landscapes, city views, historical scenes, or even the decorative arrangements of draperies that were created as wallpaper designs at the beginning of the nineteenth century.

Small scale, or "easel" grisaille and camaieu work may have originated in Northern Europe. The earliest examples are the subjects painted in that mode on the reverse of polyptychs by the great Flemish masters (pls. 59, 60). However, it has been suggested that the use of the monochrome gray scheme was motivated in such instances by liturgical rather than artistic considerations—gray, as the hue of mourning, being suitable for the season of Lent.[10] This, however, does not apply to Van Eyck's "Annunciation panels" (pls. 62, 63) with their soft golden tonality. And it cannot have been the reason for Giulio Romano's choice of grisaille to adorn his famous small sliding panel ("L'Abondance," pl. 269) probably created to protect the surface of Raphael's "La Petite Sainte Famille"– both now in the Louvre. Nor would hues of mourning have been called for in the remarkable series of sixteen miniatures in a French book of hours, circa 1510 (pl. 270) where the dramatic chiaroscuro of the black and gray oval medallions with golden borders suggests the great leaden seals used on documents, or the medals, also of lead, carried on the hats of pilgrims.

Barring such notable exceptions, grisaille in the sixteenth and seventeenth centuries reverted to its primary, purely decorative functions: as framing device, as neutral background and also as the main element in large schemes of architectural illusionism. Its cool tonality made it eminently suitable for the decoration of churches: Sainte-Marguerite, in Paris (pl. 234) or in the cathedral of Cambrai, where Marten Geeraerts painted eight monumental grisailles.

But the time came when grisaille was appreciated for its own sake, for its delicate coloristic appeal, and its subtle evocation of sculptural values. Its popularity increased at such a rate that to attempt to enumerate all the artists who took up the practice during the eighteenth century would be a labor of Hercules. The list would include not only some of the greatest names of the age but also a host of excellent painters of second rank, whose names are now only familiar to specialists, as well as a great number of anonymous practitioners.[10a]

The most significant aspect of grisaille is that it should frequently be looked upon as of dual authorship, in the sense that the painters of grisaille (and also, of course, of camaïeu) often took works of actual sculpture as their models. Thus it follows that much of the effect of the painting depends

269. *Giulio Romano (attrib.).* L'Abondance. *Paris, Musée du Louvre*

270. *French School.* Adoration of the Magi, *c. 1510. New Haven, Yale University, Beinecke Rare Book and Manuscript Library, Ms. 108*

on the choice of the sculptural model. The artist who erred in this respect might be a superlative technician, but his skill could only partly compensate for the handicap of an awkward or mediocre subject. On the other hand, when the choice was felicitous, the two talents were conjoined, and while the work of the sculptor was "duplicated," the efforts of the painter, concentrated on a worthy object, received added luster. Sometimes knowledge of the model was lost along the way and the painter received all the credit.

The earliest, or certainly one of the first, French artists of the eighteenth century to practice the art may have been François Desportes. The uncontested claim of his nephew Nicolas is on record: "M. Desportes was the first who painted [illusionistic renderings of bas-reliefs] so as to deceive even sculptors." It is also beyond doubt that Desportes the elder had begun to show imitations of marbles and bronzes as early as 1725. On that first occasion, according to a contemporary account, many reached over to touch, so as to convince themselves that the performance was bona fide. François Desportes also painted at least one *devant de cheminée* for the Marquis de Marigny, who seems to have been an avid amateur of the genre on his own, as well as the purveyor of royal commissions.

239

240

271. *Piat-Joseph Sauvage (1744–1818)*. Anacréon. *Compiègne, Musée National du Château de Compiègne*

The name of Piat-Joseph Sauvage should be singled out as the outstanding exponent of lapidary illusionism because of his sustained excellence and faultless taste in choice of themes.[11] The artist's masterpiece (pl. 271) is his so-called "Anacreon" (although the subject may be Dionysian). It was one of thirty pieces he executed for the Salle du Grand Couvert at Compiègne, commissioned by Marie-Antoinette, but better known as "Napoleon's dining room." The entire decoration of the famous apartment is illusionistic in every detail: the feigned textures of the marble and wood used in the architectural details, as well as grisaille and terra-cotta camaïeus. Sauvage was equally famed for his renderings of white-marble antique bas-reliefs—on a background of lapis lazuli for royal dwellings—and of clay, with the convincing detail of dust settled on the projecting planes of the relief. (This device found such favor that eventually a Swiss painter, François Ferrière of Geneva, would specify "feigned dust" in the descriptive titles to his trompe l'oeil paintings.)

A gifted woman artist, Anne Vallayer-Coster—elected member of the Académie de Peinture et de Sculpture at the age of twenty-three—specialized in bold and luminous still lifes. But she also made grisailles and camaïeus of outstanding quality, for which she reaped high praise when they were exposed at the Salons from 1771 to 1800.

It may seem paradoxical that Chardin, whose technique of juxtaposed touches of color foretells pointillism, was also throughout his career a skillful and apparently devoted practitioner of the radically opposed technique of trompe l'oeil. It was an illusionistic camaïeu (an imitation of a bronze relief) displayed at the Exposition de la Jeunesse, Place Dauphine, in 1732, that first brought widespread recognition to the young artist. The painting was a trompe l'oeil of a trompe l'oeil depicting a clay mold of a bronze relief by the Flemish sculptor François Duquesnoy, and it has been suggested that the clay copy may well have been given its bronze patina by Chardin himself.[12] The famous camaïeu, showing a group of eight children at play, was acquired by the painter Michel Van Loo; it was again exhibited in 1737, this time at the Grand Salon du Louvre. In 1779, at the posthumous exhibition of works by Chardin's ill-fated son, Pierre-Jean Chardin, an imitation of a wood bas-relief was included, of which it is only known that it, too, was after a relief by Duquesnoy and had as its subject some *jeu d'enfants*. Perhaps it was a variant of Chardin's own youthful work, suggested by the old artist to his son in the hope that it might help him acquire renown.

Chardin continued to exhibit camaïeus at the Salons together with the enchanting household scenes for which he is now famous. While these trompe l'oeils continued to excite the enthusiasm of the public, Diderot remarked—perspicuously, one suspects—that while the work itself was good, the choice

272. *Italian School, 18th century.* Letter Rack. *Dublin, The National Gallery of Ireland*

273. *French or Italian School, 18th century.* Letter Rack. *San Francisco, Collection Louis Pappas*

of subjects was not. Yet, Diderot added, although the models consisted of mediocre sculpture, the performance demonstrated that it was possible for an artist to prove himself a superlative colorist even while depicting the least suitable objects. Chardin's illusionistic activities also included what one authority has called "le trompe l'oeil classique": engravings and drawings depicted against wooden backgrounds.[13]

The gridlike letter racks of the previous age increasingly gave way in the eighteenth century to more casual and graceful groupings of paper ephemera (pls. 272–75). *Quod libets,* too, reflected the mood and style of the epoch.

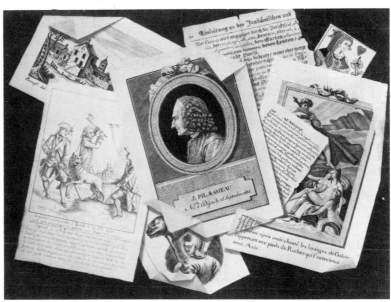

274. *French School, 18th century.* Letter Rack. *Private Collection*

275. *French or Italian School, 18th century.* Letter Rack *London, Victoria and Albert Museum*

243

276. *Jean Valette Penot (1710–1777).* Quod Libet with Self-Portrait. *Collection Frederick P. Victoria*

The delicate compositions of Jean Penot are characteristic in this respect (pl. 276). In addition to their artistic merit, they derive special interest because they are purely personal in the choice of subject matter, uninfluenced by any patron. This unusual artistic independence is attributable to Penot's total lack of success when he attempted to eke out a living as a painter in his native city of Montauban, where he had returned after studying in Italy. Forced to seek other means of supporting his family, Penot eventually established in his hometown a factory for the production of painted wall hangings of the kind he had admired in Bergamo. The undertaking brought him fame and fortune, but he continued for his own pleasure to produce small paintings on illusionistic themes. There is, however, an unmistakable hint of melancholy in all his subjects. In the example shown here, the glass pane over the framed engraving at center is broken, and one of the plaster bas-reliefs is chipped and cracked. In the same mood, a trompe l'oeil by Penot in the Museum at Montauban de-

244

picts a plaster bas-relief of the Holy Family cleft by a large crack and held together with iron clamps.[14]

Jean-Jacques Bachelier, although an excellent painter, is best remembered as a director of the royal porcelain factories of Sèvres and Vincennes. His career, like Penot's, is typical of that of many artists of the period whose talents were primarily directed towards ornamentation. Bachelier had early received official support because of his recognized merit as a painter of flowers: it is recorded that one of the artist's first offerings, in 1753, was a portrait of the King of France within an illusionistic garland of flowers besprinkled with bright dew drops. But when he was assigned a post at the Palais du Louvre, Bachelier had to be in readiness to fulfill any and all commands of his royal patron. He was frequently asked for pictorial facsimiles of hunting trophies, where he fully equalled his master, Oudry (pl. 277). What was particularly desired, however, was a record of zoological oddities—we are told, for example, of "some bizarre deer heads" and "a singular partridge." Bachelier raised at least one of these freaks to the level of a masterpiece: a multi-horned pair of stag antlers in a state of putrefaction (what huntsmen call "in velvet") immortalized by royal command (pl. 278).

277. *Jean-Jacques Bachelier (1724–1806).* Le Canard Mort. *Angers, Musée des Beaux-Arts*

278. *Jean-Jacques Bachelier.* Hunting Trophy. *Fontainebleau, Musée National du Château*

245

The taste for illusionistic accomplishments successfully weathered the revolutionary storm. In fact, the very term trompe l'oeil first came into use in the immediate aftermath of that trying period (see p. 8). And while "trompe l'oeil" appeared in print in 1803, the year VIII of the Revolutionary Calendar, it seems likely that it was current in the ateliers a few years before it was adopted into the vernacular. The first recorded use of the term was made by an adverse critic, a columnist who signed his satirical reviews of art events with the pen name of "Jocrisse" (Booby or Simpleton). Jocrisse bluntly expressed his opinion that "what was deemed trompe l'oeil utterly failed to deceive *his* eye." (Jocrisse evidently refused the minimum of cooperation that is called for on the part of a viewer.) The blow was severe, and if trompe l'oeil did not succumb, it was only because it had already effected an uneasy merger with neoclassicism. The precision of this new style brought it very close to outright illusionism and undoubtedly the most dramatic illustration of its success in this respect is found in David's grim tableau of "The Dead Marat" (pl. 279). David was well inured to such spectacles: one recalls his dispassionate sketches of Marie-Antoinette on her way to the guillotine. His memorial to the assassinated Revolutionary leader, as he appeared immediately after he had been stabbed in his bathtub by Charlotte Corday, is an extraordinarily lifelike (or rather deathlike) portrayal, and the depiction of the accessories meets with the highest standards of trompe l'oeil.

279. *Jacques-Louis David.* The Dead Marat, *1793. Brussels, Musées Royaux des Beaux-Arts*

280. *Constance-Marie Charpentier (1767–1849)*. Mlle. Charlotte du Val d'Ognes. *New York, The Metropolitan Museum of Art, Fletcher Bequest*

David's precisionist technique—and something also of his disabused spirit, cold and trenchant as hardened lava—is reflected in a work by his pupil, Constance-Marie Charpentier. Her study of a fellow student, the lovely blonde Mlle. Charlotte du Val d'Ognes (pl. 280), is set in a bare room where the window admitting a cold light on the young artist's easel is marred by a broken pane.

Other artists and literateurs—Romantics as well as Naturalists—were by no means unaware of the dramatic possibilities of illusionism. One recalls Balzac's tale of the imaginary Flemish painter driven to insanity by his relentless search for pictorial illusion (see p. 12). But in reality, the ascetic discipline, the patient skill trompe l'oeil lavished on apparently commonplace objects held little appeal for this tormented and restless generation, the orphans of the Napoleonic era, left with an unappeased longing for adventure and exotic glamour.

247

281. *Guillaume Dominique Doncre.* Ego Sum Pictor, *1785.*
Musée d'Arras

Nevertheless, the illusionistic tradition was perpetuated by such artists
as Louis-Léopold Boilly, who had inherited it from his master Guillaume Dominique Doncre (pl. 281). His renderings of broken glass were not merely indices but outright illusionistic statements. His offering at the Salon of 1800
depicted a broken glass atop a group of drawings, including his self-portrait.
Painted with characteristic Boilly bravura, the painting caused a sensation and
a rail had to be set up to protect it from the curious crowd. The example illustrated here (pl. 282) includes, in addition to the broken glass over the assemblage of pictures, a round lens and a gold louis—both as though slipped
between the covering glass and the frame. There is irony in the gold piece
placed next to the image of two lads immediately recognizable to contemporary viewers as chimney sweeps from Savoy—poorest among the poor. The
device of gold coins was a great favorite with Boilly, who often scattered his
imaginary coinage with a more generous hand: as many as nineteen in one
instance (wishful thinking?).

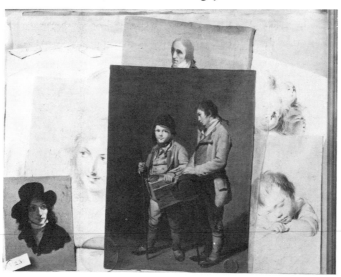

282. *Louis-Léopold Boilly (1761–
1845).* Trompe l'Oeil. *Private Collection*

283. *Louis-Léopold Boilly.* Objects on a Wall. *Private Collection*

284. *Louis-Léopold Boilly.* Crucifix. *Private Collection*

Boilly was justly renowned for his masterly grisailles, but he also delved into optical problems: he invented special lighting devices, and such tools are said to have helped him to achieve the unusual luminosity and striking relief for which his works are indeed notable (pl. 283). A special varnish, whose secret he never divulged, reputedly accounted for the undimmed freshness of coloring. He is also said to have created "transparent paintings," very likely illusionistic works, though no one knows just what these were. A latter-day minor da Vinci, Boilly, like his great counterpart did not necessarily depend on tricks for his achievements. Among his major illusionistic performances one must rank the great "Crucifix" (pl. 284)—the body of feigned ivory on a cross of ebony, a *cartellino* to the left—that was formerly in the collection at Northwick Park.[15]

249

285. *Laurent Dabos.* Peace Treaty between France and Spain, *aft. 1801. Paris, Musée Marmottan*

Another outstanding practitioner of trompe l'oeil was Laurent Dabos. His chief work is probably the famous "Peace Treaty between France and Spain" (pl. 285). Here, the symbolic significance of broken glass is irrefutable: the sarcasm is in every sense "transparent." Even more telling is that the most dangerous-looking of the fragments is aimed directly at Bonaparte. Two smaller trompe l'oeils by Dabos are not burdened with such weighty significance (pls. 286–87): each of these merely shows a playing card on a wooden board, with a flower passed through a slit (respectively, a carnation and a tulip). The two may have been part of a complete deck of cards.

250

286. *Laurent Dabos (1761–1835).* Still Life with Carnation and Playing Card. *Private Collection*

287. *Laurent Dabos.* Still Life with Tulip and Playing Card. *Private Collection*

Very little is known of the career and output of Gabriel-Germain Joncherie other than that he specialized in still-life subjects—a tradition that was carried on by his son, Hector-François, born in Paris in 1824 and his father's pupil. The elder Joncherie exposed at the Salon from 1831 to 1844, and the son began to show work in 1842. Joncherie the Elder and the Younger were honest, unpretentious painters who staunchly adhered to the ancient traditions of the French School at a most unpropitious time: the very height of the Romantic period, when nothing but exotic or archaic subjects could hope to win public applause. "La Chaufferette aux Oeufs" (color pl. 14) was probably conceived as a small *devant de cheminée,* perhaps for their own modest dwelling where they would provide for their needs on such a small portable stove as the one depicted here with its handful of glowing embers red as rubies. In the rank of the French *intimistes,* Joncherie stands midway between Chardin and Vuillard.

Flowers continued to play an important role in illusionism. The name of Pierre-Joseph Redouté evokes first and foremost his famous series of roses, although he has also glorified many other blooms, and often, one feels, with more lively originality. In his study of the "Crown Imperial" (pl. 288), the sturdy stem of the opulent bloom appears to jut beyond the illusionistic frame that surrounds it; some of the petals also overlap, and an uninhibited beetle wanders on the page, casting a most realistic shadow. Redouté, who was the art instructor to both Queen Marie-Antoinette and Empress Josephine, is chiefly associated with the eighteenth century but in fact lived and worked well into the next one, dying in 1840.

Another artist whose career also spanned two centuries was Antoine Berjon, who began in Lyon, his native city, with floral designs for textiles. And it seems as if the nacreous sheen of the silk fibers became an integral part of Berjon's subtle palette (pl. 289). He set down the tints with such

251

288. *Pierre-Joseph Redouté (1759–1840).* Crown Imperial. *New York, Pierpont Morgan Library*

289. *Antoine Berjon.* Shells and Madrepores, *1801. Lyon, Musée des Beaux-Arts*

smooth perfection that, to modern eyes, the painting reproduced here appears at first glance to be a photograph. Therefore, whether or not this famous study of seashells and madrepores was initially undertaken as a trompe l'oeil or as a still life, there can be little doubt that it has now become to all effects a trompe l'oeil. If the composition strikes us as oddly familiar, there is good reason: precisely such arrangements of tropical sea life have been worked to

252

death in our days in Caribbean travel folders, window displays of Florida souvenirs, and so forth.

In the late eighteenth century, the taste for grisaille painting—and more particularly for copies in that medium of ancient bas-reliefs—received new impetus from the strong current of neoclassicism then sweeping over Europe. This was reflected, for instance, in the decoration of the royal pavillion of Haga, near Stockholm, which was designed and carried out by a team of three French artists, Adrien Masreliez and his sons Jean-Baptiste and Louis. The murals, recently uncovered in the course of redecoration, consisted of mythological scenes and arabesques in the Pompeian style, combined with Wedgwood-like grisaille friezes. The pavillion was to have been part of a much larger residence, but the project was halted upon the death of the king in May 1792, when only the central building had been completed.

If the execution of ambitious illusionistic schemes of the kind in state apartments was entrusted only to highly skilled, professional artists, there were also occasions when the decoration of menial quarters inspired an unexpected development in "folk art." This occurred in Spain in the last decade of the century, when a number of kitchens in the region of Valencia were embellished with patently illusionistic decoration, carried out in the renowned glazed tiles made at Manises. The remarkably complete example shown here (pl. 290) was made for the Casa Dorda, Valencia. It is evident that the skill of the anonymous primitive artist fell far short of genuine deception in the rendering of the human and animal figures, but the intention is unmistakable—and a considerable measure of success is achieved in the depiction of kitchen utensils and alimentary products. [16]

Increasingly throughout the nineteenth century, architectonic illusionism was reduced to a mere adjunct of the revival of archaic architectural styles. At times, however, it might still transcend those limitations, as in the delightfully fantasque grisaille decoration of the "Porcelain Room" at the royal castle of Sintra in Portugal (pl. 291), a totally unconvincing but utterly enchanting Romantic interpretation of Flamboyant Gothic.

290. *Tiled Kitchen from Casa Dorda, Valencia. Madrid, Museo Nacional de Artes Decorativas*

291. *Decorations in the National Palace of Pena. Sintra, Portugal*

253

292. *Théodore Chassériau (1819–1856).*
Silence. *Fragment of a Grisaille Decoration.*
Paris, Musée du Louvre

In 1844, however, Théodore Chassériau painted a series of frescoes (now destroyed) for the Cours des Comptes in Paris. He included as dado a group of grisailles of which a few fragments, after a succession of mishaps, have survived (pl. 292). The poet Theophile Gautier saw these cool, gray personifications of Silence, Study, and Meditation as a planned overture, a preparatory introduction to the impact of the more dramatic works in color.[17] Chassériau had, at any rate, assigned to the grisailles their ancient function as an honored and significant auxiliary of architecture.

But in spite of such exceptions, during this period the tradition of illusionism peristed on the whole in graphic examples of a reduced scale, rather than in the monumental schemes of yore. A typical example is "Ferns, Grass, and Flowers" (pl. 293), a small gouache painting by the English Pre-Raphaelite aquarellist William Henry Hunt. John Ruskin commented that this artist was, "take him for all in all, the finest painter of still life that ever existed." The minutious attention to detail that won him such unreserved eulogium was motivated primarily by the painter's keen interest in the natural sciences, which also had the effect of bringing his works to the very verge of trompe l'oeil. The almost miniature-sized studies are kindred in mood and technique to medieval illustrations. In this particular work, the unusual shape of the rectangle surmounted by an arc has the inevitable effect of suggesting an opening as of a small window, beyond which one glances this verdant bit of garden.

Similarly, in "The Song of the Tea-Pot" (a music sheet cover illustration by an anonymous artist, circa 1840, pl. 294) the evocation of domestic bliss is viewed beyond an arched opening, window, or loggia. However, here more emphasis is laid upon the architectural setting—an epitome of neo-Baroque magnificence, in contrast to Hunt's narrow, severely plain molding. But the basic purpose in both instances

254

293. *William Henry Hunt.* Ferns, Grass, and Flowers. *New York, Collection of Mr. & Mrs. James Biddle*

294. *"The Song of the Tea-Pot," 19th century music sheet. Private collection.*

is essentially the same: the raising of the "space curtain" is suggested, if not actually accomplished.

With the rise of Impressionism, illusionism unquestionably underwent a major eclipse. The new school had little use either for the "castles in Spain" of illusionism or the self-effacement of trompe l'oeil. Yet we owe to the Father of Impressionism himself at least one undoubted illusionistic milestone: Manet's "Dead Toreador" (pl. 295) should properly take its place in the macabre but rarified category that includes Mantegna's "Dead Christ" (pl. 88), Holbein's "Christ in the Tomb," and David's Dead Marat" (pl. 279). (And one should perhaps add to the list the masterpiece of the Flemish romantic visionary Anthonie Wiertz, "Premature Burial.")

Spasmodic, isolated performances—frequently by gifted amateurs—are still found intermittently during this period of illusionistic dormancy in Europe. Admittedly, these seldom rose to the level of Thiaucourt's study of a chunk of peasant bread placed on a folded napkin (color pl. 18), dated 1880. An inscription on the *cartellino* in the left corner, as if between the painting and the frame, sets the mood of deadly seriousness. It reads in part: "To my friend . . . the password of hunger. . . ." That password is, of course, "du pain!"—echo-

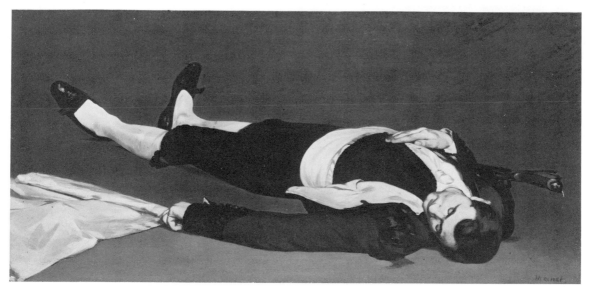

295. *Eduoard Manet.* The Dead Toreador. *Washington, D.C., National Gallery of Art, Widener Collection*

ing precisely that of the Revolutionary masses of the previous century. If trompe l'oeil had lost its artistic supremacy, it was still exercising its chosen function of social commentary. Beyond this pathetic implication of dire personal need and the call for proletarian solidarity, there is also an undeniable sense of religious solemnity in the presentation of the staff of life; the plain deal table assumes the sacredness of an altar.

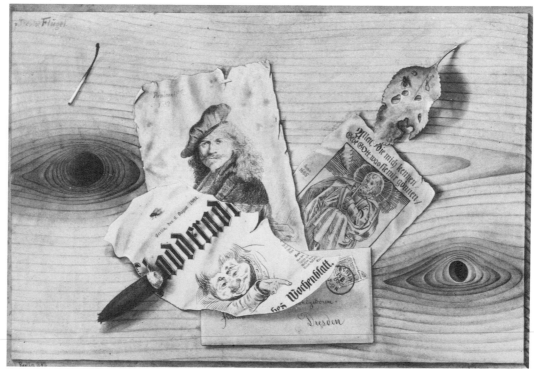

256

296. *Theodor Flügel.* Letter Rack. *San Francisco, Collection Louis Pappas*

Overflowing *gemütlichkeit* and the touch of the spiciness of Berlin wit bubble up in a pair of quizzical trompe l'oeil aquarelles painted by Theodor Flügel in 1882 (pl. 296). The illusionistic background of wooden planks supports a grouping of various prints and paper scraps bearing humorous messages. The addition of a leaf with a drop of dew and of a meandering fly further adorns these slightly delayed examples of "papyromania."

The lowering of the curtain over the pageant of European illusionism was carried out literally as well as symbolically, and in a proper climax of grandeur, with the famous curtain designed by Jean Louis Charles Garnier in 1874 for the Paris Opera House (pl. 297). An overwhelming display of sumptuous draperies—fringed, tasselled, embroidered, opulently overlapped, and looped up with heavy golden cords—was painted on the flat surface of the functional stage curtain. All this intricacy certainly did not "deceive" anyone in the strict sense, but instead provided a kind of hors d'oeuvre for the spectators awaiting the main entertainment. Viewers of the Garnier curtain—and of its many imitations—echoed at a distance of three millennia the wonderment of the ancient Athenians who had marvelled at the curtain of Agatharcos. Illusionism, one might say, ended as it had begun.

297. *Jean Louis Charles Garnier. Painted Curtain for the Paris Opera House, 1874.*

257

298. *John Mare (1739–1768).* Portrait of John Keteltas. *New York, Courtesy of the New York Historical Society*

7

Trompe l'Oeil in America

I. The Precursors

The earliest recorded instance of illusionism in America is found in the work of an artist about whom little is known besides the fact that, unlike most of the Colonial painters of the first half of the eighteenth century, he was a native American. John Mare was long known solely for his portrait of John Keteltas (pl. 298). About twenty years ago, a second and more ambitious work was discovered: a full-length portrait of a young man. What we are concerned with here, however, is a third, unheralded "portrait": that of the fly which the artist chose to depict on the cambric shirt cuff of John Keteltas.

Of all the foreign artists then practicing in America—the Englishmen, Wollaston, Blackburn, Smibert; the Swede, Hesselius; the Swiss, Jeremiah Theus, to name but a few—none was of the first rank but all were competent, well-trained professionals acquainted with the history and the production of European art. On the contrary, John Mare, born in New York in 1739, appears to have been self-taught. It is not impossible, therefore, that the idea of depicting the fly illusionistically, as a whimsical touch, may well have been an original inspiration. Still, Mare could have been familiar with the legendary anecdotes of trompe l'oeil which were of the sort that made the greatest impression on untutored minds. He may have known about these from his brother-in-law, the versatile, provincial English painter, William Williams, "sailor, painter-novelist, musician and wanderer."[1]

Whatever the reason, there is humor, independence, perhaps even a touch of imprudence, in the artist's daring decision to sport thus with his rather

299. *Winthrop Chandler (1747-1790).* Shelf of Books. *Shelburne Museum, Inc.*

formidable patron, for we may feel certain that the worthy John Keteltas did not fail his appointed and slightly ridiculous role of dutifully attempting to brush away the fly upon viewing the finished painting. The depiction of the insect in European examples does not usually suggest a comparable infringement of human dignity. Giotto played a light-hearted prank on his master (see p. 56) but did not introduce the fly as a permanent feature of a formal portrait. In religious pictures, and later in the gloomy symbolism of the Vanitas (e.g., pl. 69), the insect served the very earnest purpose of alluding to the evanescence of life and the insignificance of man. Yet, in his own homespun way, John Mare may have intended to put across much the same message. It is difficult to believe that his only intention was trickery and a display of skill. Illusionism and symbolism have always gone hand in hand, and the association was continued in America where allegiance to reality—pragmatism, as it would later be called—surfaced early, proved a tenacious undercurrent, and was finally and fully embodied by illusionists in the visual parables of the nineteenth century, by Harnett, Peto, Haberle, and their numerous followers.

But still in the eighteenth century another unequivocal trompe l'oeil was executed by Connecticut-born Winthrop Chandler, by profession a house painter (although he may have studied in Boston with Copley) and now famed for his portraits, hieratic giants a century ahead of those of Erastus Field. His "Shelf of Books," created to adorn a Connecticut home (pl. 299), is a naive version of earlier European treatments of the same theme. However, in addition to the possibility that the "Shelf of Books," like Mare's fly, may have been an original conception, the painting derives further interest from its close stylistic relation to Chandler's settings for his portraits, which are undoubtedly illusionistic in purpose. This ambition is evident, for instance, in the "Portrait of Mrs. Chandler" (pl. 300)—the wife of Captain Samuel Chandler—where an overwhelming sense of both the veracity of the artist and the personal dignity of the sitter redeem from naiveté this touchingly gauche embodiment of Colonial gentility—even to the awkward flounces that frame the book-laden shelves in back of the sitter.

300. *Winthrop Chandler.* Mrs. Samuel Chandler. *Washington, D.C., National Gallery of Art, Gift of Edgar William and Bernice Chrysler Garbisch*

301. *Ralph Earl.* Portrait of Roger Sherman, *c. 1775–79. New Haven, Yale University Art Gallery, Gift of Roger Sherman White*

A more skillful American portrayal that must have appeared extraordinarily lifelike at the time, and that remains today an impressive "presence," is the masterly portrait of Roger Sherman, painted circa 1777–1779 by Ralph Earl (pl. 301). What has been justly characterized as "the architectonic decorative power" of Earl brings his brand of portraiture very close to the drama of illusionism. The same traits are evident in the stagelike setting of the portrait "Mrs. Benjamin Tallmadge with Two Children."

Similar characteristics also mark the early (so-called American) work of Copley. One thinks particularly of his scrupulous attention to the minutiae of texture: shimmering satins, high-gloss wood veneers, and best of all, the wonderful rendering of the silver teapot and tools of the silversmith's trade reflected in the lustrous surface of the foreground table in Copley's portrait of Paul Revere (pl. 302). Such details, along with its volumetric density and brooding mood, irresistibly evoke Antonello da Messina. Indeed, the portrait of Paul Revere is a tantalizing echo of the great illusionistic portraits of the High Renaissance, and one is tempted to speak of an American continuation of the tradition. But Copley, in his later years, when he acquired the cosmopolitan polish Reynolds had preconized for the young provincial, also lost much of the weightiness and thoughtfulness, as well as the archaic precisionism, that had first brought him so close to illusionism.

Charles Willson Peale, on the contrary, who eventually became the first American illusionist of stature, did not exhibit in his early works an innate bent towards illusionism. The series of portraits done during the first half of his career—from 1765 to 1795—are conventional likenesses, uniformly marked by what has been called the artist's own "quiet affability."[2] His success as a portraitist may well have been due to his pleasing blandness, for

> when Peale casts the conventions aside in a large piece, it is . . . in a work outside his professional career and within his own family. The conventions had to be sacrificed in order to perfect that other, essential artist's purpose, the illusion of reality. He painted his sons in the famous "Staircase Group" [pl. 303] to show the young men of the Columbianum what a painter of thirty years' experience could do, and the result was a triumph indeed, for General Washington took off his hat and bowed to it.[3]

302. *John Singleton Copley (1738–1815).* Portrait of Paul Revere. *Courtesy, Museum of Fine Arts, Boston, Gift of Joseph W., William B., and Edward H. R. Revere*

303. *Charles Willson Peale.* Staircase Group, *c. 1795. Philadelphia Museum of Art, George W. Elkins Collection*

The last phrase is to be taken in the literal sense: the Father of His Country was actually "deceived" by the painting and saluted the two figures, whom he took to be the models. We would probably doubt the anecdote, if it had not actually been fully documented by Rembrandt Peale, one of the artist's four sons, who lived until 1860 and wrote:

> My father had invited the General to see some Indian figures
> dressed in their proper habiliments. A painting which he had
> just finished was placed in the room leading to the Indian Depart-
> ment of the Museum in Philadelphia. The picture represented my
> elder brother, with palette on hand, as stepping up a stairway,
> and a younger brother looking down. I observed that Washington,
> as he passed it, bowed politely to the painted figures, which he
> afterwards acknowledged he thought were living persons.[4]

The models for the "Staircase Group" (pl. 303) were the two sons of the artist whom he had named Raphaelle and Titian. (The other two had been called just as buoyantly Rembrandt and Rubens, while one of the daughters was christened Angelica Kauffmann—a true roll call of the artistic pantheon.) Two younger daughters were placed under the patronage of, respectively, Sophonisba Anguisciola and Rosalba Carriera. The "Staircase Group" was displayed at the first Columbianum (or "American Academy of Painting, Sculpture, Architecture, and Engraving") held in the Senate Chamber of the old Congress Hall in Philadelphia, on May 22, 1795.[5] It was then "framed" in an actual doorway with one additional wooden degree added to the painted steps, a setting that would certainly be conducive to the illusion. Was the conception itself entirely original—if anything indeed ever is? It may be only a coincidence, but a painting at the Castle Sant' Angelo in Rome depicts a cavalier as if stepping up a stairway.[6] Numerous English travellers, many of them artists, were then making the "grand tour," and such a curiosity would certainly have enchanted them. Knowledge of the work may eventually have reached Peale's ears during his stay in England as pupil (and guest) of Benjamin West. This can be only a supposition, not likely to be verified, but it would establish a most interesting link between European and American illusionism, and one not unlikely in view of Peale's keen interest in Italian painting, particularly the Venetians.

Almost three decades later, the eighty-four-year-old artist reverted to the staircase theme for a self-portrait which he had been asked to contribute to the museum managed by his son Rubens in Baltimore. He chose for this ambitious project, his swan song, a very large canvas (102 x 78 inches) set within an elaborate door frame. The accessories depicted symbolized his career and his life: a saddler's hammer, representing the painter's earliest avocation, on the lowest step, and a view of the museum in the background. Unfortunately nothing remains of this painting but the descriptions in the painter's letters; the great canvas, which excited much admiration, is believed to have been destroyed, along with so many irreplaceable relics of American art and history, in the fire of Barnum's American Museum. Peale recorded the public reaction to his "Self-Portrait" at some length.

> Mr. Sully, the famous painter, and his family came to see it yesterday . . . And what surprised him was my carpeting. He said that I ought to send you a piece of the same carpeting on the lower steps to supply you when that shall by spoiled. "How can I do that? Can I send painted steps?" "Painted steps. Bless me, I am completely deceived!"
>
> To Rubens Peale, August 25, 1823

304. *Charles Willson Peale*. The Artist in His Museum, *1822. Philadelphia, Courtesy of the Pennsylvania Academy of Fine Arts*

> This morning 13 artists came to see it and every one of them pro-
> nounced it to be the best picture which they had ever seen from
> my pencil, and what is extraordinary, everyone is deceived by
> some part of the picture. The truth is that I had determined from
> the commencement of it to make as much as I could in it to de-
> ceive the eye of a critical observer.
> To Mrs. Samuel Morris, September 19, 1823[7]

We may draw at least a general idea of the lost painting by mentally combining the "Staircase Group" with the equally famous "The Artist in His Museum" (pl. 304). The latter was painted a year before the self-portrait, and the grand old man of American art elected to depict himself (upon pressing request from the trustees) as if at the threshold of the museum's huge main hall, in the act of raising a rich drapery to reveal a plunging vista of the long gallery with tiers of shelves, or compartments, housing his precious zoological specimens. To understand the picture, it is necessary to recall that Charles Willson Peale was an important figure not only in the history of American art but of American cultural life. He had originally pursued a number of crafts (saddler, watchmaker, silversmith) before deciding to become a painter. Although he achieved immediate success as a portraitist, he was still not satisfied, but felt drawn to the natural sciences, and did in fact pursue dual careers as both scientist and artist. He founded the first American museum of science; the displays in the rows of superimposed cases had been gathered and prepared by him from the smallest specimen to the colossal *pièce de résistance,* the giant skeleton of the mastodon.

Himself larger than life, and in a sense "prehistoric," the elder Peale was the initial archetype of the American self-made man. His optimism and energy, his literal belief that "where there is a will, there is a way"—on one occasion he expressed the conviction that anyone could become an artist who really *wanted* to—these were precisely the qualities that led Peale to attempt illusionism, even if the essential basis of his efforts was his unreserved allegiance to Nature. As he oddly but expressively put it, "Nature is very perfect, and a juditious Painter cannot finish too high."

This injunction was obeyed by Charles Willson Peale's own children, all artistically gifted, as if they could hardly escape the contagion. Art was virulent in the Peale household. The younger son, Titian, portrayed in the "Staircase Group" in 1795, was by 1822 his father's trusted assistant in the execution of the great Museum portrait:

> To make trial of the effects in perspective in the Long Room, I drew the lines with my machine and set Titian at work to fill it up with his water colors, and he has nearly finished an admirable representation of the Long Room. The minutia of objects makes it a laborious work. It looks beautiful through the magnifiers. Coleman, seeing it yesterday, says that it deceived him. He thought he was viewing the Museum in the looking-glasses at the end of the Museum. He thinks it might be a good deception to see it in another room and would have a good effect on visitors.
>
> To Rubens Peale, August 4, 1822[8]

Thus the creation of one great illusionistic work immediately gave rise to a second: Titian Peale's representation of the Long Room. Even more notable than this process of emulation is the pragmatic appreciation by the elder

Peale that illusionism is essentially good spectacle.

Among the elder Peale's descendants, the mantle of illusionism fell unaccountably on the shoulders of Raphaelle Peale (1774–1825). Raphaelle had been the alert and assured young man depicted as the chief figure of the "Staircase Group"—once his father's brightest hope; now, belying his name, a fallen angel, a bohemian vagabond, and an alcoholic. Yet the splendor still glimmered through: there is a subtle, inimitable character in even his poorest works that seems to have been far beyond the reach of the rest of the brood, even the good industrious Rubens, or the upright Rembrandt (who was singled out to paint Washington from life). Rembrandt, one should add, did evince some occasional interest in illusionism: his portrait of Chief Justice Marshall in particular (pl. 324) is notable as an original and attractive variant of the lunette, or cartouche type, in contrast to the rather vapid, noncommittal oval then used by fashionable portraitists.

The early extant examples of trompe l'oeil by Raphaelle Peale—the "Deception" of 1802 (pl. 305) or the "Patch Picture for Dr. Physick," circa 1806—are conventional in subject matter but, like all of Raphaelle's produc-

305. *Raphaelle Peale.* A Deception, *1802. Private Collection*

tions, are raised above the ordinary by a severely abstract quality that recalls the works of the Spanish artists / mystics. This is true particularly of Rapha-elle's rather somber but dramatically highlighted, sharply outlined still lifes (pl. 306) in the hard-edge style of Floris van Schooten's "Dessert Table" (pl. 165) which only miss trompe l'oeil for the same reason that invalidates the Dutch master's picture: Raphaelle Peale's still lifes are also table*tops* or table*corners*. (See pp. 154–55.)

306. *Raphaelle Peale.* Still Life with Red Pepper. *Hartford, Courtesy Wadsworth Atheneum*

It is known that in 1812 Raphaelle Peale sent the Pennsylvania Acade-my of Art a painting, now lost, with the title "Catalogue for the Use of the Room—A Deception." Not only is the title self-descriptive and clearly indica-tive of the illusionistic nature of the picture, but there also exists a picture bearing the same title by Margaretta Angelica Peale (pl. 307), Raphaelle's niece, which is in all probability a copy of the original by him. He also painted such a catalogue "deception" on the wall of the Peale Museum, and many visitors are said to have bruised knuckles as they tried to pick up the leaflet apparently hanging from a nail on a long string.

In 1823, at the very same time that the partriarch was painting the "Staircase Self-Portrait," Raphaelle emulated his father's illusionistic achieve-ments by producing what was also certainly the masterwork of his own ca-

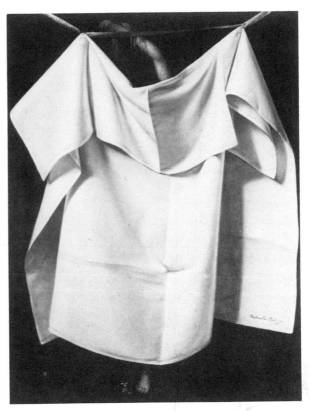

307. *Margaretta Angelica Peale (1795–1882).* Catalogue Deception. *Collection James O. Peale*

308. *Raphaelle Peale.* After the Bath, *1823. Kansas City, Mo., William Rockhill Nelson Gallery of Art, Atkins Museum of Fine Arts*

reer. This was the prankish, but artistically serious, "After the Bath" (pl. 308). The painting represents a white towel, freshly unfolded and still marked with sharp creases, which has been stretched across a room to provide privacy for a bather. The white drapery stands out starkly against a dark ground, almost filling the entire space of the canvas. Only a hint is furnished of what it conceals: a pretty hand and graceful arm at the top, and a slender foot and ankle peeping below the margin of the cloth a few inches above the ground. The wife of the artist, we are told, was the first to be taken in by the deception and felt properly outraged—only slightly less so when she found out that it was after all, only a playful fantasy of her artist husband.

There is an unmistakable prophetic dash of romanticism in this conception but also a great deal more; it offers a hint of the originality and imagination that might have led Raphaelle to a greater and stronger art than either portraiture or still life. It may be that the climate was not favorable to this development. Or perhaps Raphaelle Peale, brilliantly gifted and hypersensitive, may in some measure have been the victim of a situation now defined by modern psychology: the pitching of the clay pot against the iron vessel, of the dutifully filial introvert against the forceful extrovert father. "After the Bath" may represent Raphaelle's only meaningful escape from a life of re-

269

270

309. *Major Andre [?].* British Grenadier. *Philadelphia, The Historical Society of Pennsylvania*

pression. What is beyond doubt, regardless of personal considerations, is that in its unadorned simplicity and taut, understated pathos it is the foremost achievement of American illusionism of that age.

The catalogue of the first Columbianum includes a rather puzzling item: "Five flower pieces in imitation of enamel by a japanner." Another entry, however, was less equivocal. It was in the opinion of a contemporary critic, "a remarkable example, privately owned, with the signature of the Boston portraitist, John Johnston, which testifies to the prevalence of illusionistic intention— its bee and caterpillar among peaches and grapes shedding drops of water are a fitting pictorial succession to John Mare's fly."[9]

If American artists of Colonial and Revolutionary times lacked both the leisure and the opportunity to acquaint themselves as fully as their European counterparts with artistic tradition, they made virtue out of necessity and compensated for the lack by native creativeness. Nevertheless, they were not quite as destitute of models or inspiration as is often thought. Considerable "intelligence" did make its way to the American backwoods. There is evidence, for instance, that the fad of *chantourné* figures that had journeyed from Holland to England next made its way to the "rebellious colonies." A painted life-sized figure of a British grenadier (pl. 309) is believed to have been the work of a gifted amateur, sadly famed in American and British annals: the unfortunate Major André, who is said to have created the figure "to answer the purpose of an advertising poster" for the old Southwark Theatre in Philadelphia, which had been reopened when the British occupied the city in November 1777.[10] The life-sized figure may also have filled a decorative purpose and was probably not a figure alone but part of a group forming a mock guard of honor. At any rate, the diary of a daughter of a distinguished Philadelphia family recounts the role played on December 12, 1777, by precisely such a grenadier figure, if not this very one. If Miss Sally Wister is correct, and there is not the slightest reason to doubt her, this would be the first illusionistic practical joke played on the American continent:

> We had brought some weeks ago a British grenadier from Uncle
> Miles' on purpose to divert us. It is remarkably well executed,
> six feet high, and makes a martial appearance. This we agreed to
> stand at the door . . . with another figure, a Turk, that would add
> to the deceit.

Then the gentlemen were called by a servant who advised them that they were wanted at the door. The chief victim of the prank was to be a certain "Captain Tilley," a likable fellow but rather pusillanimous.

They all arose, and walked into the entry, Tilley first. The first object he saw was a British soldier. Then a thundering voice said— "Is there any rebel officer here?" Tilley darted like lightning at the front door, through the yard and over the fence. Swamps, fences, thorn-hedges and ploughed fields no way impeded his retreat. He was soon out of hearing. The woods echoed with "Which way did he go? Stop him! Surround the house!" We females ran down to join in the general laugh. Figure to thyself this Tilley, of a snowy evening, no hat, shoes down at the heel, hair unty'd, flying across meadows, creeks, and mud-holes. Flying from what? Why, a bit of painted wood."

310. *Benjamin Henry Latrobe.* Letter Rack, *1795. Baltimore, Maryland Historical Society*

The ill-used Tilley, we are told, took the joke in good part and forgave his tormentors. No one, however, thought of pinning a medal on the stalwart chest of the star performer.

One hesitates to term the distinguished architect and engineer Benjamin Latrobe an "amateur"—the Maryland Historical Society alone possesses a treasure trove of 325 paintings and drawings of extraordinary charm and undoubted professionalism, including what may be the best portrait of Thomas Jefferson. Yet trompe l'oeil was hardly Latrobe's favorite avocation. But to while away the hours during the long sea voyage that brought him to America in 1795, he executed a casual illusionistic exercise that combines the features of letter rack and *quod libet* (pl. 310).

311. *"Nathaniel Peck."* The All-Seeing Eye. *Hartford, Courtesy Wadsworth Atheneum*

One of the most famous American trompe l'oeils is "The All-Seeing Eye" (pl. 311), so titled because the intriguing symbol depicted at the top is probably of Masonic inspiration, although the eye here is not framed in the symbolic triangle of the Craft. The precisionistic excellence of the picture alone would be sufficient grounds to justify the appellation: the eye of the artist was indeed "all-seeing." On the sole evidence that the name "Nathaniel Peck" appears on an envelope in the composition, the unknown artist has tentatively been identified with him. But this is by no means conclusive, any more than is the dating of the picture to 1827 because a calendar bearing that date is included. Valued letters and other outdated material were often included in such arrangements. To cite the example at closest range, Raphaelle Peale's "Deception" of 1802 included an invitation card to "the President's birth night" of 1795, and the "Patch Picture" of 1806, an 1893 directory. What does seem likely, however, is that the artist probably was a denizen of New York and possibly lived (or summered) in Flushing, Long Island, since envelopes bearing New York and Flushing addresses are part of the letter rack and the painting was discovered in Flushing

No such uncertainty exists regarding the portrait painter Charles Bird King, who in his youth had been one of the last students of Benjamin West in London. Brilliantly gifted and a most receptive pupil, the young man used his stay abroad to acquaint himself with the best of the European tradition, old and new. Something of this is reflected in his two superlative trompe

273

312. *Charles Bird King.* The Poor Artist's Cupboard, *c. 1815. Washington, D.C., Corcoran Gallery of Art*

l'oeils in the Dutch style: "The Poor Artist's Cupboard" (pl. 312), dated circa 1815, and "The Vanity of the Artist's Dream" (pl. 313), which is assigned to the year 1830. Charles Bird King is beyond doubt the most painterly of all American practitioners of trompe l'oeil in the pre-Harnett period. It is evident, however, that in the poetic pathos of his themes and the noble lyricism of his style—in perfect antithesis to the drypoint precisionism of "Nathaniel Peck"—he is far more European than American in mood.

Contrary to appearance, the two trompe l'oeil paintings by King are not a pair, since in execution they are separated by an interval of fifteen years. It seems rather strange that at such a distance in time the artist should have adhered not only to what is basically the same theme but even to the same diagonal composition (the roll of paper that slants across from left to right in one instance is merely reversed in direction in the other); to a very closely related choice of accessories (the book with titles suggestive of the only pleasures—of "hope" and "imagination"—that are within the reach of an unmoneyed artist, the bread, symbolic of abstemious fare, on the same round plate with jutting knife); and even also the eloquent device of the "sheriff's sale" broadsheets. But where the two paintings differ considerably is in the effect of depth. "The Vanity of the Artist's Dream" presents the assemblage of objects within a square frame and rather shallow recession, even though the composition includes a strongly plastic piece of statuary. In "The Poor Artist's Cupboard" the medley is displayed within a deep niche. It is also more luminous in tone, suffused with a vermeil glow: although the water glass retains crystalline and colorless purity, the bright red of the cover in the foreground is reflected in the enamellike surface of the tropical seashell above, which, in sophistication of pictorial rendering is certainly not inferior to that pictured by Berjon (pl. 289).

If Charles Bird King was indeed "a painter's painter" and set the highest possible standards for American illusionism, Goldsborough Bruff was by nature and schooling a graphic artist. He was trained at West Point as a cadet but never pursued a military career. At West Point, however, he attended the art classes organized by General Tadeusz Kosciuszko—himself a portraitist and landscapist of merit, as well as a fortifications engineer—and was next heard of as draftsman in the Washington office of the Topographical Engineers. His

313. *Charles Bird King.* The Poor Artist's Cupboard, *c. 1815. Washington, D.C. Corcoran Gallery of Art*

watercolor trompe l'oeil, "Assorted Prints" (pl. 314), faithfully reflects this training, as well as it does the artist's varied interests and his many-faceted personality. The composition not only includes his own "business card" but presents a complete sampling of his professional accomplishments as cartographer, illustrator, heraldist, ornamentist, etc. The envelopes do not bear postage stamps, and therefore the picture must have been done before 1847 (when stamps were introduced in America), although perhaps as late as 1845. The purpose was so clearly illusionistic, in spite of the medium, that "the outside edges of the paper are painted to resemble the cross section of the board on which cards, letters, drawings and prints are placed."[12]

Charles Fraser, born in Charleston in 1782, was a childhood friend of Thomas Sully, the portraitist. Fraser must have been conscious of his own limitations, for he had the wisdom to study law and accumulate "a modest competence" in this profession, reserving the pursuit of art as an avocation. He was also a poet, was active as an art critic of sorts (in the moralizing tone of the period) and held an exhibition of his paintings in 1857 "at the Fraser Gallery," which one presumes to have been a sort of private museum.[13] The list of works on display is of considerable interest: in addition to many that are clearly still lifes, several titles imply illusionistic treatment. There can be no doubt, for instance, about number 68 on this list: "Imitation of wood,

314. *Goldsborough Bruff.* Assorted Prints, *c. 1845. Private Collection*

276

315. *William Aiken Walker.* Blue-Winged Teal
Drakes, *1860. New York, Collection Gerald Paget*

316. *William Aiken Walker.* Dollarfish and Sheepshead, *1860. Courtesy, Museum of Fine Arts, Boston,
M. and M. Karolik Collection*

with a nail painted on it," ot which, unfortunately, no trace remains. Some
of the still lifes of game may perhaps have been painted against a background
of grained wood, precisely as was done a few years later by another Charleston
artist.

This was William Aiken Walker who, born in 1831, was already exhibit-
ing as a child prodigy in 1843. In 1860 Walker produced two still lifes of
game birds against a background of wood panelling. It seems probable that
the two artists must have been acquainted, if only because Fraser, the art
critic, would be likely to have taken an early interest in the local prodigy.[14]
In later years, Walker devoted most of his energy to depicting the life of plan-
tation workers in the cotton fields. In the year 1860 alone, Walker painted in
addition to two hunting trompe l'oeils ("Blue-Winged Teal Drakes," pl. 315;
and "Duck, Bob-Whites, and Rails"), a tabletop frieze, "Still Life with a Bottle
of Cognac, Crab, and Prawns," and the beautiful "Dollarfish and Sheepshead"
(pl. 316) on a luminous background of golden Southern pine. His interest in
illusionistic studies of fish never abated, and his career is marked with recurrent portrayals of the creatures of the sea that had a double appeal for him,
both as an artist and as a sportsman. Many were done on the Florida Keys in
the early 1900's when he accompanied his friend "Mr. Gamble" (one of the
founders of Proctor and Gamble) on piscatorial expeditions in what was still
unexplored wilderness.

277

317. *Martin Johnson Heade and Frederick E. Church.* Gremlin in the Studio. *Collection of Dr. and Mrs. Irving F. Burton*

Walker's unusually precocious career and long life (he died in 1921) make him, in the strict chronological sense, a contemporary of both Washington Allston and Jackson Pollock. In relation to American illusionism, it is not always realized that he antedated Harnett and the other members of the Philadelphia School by a decade.

Martin Johnson Heade (1819–1904) is famed for his exquisite renderings of hummingbirds in their natural habitat, made during his travels in South America and particularly in Brazil. Heade has been called the creator of a new species of illusionism—illusionism "as a medium for the student of natural history.[14a] This is precisely what the miniature scenes are, for the faethered actors are seen through a realistically painted tunnel of verdure in the immediate foreground.

Unlike any of these works, however, and a phenomenon for which it is difficult to find a proper classification, is the painting originally titled "Overflowing River Landscape" and renamed in our times "Gremlin in the Studio" (pl. 317). While this odd picture appears solely under Heade's name, it is said to represent the result of a cooperation between this artist and Frederick E. Church. The upper part of the picture is taken up by a conventional landscape, signed by Heade in the lower left corner, and which appears to be standing on some rude wooden horses. All is well so far, but one then notes

278

that a shallow pond depicted at the center of the landscape is overflowing the border of the canvas and draining in a steady trickle on to the studio floor. Next to the small waterfall, a fantastic, Bosch-like little creature is disporting itself joyfully, as if congratulating itself for having brought about the weird occurrence.

The setting of the trestles and the figure of the gremlin were the contribution of Frederick E. Church,[15] who, it will be recalled, was famed as the great landscapist of South America. But beyond the phantasmagory of "Gremlin in the Studio," the interpretation of two worlds, one real and the other of the imagination, heralding surrealism, there is one more puzzling element: the fact that painting signed by Heade is actually characteristic of Frederick E. Church—so that the deception persists even in the realm of style.

Church perpetrated yet another prank of trompe l'oeil, if not this time *trompe l'esprit*. This is "The Letter of Revenge" (pl. 318) which, according to Alfred Frankenstein

> was presented in Oberlin College in 1904 by a gentleman named Olney who had acquired it from the artist and who claimed, apparently with good reason, that it had been "painted to deceive a friend who made the statement that a work of art is meritorious only as it may be mistaken for the original"; consequently Mr. Olney gave the picture the title *The Letter Revenge*.[16]

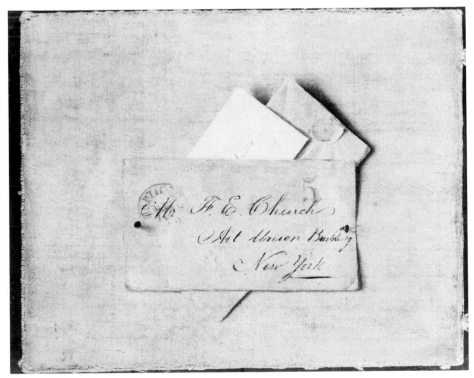

318. *Frederick E. Church*. The Letter of Revenge, *before 1892. Oberlin, Ohio, Oberlin College, Allen Memorial Art Museum*

319. *Constantino Brumidi. Frieze of the Capitol Dome, Washington, D.C.*

"I fail to understand," Mr. Frankenstein adds, "just why Church should have been regarded as having taken revenge on his friend when he embodied that friend's esthetic principles on canvas." But one cannot help but feel that the friendly "statement" might have been much in the nature of a taunt, implying that Church was not capable of painting an object so that it might be "mistaken for the original." The artist very likely picked up the gauntlet and achieved not only an artistic triumph but also a personal revenge for the slight on his technical capacity.

So much contumely has been heaped on Constantino Brumidi's ambitious, but uninspired, decorative scheme of the Capitol dome in Washington that what is probably the sole praiseworthy element of this ensemble has been lost in the condemnation. Yet the Italian artist deserves commendation at least for the trompe l'oeil frieze in grisaille because of its great simplicity and the aptness of both style and subject matter (pls. 10, 319). The frieze, depicting highlights of America's early history, was to have skirted the entire perimeter of the base of the cupola—three hundred feet in length by nine in height. It would have been architectural illusionism on an hitherto unprecedented scale—certainly never attempted on this continent. Brumidi died before completing the task, but it was continued by his assistant Filippo Costaggini until about two thirds had been done. Then, regrettably, the powers that had stoutly supported Brumidi chose to withdraw that support precisely at the time when it would have brought worthwhile results. The illusionistic frieze remains unfinished to this day.

Erastus Field's "Historical Monument of the American Republic" (pl. 320) was never even begun, but it undoubtedly deserves the palm for imaginary architectural illusion, and this is the category to which it is here assigned. Yet, unlike its famous predecessors by Thomas Cole—"The Architect's Dream" (pl. 321) or the even more fantastical "Titan's Goblet," which were presented as the visions of a poet—Field's masterwork was conceived in its entirety, from cyclopean base to aerial railroad linking the topmost towers, as a sober architectural plan for the "historical monument" of the title. The

320. *Erastus Salisbury Field.* Historical Monument of the American Republic, *1874. Springfield, Mass., Museum of Fine Arts, The Morgan Wesson Memorial Collection*

321. *Thomas Cole.* The Architect's Dream, *1840. Toledo, Ohio, Toledo Museum of Art*

project is believed to have been undertaken in 1874 as an entry in a contest for the design of the central building at the Philadelphia Centennial Exhibition.

Grandiose as the winning design turned out, it was mere play compared to the monster envisioned by Field. Never realized and probably not realizable, the visionary "Historic Monument" is adorned with a multitudinous wealth of grisaille and bronze camaïeus—somewhat disappointing at close range, but of ravishing grace and jewellike delicacy as a whole.

Field's sole realized venture in the field of trompe l'oeil was the decoration of frames for his own painting (pl. 322), which he embellished with feigned enamelling or incrustations of naive sumptuosity—rich carbuncles or faceted gems, echoing at a distance of two millenia the Greek painting mentioned by Philostratus: "The artistry of the painting must be praised first, because the artist in making the border of precious stones, has used not colours but light to depict them, putting a radiance in them like the pupil in the eye. . . ."[17] Kindred practices by the *pointillistes* and the *tachistes* differ both from those of the recorded Greek artist and from Field's in that all that was attempted at this later date was basically texture imitation of the painted canvas itself, with a view of doing away with the limiting effect of a frame by means of finer or coarser speckling. In addition to the actual imitation of the gemmed borders for their own sakes, Field went one step further by creating an effect of depth by means of various optical devices: in "The Embarkation of Ulysses" (pl. 322), the painting appears as if boxed, although the frame is actually rather flat, because the stripes on the inner border all slant towards the vanishing point.

282

322. *Erastus Salisbury Field.* The Embarkation of Ulysses. *Springfield, Mass., Museum of Fine Arts, The Morgan Wesson Memorial Collection*

323. *George Washington Marks.* Young Girl at a Door, *c. 1845. Dearborn,
Mich., Collections of the Greenfield Village and the Henry Ford Museum*

The purpose of another imaginative American artist of the mid-nine-
teenth century was not merely illusionistic but spectacular in the grand Peale
tradition and in the literal meaning of the term. George Washington Marks
created a life-sized trompe l'oeil of a small girl peeping through a large open
wooden door specifically for public exhibition and for the express purpose of
"deceiving the eye" for profit (pl. 323; color pl. 15). He is said to have succeeded
in achieving both purposes in his own day, as well as a third for posterity: while
the portrayal now appears somewhat aloof, the shy maiden nevertheless retains what a modern critic has defined as the charm of a rose pressed in a
book. But what is perhaps most interesting is Mark's evocation—conscious or
not—of the great tradition of Renaissance architectural illusionism. We need

283

324. *Rembrandt Peale.* Chief Justice Marshall, *c. 1826. Washington, D.C., U.S. Supreme Court. Courtesy Supreme Court Historical Society*

only compare his little girl to the young lady entering a room through the painted door in Veronese's fresco at the Villa Maser (pl. 112) to see how the conceit has travelled over three centuries. Even more ingenuously illusionistic than this superannuated evocation, but surprisingly effective, is the keyhole glimpse of a Quaker meeting by an anonymous American artist of the nineteenth century (pl. 325). Scaled down, and in a far more modest mood, this is nevertheless a legitimate kin—one might say a country cousin—of Rembrandt Peale's romantic portrait of Chief Justice Marshall (pl. 324), as well as of an even more famous example, Gilbert Stuart's "porthole" study of Washington.

An intriguing object known as "The Mount Brothers' Music Stand" (pl. 326) is decorated on the faces of the lectern with sheets of music in casual disarray. The painting is the work of William Sidney Mount, the most gifted member of a family of American painters, comparable to the dynasty of the Peales. "The Mount Brothers' Music Stand" is interesting not only as a reincarnation of an ancient theme—the Renaissance music desk with intarsia decoration (pl. 57), the painted "Open Book" (pl. 58), and the *devant de cheminée* (pl. 250)—but also as one more instance of illusionistic activities by American artists who had formerly not been connected with this style at all. Among them one may now rank William Sidney Mount, not only on the strength of "The Music Stand" but because of his close connection with an undoubted American illusionist, the Long Island artist William M. Davis, resurrected in our own days by the discoverer of Harnett, Alfred Frankenstein.[18]

284

325. *American School, 19th century*. Quaker Meeting. *Boston, Museum of Fine Arts, Bequest of Maxim Karolik*

326. *William Sidney Mount (1807–1868)*. The Mount Brothers' Music Stand. *Courtesy of the Museums at Stony Brook, Long Island, New York*

285

William M. Davis, whose life spanned almost a century (1829–1920) was a Union supporter during the Civil War and is known to have created at least two paintings, now lost, expressing these sentiments in 1862, both foretelling the defeat of the Southern cause: "The Neglected Picture" and "Hic Jacet Secesh." As the latter included a representation of a grave headstone, it may have been an ambitious illusionistic still life rather than a trompe l'oeil. No doubt exists, however, about "The Neglected Picture," which was minutely described in a contemporary publication:

> . . . an old, dirty, stained lithograph [of Jefferson Davis] in a dilapidated, mahogany frame, with the glass broken. The edges and points of the broken glass look remarkably keen, appearing as if ready to fall from the picture. The frame, one corner covered partially with cobwebs, in which several flies have become imprisoned, seems ready to drop apart and the business cards of "Justice and Co." and "B. Happy" in the corners are so accurately delineated that it seems almost impossible that the representation is on a piece of canvas.[19]

"The Neglected Picture" may be the earliest instance of the theme of broken glass in American art. William M. Davis was an untutored genius who combined extreme painterly sophistication with almost childish naiveté. Both are evidenced in "A Canvas Back" painted circa 1870 (pl. 327), showing the reverse of a painted canvas on a stretcher. Several letters are tucked at bottom between the wooden support and the linen material. A label at top bears the whimsical indication: "A Canvas Back By Kro Matic." The odd title is actually a pun: a "canvas back," the back of a canvas; and a "canvasback," a North American duck, so named from the color of the back feathers. Davis was poking fun at the current vogue for hunting trophies with enumerative (and deadly dull) titles—"Blue-Winged Teal Drakes," "Duck, Bob-Whites, and Rails," and the like. In addition, the jocose purpose was to incite the curious viewer to turn over the picture to see the "canvasback," when all that would meet his eye would be the real verso of the canvas on which the feigned one had been depicted.

Notwithstanding this cumbrous weight of allusion and facetiousness, the picture is excellent—unquestionably worthy of comparison with Gysbrechts' great early classic of the same genre (pl. 154). Yet it seems highly unlikely that Davis, of all American artists of that time, would have known about this. One should recall that awareness of the oeuvre of Gysbrechts, most of it kept in Scandinavia, was not widespread at any time, even in professional art circles in Europe, and least of all during the long eclipse of Gys-

327. *William M. Davis.* A Canvas Back, *c. 1870. Courtesy of the Museums at Stony Brook, Long Island, New York*

brechts' fame that came to an end only in our own days.

It is unlikely that William Sidney Mount, whose taste was chaste and severe, approved such quips. He certainly disapproved of another trick by Davis, who had directed that one of his paintings on view at the National Academy should be retitled "Four Apples and a Pare" [*sic*] instead of "Fruit," whereas it actually represented four oranges and a lemon.[20] Davis slyly expected reviewers to pounce on the error and at least mention his picture. But this, Mount commented, "was courting notoriety at the expense of truth." He apparently forgave Davis, for he could not find it in himself to deny recognition to such outstanding skill on purely moral grounds. Mount actually went to the trouble of writing an article which was read as a preface to an auction sale of a large number of Davis' paintings held in Port Jefferson. The text of this has not been preserved, which is unfortunate, for although it was presumably an appreciation of Davis' works, it may have incorporated some thoughts of William Sidney Mount on the larger subject of illusionism.

287

328. *De Scott Evans*. The Parrot, *c. 1877. Los Angeles, Collection of Mr. & Mrs. Oscar Salzer*

The Davis Sale took place in 1865. The next known example of broken glass in American illusionism was probably "The Parrot" by De Scott Evans (pl. 328; color pl. 19), most likely executed in France. The story connected with it is very different from the homespun tale of Davis. De Scott Evans was born in Boston in 1847 and is known to have been active in Cleveland, Ohio, in 1874. In 1877, however, he was a pupil of Bouguereau, in Paris, and upon his return to Cleveland, probably during the next year, Evans became an art teacher. He was lost in the shipwreck of the *Bourgogne* in 1898, which he had boarded on his way once more to Paris, where he had been commissioned to carry out some ceiling decorations, presumably illusionistic. His delightful and touching "Parrot" was most likely a product of his student days in France. The inscribed card within the box reads (translated from the French):

> This parrot was found in South America, whence he was brought
> to Paris, where he learned to speak French, [a talent he practiced]
> for many years. He died at the age of twenty, was stuffed, and
> here you see him now.
>
> [Signed] Pierre Gastereau

No doubt the bird had occupied his transparent cenotaph for a long time before an accident broke the protective seal. Without repair, the parrot's afterlife would soon have come to an end. Whether for this or any other reason, thanks to De Scott Evans, he has been granted a reprieve.[21]

The wreath of flowers and fruit set against a stone wall by the brilliant and sensitive John La Farge (pl. 329; color pl. 17) is undoubtedly a trompe l'oeil. The delicate style is supremely suitable for what is in effect both an epitaph and an elegy. The inscription, painted in red Greek characters, reads: "As the summer was just beginning . . ." Except for the vivid sparkle of the flowers, only the subtle texture of the wall, the shadow of the wreath, and the slight bevel at bottom bring plastic drama to this poetic conception, so surprisingly modern that it is hard to believe that it was painted in 1866.

329. *John La Farge.* Love Token, *1866. Washington, D.C., National Collection of Fine Arts*

289

290

330. *William Harnett.* After the Hunt, *1883. Columbus, Ohio, Columbus Gallery of Fine Arts, Gift of Francis C. Sessions*

8

Trompe l'Oeil in America

II. The Second School
of Philadelphia

Philadelphia had been the Athens of America when New York was little more than a trading post, but by the middle of the nineteenth century, New York had become capital of the nation in every sense other than governmental. Above all, it was recognized as its art center: not only was New York the distribution point for European imports but the ateliers were there, the Bohemian life, the power and the glory too. Yet it was still in the Quaker City that a development was to take place that would profoundly affect American culture and of which the repercussions have not been fully felt until our own day.

The development resulted in a virtual renaissance of illusionism in the New World' The movement is now known as the "Second School of Philadelphia," a convenient but somewhat illogical appellation, since the three artists that spearheaded it worked independently, and one of them actually had no connection whatever with Philadelphia. The great triad consisted of William Harnett, John Peto, and John Haberle—names that are now familiar but which had sunk into oblivion for nearly half a century until they were rediscovered and restored to high honor by Alfred Frankenstein. In his important work, *After the Hunt* (1953), Frankenstein brought back to light not only these three masters but also a host of minor, yet by no means negligible, imitators and followers. The book not only presented the results of the author's scholarly chase but its title is doubly apt, for it refers as well to the *pièce de résistance* of the movement, the famed trompe l'oeil by Harnett bearing that same title (pl. 330).

331. *William Harnett.* After the Hunt, *1885. San Francisco, California Palace of the Legion of Honor*

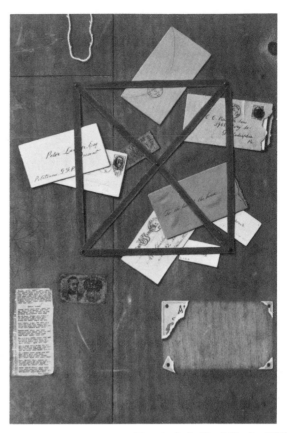

332. *William Harnett.* The Artist's Card Rack, *1879. New York, The Metropolitan Museum of Art*

333. *William Harnett.* Golden Horseshoe, *1886. Collection Mr. and Mrs. James W. Alsdorf*

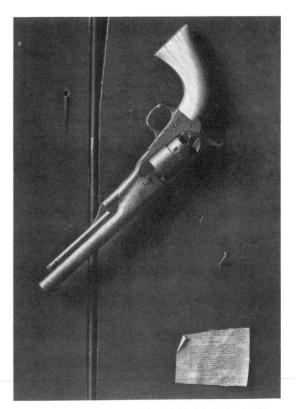

334. *William Harnett.* The Faithful Colt, *1890. Hartford, Courtesy Wadsworth Atheneum*

William M. Harnett is indeed entitled to pride of place if only because he was first of the three to be resurrected and, due at least in part to this early start, his name still commands more prestige than those of the others. But the far greater precision and delicacy of his style also plays a significant role; it is the sort of technique that would draw "ohs" and "ahs" even if it were not the vehicle of a true artistic message. Harnett's sensitive awareness of textures and of the fine points of good workmanship, so faithfully reflected in his renderings of the objects he called his "models," might also be termed a birthright, for the artist came from a family of Old World artisans. While it is possible to find a certain lack of taste in the somewhat cluttered still lifes of his middle and late periods, his technique is invariably impeccable, and his trompe l'oeil paintings without exception are marked by admirable sobriety and understated drama. If it is permissible to make such a heretical statement, Harnett would have been an even greater artist had he painted half as many pictures, or else twice as many, spreading out the subject matter more thinly. Either way, what would have remained towering in uncontested majesty would be the few illusionistic masterpieces that are milestones of his career: the early "Artist's Card Rack" of 1879; the peerless "Golden Horseshoe" and "Old Violin," both of 1886; "Mr. Huling's Rack Picture" of 1888; and the last great work, "The Faithful Colt" of 1890 (pls. 332, 333, 334). All these are imbued with that same uniquely noble, transcendental quality—the result of self-imposed limitation to monumental essentials—that is a common trait of the great illusionists.

It may bear repeating here that nothing was ever further removed from either realism or reality, and nothing closer to high poetry, than trompe l'oeil as practiced by the true masters of the art. Harnett once commented on still life—and of course the statement applied to trompe l'oeil as well—that "In painting from still life I do not closely imitate nature. Many points I leave out and many I add."[1]

Nothing could have been more categorical, but he went even further and itemized some of his exacting requirements. For instance, Harnett told how, in depicting a flute, he sought for subtle tints of old ivory not found in the rather ordinary model he had before him, and how he also added to the brass mounting rings additional glints of gold, which he had studied on the edge of a gold coin. Yet all these efforts were ignored, and one writer, when describing Harnett's paintings, felt justified in placing the expression "works of art" in quotes. Later, an American critic would speak even more slightingly of "painting by recipe."[2] These unjust comments must have rankled in spite of the calmly dignified front the artist put up, answering fellow students who jeered at his "realism" that he "would change his style as soon as he stopped selling." In spite of this brave show, he was actually the least mercenary of artists and was undone solely by the very subtlety of his style, which was, in painterly terms, an equivalent to Proustian or Jamesian refinements.

A telling incident involving another famed American painter, William Meritt Chase, took place in Munich, probably at the time when both men were students there. It reflects the general climate of scorn that was prevalent towards illusionism.

> Discussions concerning the old and new ideas were rife in those days. Chase recalled one that had an amusing result. He had been insisting that the exact reproduction of nature had nothing in common with art. (I remember well the harassed frown with which he used to say to his students: "You have all heard of the picture of the fruits which was so natural that the birds flew down to peck at it? I do not need to see that canvas to know that it was a Terrible Thing!") Talking, no doubt, along some such line as that, another student challenged Chase with the remark that whether art or not, such painting represented skill of a sort, and that Chase himself was no doubt unable to paint an object that could deceive anyone. As a result of this friendly contention, the student agreed that if Chase could perform the feat, he would give all the students a dinner. Chase accepted the challenge.
>
> The next day, when Professor Raab arrived to criticize his pupils, he turned upon entering to hang his hat on its usual peg on the wall. The hat, before the eyes of the waiting class, fell to the ground. The professor picked it up and tried again, thinking he had missed the nail; but again his hat fell to the floor. When the same thing happened a third time, the old German looked intently at the wall, then without a change of expression laid his hat upon a chair and began his criticism. After his departure, the class gathered to examine the highly successful imitation painted upon the wall by William Chase in place of the real peg of which he had painstakingly removed all traces. That night the students enjoyed an excellent dinner at their favorite *Kneipe*.[3]

Thus the wheel had gone one full round: skill that once would have won fame for its owner now was laughed down as mere sleight-of-hand, unworthy of serious consideration. These were also the high-spirited days when Piloty, Chase's own teacher, did not hesitate to predict that the next great development in art would take place in America. Chase readily agreed, but we can feel sure that the brilliant young student never dreamt for an instant of the major role that would be played by those very illusionists to whom

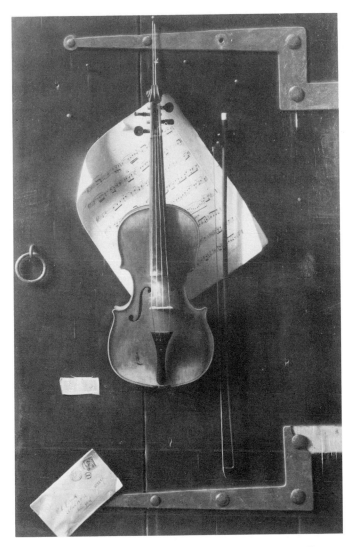

335. *William Harnett.* The Old Violin. *Cincinnati, Collection Mr. and Mrs. William J. Williams*

he denied even the slightest measure of artistic merit. Yet Chase himself would probably have been a greater and a deeper artist if he had been able to understand how much more there was to trompe l'oeil than the clever trick of painting a peg on a wall.

One does not wonder that the Reverend Doctor F. T. Gates should have pontificated that "The Old Violin" (pl. 335) was "unworthy because its purpose is low and selfish . . . just nothing else than to make you admire the man who could depict it so vividly."[4] It seems inexcusable that artists of high rank should have joined the hue and cry. Thus, George Inness: "A picture without passion has no meaning, and it would be far better hat it never been painted. Imitation is worthless. Photography does it much better than you or I . . . The only charm of the picture is in deceiving you."[5]

Today we do find "passion," and of a far more intense pitch than Inness himself could ever muster, in Harnett's brooding portrayals of commonplace objects. As to photography, it is no more the miracle it appeared to be then; we have long ago been disabused of its vaunted powers. What "imitation" meant for Harnett, as for all great illusionists, was *distillation, epuration*: he never relented in his efforts to achieve this rarefied perfection.

Harnett began painting in 1874, and during this early period, the year 1879 is notable for a succession of epochal works ranging all the way from the delightful "Thieves in the Pantry" (now known only from a photograph), an American equivalent of Susio's "Dessert Piece with Mice" (pl. 20) to the "letter-rack" trompe l'oeil, "The Artist's Card Rack" (pl. 332), remarkable for its boldness of coloring: of the envelopes displayed there, two are intense yellow, one is lavender blue, and another is shell pink—a daring range of tints in letter paper for that age. The still lifes of this period (pl. 7) are also simply and excellently composed, without the excess of bric-a-brac that would later burden some of Harnett's canvasses.

In the early 1880's his now world-famous "After the Hunt" brought the painter recognition and fortune. This is a theme that he treated no less than four times with minor variations, and for which he drew his inspiration from the photographs of a camera pioneer, the Alsatian Adolphe Braun.[6] It is illuminating to compare the initial 1883 treatment of "After the Hunt" (pl. 330) with the 1885 version (pl. 335), which far surpasses it for a number of reasons: the bold and delicate curve of the great horn in place of the rather amorphous instrument of the first version, together with an all-over tightening and simplifying of the design. This late version is also furthest removed from the Braun photograph, and it includes an incontrovertible confirmation of Harnett's purposeful transcending of mere realism: it has been noted that the alpenstock, which furnishes the all-important diagonal axis of the composition, could not remain in that position, where it openly flouts the laws of gravity.

Harnett's interest in illusionism was evidenced early, but contrary to what was first believed, it was stimulated by his familiarity and sympathy with the works of the quattrocento and cinquecento. A miniature watercolor of 1873 is an exact copy of Luca Signorelli's portrait of Dante at Orvieto, where the poet is shown within a deep square niche (pl. 336). In that same year, the young artist executed a work of sculpture: a profile head of Dante, also miniature in scale and again inspired by Signorelli. The same sculptural mastery is displayed in Harnett's youthful drawings in charcoal or crayon, done at the art academy, in all likelihood from plaster casts (pl. 337).

336. *William Harnett.* Dante in His Study *(after Luca Signorelli), 1873.*
New York, Courtesy of the Kennedy Galleries

337. *William Harnett.* Bunch
of Plums, *1873. New York,*
Courtesy of the Kennedy Gal-
leries

297

It is tantalizing to be told of "a singular masterpiece of trompe l'oeil" by Harnett which was "seen by David Gibson in Munich":

> It was a portrait of a man; but portraiture like this was never taught at the Pennsylvania Academy of the Fine Arts, nor yet by Professor Kaulbach: You could walk up to it and pull the necktie from the subject's vest.[7]

Other illusionistic feats by Harnett embroiled him in difficulties with the Treasury Department: he was seriously suspected of being "Jack the Penman," a famous counterfeiter, because of his uncanny, although totally innocent, rendering of American currency. In the same mood, bets were laid that the objects depicted in "After the Hunt" were not painted but real. On another occasion, there was much incredulity expressed about whether a tag apparently affixed to a painting was an illusionistic rendering, as claimed, but when an unbeliever tried to remove the pretended tag, it proved to be an honest deception. The usual run of anecdotes.

One of the most interesting aspects of Harnett's work perhaps is his musicianship, which resulted in faultlessly accurate, illusionistic renderings of musical texts (pls. 335, 338). Indeed, spurious Harnett's have been detected solely on that "score," if one may be permitted the pun.

In his search for total pictorial illusion, Harnett, early in his career, had attempted to duplicate textiles by piling layers of paint to mimic the relief of weave. (One recalls that Bettera also had not been above this; pl. 200). He abandoned this meretricious practice after 1800, but whether the attempt was cause or effect, the fact is that the depiction of textile was never his forte. Almost anything else, however—wood, marble, metal, paper, ivory and horn, pottery—is rendered with superlative excellence. Yet, contrary to what one might expect, this delicate and meticulous work was executed swiftly and apparently effortlessly. All the labor went into the advance conception of the themes, the subtle balancing of compositional elements into a faultless whole. Yet this thoughtful planning was precisely what he had been consistently accused by unjust critics of neglecting entirely for the sake of a soulless duplication of "reality."

To the now forgotten French journalist Louis Enault belongs the credit of having early recognized in Harnett's works "a crispness and vigor attaining trompe l'oeil." But even more important is the unusual use of the term trompe l'oeil in a laudatory sense. When trompe l'oeil had been at the height of favor, in the eighteenth century, the term itself did not yet exist; in the next age, it soon came to be used at best in a decorative, at worst in a pejorative sense.

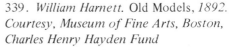

339. *William Harnett.* Old Models, *1892. Courtesy, Museum of Fine Arts, Boston, Charles Henry Hayden Fund*

338. *William Harnett.* Music and Good Luck, *1888. New York, The Metropolitan Museum of Art Purchase, 1963, Catharine Lorillard Wolfe Fund. The Catharine Lorillard Wolfe Collection*

John Frederick Peto (1854–1907), the second of the Philadelphia triad, possessed neither Harnett's aloof dignity nor his brooding lyricism. Indeed, Peto combined artistic bravado with pessimism of the darkest dye. A contemporary of Harnett and his fellow student at the Pennsylvania Academy of the Fine Arts, Peto had followed the career of his colleague and did adopt some of Harnett's "models," particularly in trompe l'oeil. Yet this was never anything more than an incentive, perhaps a challenge, for Peto approached these subjects in a radically different mood. He never had the pious respect for matter that one senses in all of Harnett's renderings; rather, a scornful acceptance of it as a hateful necessity. But Peto's oeuvre resembles Harnett's in that both are divided between trompe l'oeils and illusionistic still lifes, mostly of the table-corner and shelf-top variety. Peto, however, is undoubtedly far more at ease when portraying disorder and decay than clarity and freshness. It is probably symptomatic that, whereas Harnett titled one of his paintings "Old Models," (pl. 339), a work by Peto is dubbed "Old Scraps." [8]

299

340. *John Peto.* Old Scraps, *1894. Collection, The Museum of Modern Art, New York, Gift of Nelson A. Rockefeller*

342. *John Peto.* Office Board for John F. Peto, *1904. Los Angeles, Collection Mr. & Mrs. Oscar Salzer*

341. *John Peto.* Old Time Letter Rack. *Courtesy, Museum of Fine Arts, Boston, Bequest of Maxim Karolik*

343. *John Peto.* Memorial Tablet. *New York, Courtesy of the Kennedy Galleries*

Peto's best-known trompe l'oeil is precisely the "Old Time Letter Rack" (pl. 341), if only because it shares with Harnett's "Old Models" the honor of being one of the only two illusionistic paintings reproduced on U.S. postal stamps. "Old Time Letter Rack" was long assigned to Harnett, although there are major differences of style as well as mood between this composition and Harnett's "Artist's Card Rack" (pl. 332); the frayed and worn tape that serves as the rack in Peto's painting is in strong contrast to the neatness and freshness of Harnett's rose-colored ribband, reminiscent of the earlier Flemish and French racks. Harnett uses as a background smooth wainscotting, professionally jointed; Peto, more often, rough boarding, crudely nailed in place. (Harnett had indeed used unfinished boarding, where he thought it fitting: as background for the horseshoe which was presumably displayed on a barn door; pl. 333). Peto's letter rack consists of patently worthless ephemera and incorporates what was eventually to be recognized as his trademark: the small picture of Abraham Lincoln. Harnett's card rack was intriguing, intellectual, one might even add "gentlemanly": on one of the envelopes, addressed to "Peter La——, Jr., Esq.," appears the quaint indication "Politeness G. F. P.," no doubt a variant of our current "Courtesy of . . ." In Peto's letter rack, there are no such niceties. The date "94" carved on the wooden plank close by the portrait of Lincoln suggests a veteran of the Grand Army and that the painting might as well have been entitled "Thirty Years Later." Everything suggests the shabbiness and loneliness associated with destitute old age—with a pathetic implication to be found in the placement of the dinner ticket above Lincoln's picture, an image that had symbolized the idealism and higher aspirations of youth.

The recurrent motif of illusionistically carved lettering is a major element of Peto's trompe l'oeils. At times, typographical characters furnish the entire subject matter, for instance in "Office Board for John F. Peto," 1904 (pl. 342), where trompe l'oeil is indeed a most suitable medium, for the office never existed. In this example, as well as in the solemn "Memorial Tablet" for his father (pl. 343), the lettering style recalls that of a professional sign maker. On the contrary, in the quizzical "The Cup We All Race 4" [sic], the facetious comment that has given the painting its title has been rendered as if scrawled on hurriedly by a prankster.

Little is known about Peto either personally or professionally, since he exhibited rarely, did not seek publicity, and was as secretive as Harnett, though far more elusive. And whereas Harnett's works were acceptable to the public, if not to the critical elite, Peto was considerably more avant-garde, and it is not likely that he would have met with greater favor even if he had striven harder for recognition. That his merit did not go entirely unrecognized, however, is indicated by an article that appeared in the French-language paper, *L'Abeille de la Nouvelle-Orléans*, Sunday, May 30, 1886. Entitled "A Painter's Freak" and signed by a critic with the euphonious and typically creole name of "L. Placide Canonge," the article is highly laudatory:

> One reaches out to touch the canvas as if in spite of oneself. Yes, in looking at this strange composition—if it is a composition— the eye is deceived throughout. The hand longs to play with that string, which seems to move and flutter. One would like to unfold and read that copy of the *Picayune*. One is seized with the notion of extracting those stumpy nails, of denuding the picture of its objects. In short, if you put this board in the right light, the illusion is complete.

The article describes a Peto painting whose present whereabouts are unknown. It is notable also for the use of the expression "the eye is deceived" and for the perspicuous remark that even such a superlative example of illusionism requires placement "in the right light" to achieve the optimum effect. Nevertheless, criticism of this kind, with the full emphasis brought to bear on "trickery" as the chief merit of the paintings, may have done more harm than good to the cause of illusionism.

The third member of the Philadelphia group, John Haberle (1856–1933), exemplifies to an even higher degree the special American gift of concentration on the most ordinary objects. What seems to have been necessary was what one might call a clean artistic slate: a truly "new world" in the cultural as well as the geographical sense. It also explains why, although American trompe l'oeil is not far removed in subject matter from European trompe l'oeil, it is nevertheless unmistakably native. Yet the artists of the Second School of Philadelphia are as dissimilar in style as in regional origin. John Haberle's allegiance to Philadelphia is purely hypothetical. Harnett and Peto both studied at the Academy in Philadelphia, whereas Haberle was a pupil at the Academy of Design in New York He was born in Connecticut and eventually became a member of the staff of the paleontological museum at Yale University. It has been conjectured that he may have done some scientific drawings for the University's famed paleontologist, Professor Othniel C. Marsh. But since there are no records to that effect, it seems more likely that his duties were limited to those of "preparator"—caring for and displaying the various specimens. This may have been valuable experience: handling the relics surely helped to hone his inborn sensitiveness to formal values under the most unexpected shapes.

Whether his acquaintance with science played a role or not, Haberle was the only one of the great triad who chose trompe l'oeil exclusively and

344. *John Haberle.* Changes of Time, *1888. Ferndale, Michigan, Collection Mr. and Mrs. Marvin Preston*

avoided that halfway means, still-life painting. What is more, his subject matter was so personal that it was never possible to perpetrate the usual fraud by replacing his signature with that of Harnett, as was frequently done with Peto. The sole exception to this might be his trompe l'oeil work on the "currency" theme (pls. 344, 345), where originality is subjugated to technical skill. On

345. *John Haberle.* A Bachelor's Drawer. *New York, Collection Mr. & Mrs. J. William Middendorf, II; Photograph courtesy The Metropolitan Museum of Art*

346. *William Harnett.* For Sunday's Dinner, *1888. Courtesy of the Art Institute of Chicago*

304 347. *John Haberle (1856–1933).* Grandma's Hearthstone, *1890. Courtesy of the Detroit Institute of Arts*

assurances received from no less a judge than the distinguished painter Eastman Johnson, who had actually examined such a "currency" painting by Haberle, the art critic of the contemporary *Chicago Tribune* felt safe in asserting that the bills included in Haberle's pictures were not painted at all but were in fact actual notes pasted onto the painted ground. Haberle, justifiably incensed, left for Chicago at once and forced a retraction from the imprudent critic. (Before we condemn Eastman Johnson, let us recall that in our own time Marcel Duchamp took the same stand in regard to the sheet music depicted in Chalfant's paintings and was similarly discomfitted, see p. 322.

We may presume that the controversial "currency" trompe l'oeil profited from the publicity and most likely went on view in a "saloon"—even as Harnett's "After the Hunt" and many of Peto's finest works did in their time. "Saloon" in those days was still an accepted synonym for "salon," in the double sense of art gallery and drawing room. Harnett himself referred to the Paris Salon of 1884 as "the current saloon." As the gathering place where good fellows met, the "saloon" was a clubroom, a forum where judgment was passed on matters artistic as well as political and social. It was the logical successor to the tavern where patriots of the Colonial period had gathered; its nineteenth-century equivalents were the drugstore and the department store. Art museums were then few and far between, and it was therefore quite acceptable to the American mind that Harnett's great trompe l'oeil "For Sunday's Dinner" (pl. 346) should have been shown for the first time not in the hushed, velvet-draped precincts of an art gallery but in a busy Philadelphia drugstore—and at a time when the artist was at the very apex of his fame.

Thus Haberle received what would then have been considered the supreme accolade to his talent when he was commissioned to execute a major work for a "saloon" in Detroit, Michigan—a princely commission for the new painter-laureate of the American people. The model was nothing less than a mantelpiece and fireplace from an old Massachusetts farmhouse which was transported to the artist's studio. The final product was a sort of American *devant de cheminée*, far more extensive and variegated than its European predecessors, though never intended to fulfill their utilitarian purpose. The painting was two years in the making—not surprisingly, since "Grandma's Hearthstone" is eight feet high by five and a half wide (pl. 347). It is a moot point whether we should look upon this magnum opus as trompe l'oeil or as architectural illusionism, not only on account of the large size but because it was planned to be inserted in a specific location. Under either appellation, "Grandma's Hearthstone" is a superb example of Haberle's scientific precision. A noted critic, however, has drawn attention to the bowl of flowers on the mantelpiece as perhaps the most notable feature of the work—very justly point-

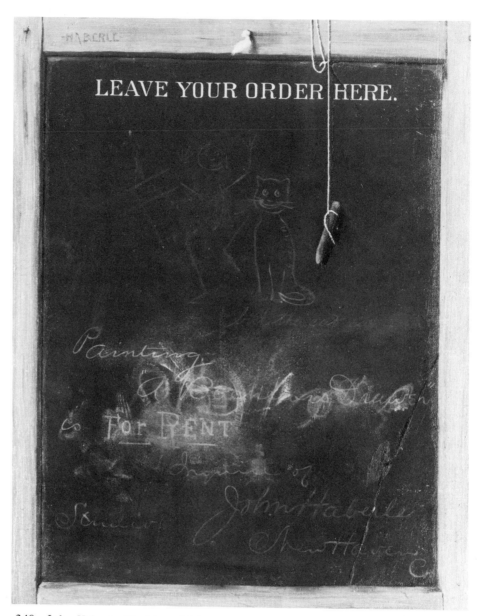

348. *John Haberle.* Blackboard I (Leave Your Order Here). *New York, Courtesy of the Kennedy Galleries*

ing out that blossoms lack the "tactilely perceptible" forms best suited for trompe l'oeil performances.[9]

Though Harnett and Peto are justly famed for their card racks, the foremost "paper man" was undoubtedly Haberle, who seems to have loved paper for its own sake, beyond its special suitability as a model. But Haberle's "papyromania" extended to other, more modern, writing surfaces: "The Blackboard—Leave Your Order Here" (pl. 348) is a glorification of grafitti well in advance of Dubuffet.

In "Time and Eternity" (pl. 349), the watch and the odd, rosarylike string of beads (with its strange, almost cruciform pendant) clearly symbolize modern science and ancient faith, while the clipping relating the activities of Ralph Ingersoll, crusader of atheism, suggests the conflict then raging between the atavists and the modernists. The theme is ponderous, but the execution is nothing less than ravishing. In the same vein, "Changes in Time" (pl. 344) is oddly reminiscent of the border of coins on a page from the Book of Hours of Catherine de Clèves (pl. 73). Haberle here combines deception with decoration so that it is difficult to know to which he assigned greater importance. This is far removed from Harnett's simpler purpose—if no lesser skill—in depicting a gold coin on the floor of a barroom so deceptively that it was said "that men did not even need a beer to try to pick it up."

349. *John Haberle.* Time and Eternity. *New Britain, Conn., New Britain Museum of American Art*

Mr. Frankenstein has pointed out the incredible refinement of technique displayed in one particular detail of this picture:

> The small corner of the letter which protrudes from the envelope [bottom right] is one of Haberle's most delicious feats of virtuosity; one can almost hear him chuckle with delighted self-approval as one studies it. No complete words are legible, but it is nonetheless apparent that the more boldly stroked letters are in mirror writing, while the interlined fainter letters are not. In other words, the paper is quite thin, the mirror writing is on the reverse side of the first sheet, and the fainter letters are on the obverse side of the sheet beneath. "Entirely with the brush and with the naked eye!"[10]

The last phrase is Haberle's own characterization of his work, as an illusionist / miniaturist. That he was not limited solely to such minutiae, however, is evidenced by the magnificent rendering of the curtain in "Night" (pl. 350), where he has endowed the ancient device of illusionistic drapery with unparalleled mellowness and richness of texture.

350. *John Haberle.* Night, *1909. New Britain, Conn., New Britain Museum of American Art*

351. *John Haberle.* Torn in Transit. *Amagansett, N. Y., Collection Amanda K. Berls*

Haberle's pixyish character—what Frankenstein has so well called his "sly flamboyance" and "hell-on-wheels spirit"—was only equaled by his versatility. This perhaps worked to his disadvantage, since he might have been taken seriously far earlier if, instead of bounding from one imaginative concept to another, he had, like Harnett (and even like Peto, though to a lesser degree), become identified with a limited number of themes. But he would not make things quite that easy: witness his quizzical "Torn in Transit" (pl. 351) or "Bachelor's Drawer," neither of which can easily be categorized any more than can his other productions.[11] It may well be, therefore, that Haberle was the illusionist par excellence because his artistic abnegation was so complete that he was literally annihilated by the illusion he fostered.

The sensational success of Harnett's "After the Hunt" led to a plethora of imitations: hunting pieces that are often fully the equal of Harnett's famous work in precisionism of technique but somehow lack the magic element. The photographs by Adolphe Braun, which are thought to have supplied the initial theme, were in the public domain and continued to furnish, if not inspiration, at least incentive to many competent artists who were eager to fill the demand for such subjects. But only Harnett, it seems, had the ability to render acceptable these archaic Black Forest cynegetic themes—perhaps because they had aroused his sincere enthusiasm as a young student and supplied an ideal vehicle for his latent romanticism. Otherwise, the innumerable hunting trophies of this period are only redeemed in the few instances where they are imbued with an American tang that gave new life to the exhausted theme.

The initiator and foremost practitioner of the hunting piece with a Wild West flavor was George W. Platt, a gifted painter who had been a fellow student of both Harnett and Chase—and also perhaps of Peto. His most famous work (now lost) was entitled "Vanishing Glories," a nostalgic echo of the romance of the frontier, already then nearly vanished, as were the teeming herds of buffalo that had once roamed the great plains. And a huge buffalo skull had been the central element of "Vanishing Glories." This painting attracted so much interest and received such wide publicity that, on the strength of this achievement, Platt was in demand again and again to deliver a lecture with the intriguing title "Illusions in Art," of which regrettably no record whatever appears to have survived. A Pennsylvania artist, George Cope spent some time in the Far West in the late 1870's and found inspiration there for some works akin in mood to Platt's. "The Hunter's Yellow Jacket" (pl. 352) is a representative example. His best known subject, however, "Buffalo Bill's Trap" survives only in a photograph.

One artist who contributed a noble share to American trompe l'oeil nevertheless considered himself an amateur. This was J. M. Shinn, who demonstrated with one remarkable work with a self-descriptive title, "The Old Barn Door," that he would have been in the forefront had he turned a cherished avocation into a profession.[11a] Shinn was Harnett's fellow student at the National Academy of Design. Another notable illusionistic accomplishment is the painting by William Keane, entitled "The Old Banjo" (pl. 353). Although this has sometimes been looked upon as a satire of "After the Hunt," it appears rather as an adaptation of the formula to a different mood.

The most versatile personality of the post-Harnettian period was probably Alexander Pope. This Boston artist did turn out his share of conventional hunting trophies, but it would be a grave injustice to gauge him solely by these. Above and beyond this pedestrian aspect of his work, we are indebted to him first of all for his great "Trumpeter Swan" (pl. 354), which has now acquired additional significance and undertones of high tragedy because of the extinction of the species. It is also one of the milestones of American illusionism. Indeed, when first shown in the artist's studio, the work created a sensation. According to a reporter in the *Boston Sunday Post* of November 2, 1902, to behold this painting was "to be startled out of ordinary complacency and to almost believe the days of sorcery have returned." Pope would not have been able to create this moving work if he had not from the start approached the theme with a poetic sensitiveness that distinguished him from less inspired practitioners.

Pope's talent as an animalier was not limited to birds. And in one instance, when he applied it to quadrupeds, the talent was put to rather start-

310

352. *George Cope.* The Hunter's Yellow Jacket, *1891. New York, Collection Victor D. Spark*

353. *William Keane.* The Old Banjo, *c. 1889. San Francisco, California Palace of the Legion of Honor*

354. *Alexander Pope.* Trumpeter Swan, *1900. New York, Collection Mr. and Mrs. J. William Middendorf II.*

355. *Alexander Pope.* Pups in Transit. *Stonereath Farms, Paris, Ky., Collection Mr. & Mrs. Samuel C. Register*

ling use: his painting of a lion in a cage was displayed and received with great applause in the hall of the old Plaza Hotel in New York City—not in a conventional frame, but behind bars. A domesticated version of this theme is the small painting "Pups in Transit" (pl. 355). We do not know how the problem of arrested movement—one *sine qua non* of trompe l'oeil—was resolved in the feral subject at the Plaza, but in "Pups in Transit" one of the animals is sound asleep and therefore motionless, while the others appear to be gazing out of their makeshift cage with the peculiar stolid solemnity of puppyhood awaiting its fate.

Among the few artists at the turn of the century who were able to treat the theme of "After the Hunt" with new freshness, Richard La Barre Goodwin (1840–1910) is notable for his total abandonment of the lingering overtones of neoromanticism. His famous "Theodore Roosevelt's Cabin Door" was inspired by a view of the actual door of the hunting cabin occupied by Roosevelt during his ranching days in South Dakota, when it was exhibited at the Lewis and Clark Exhibition of 1905 in Portland, Oregon. Goodwin arranged for the loan of the door and at first used it as a background for conventional game pieces (pl. 356). He then achieved a more meaningful composition by placing the emphasis on the Rooseveltian presence. This led to inclusion of the muzzle-loading fowling piece that had been used by Phil Sheridan and, finally, the familiar Roosevelt soft hat and boots. Although a string of plumaged ducks remains the central feature of the composition in the several versions, the true significance shifted to the historical accessories. In addition to the various cabin doors for which he is best known, Goodwin's "Kitchen Piece" (pl. 357) hovers halfway between still life and trompe l'oeil and could easily hold its own next to the best seventeenth- or eighteenth-century work of this kind.

A grisly panorama entitled "Doughboy's Equipment" (pl. 358) presents us with a different kind of variation on the "After the Hunt" theme. Painted in 1920 by Charles A. Meurer, this work visualizes the soldier's experience in World War I. It brings together the doughboy's "tools" (gun, bayonet, hand grenade); his accoutrements (helmet, fatigue cap, gas mask); his comforts (canteen, a letter from home); and his reward (a medal). All of this is symbolically displayed against a bolted door. Meurer, who died in 1955, has been called "the last living member of the great school of American trompe l'oeil painters."[12] But "Doughboy's Eqipment" is an exception, for Meurer's work was not usually outright trompe l'oeil. However, he was the first to practice what Alfred Frankenstein has dubbed "the editorial sanctum still life," that is, the paraphernalia of an editor's desk. Meurer turned out a number of paintings on this subject, though in a rather posterlike style. Yet the artist was by no means a self-taught primitive: he had studied in Cincinnati with Duveneck, and perhaps with Chase, and abroad in Paris and Lyon. He had greatly admired Harnett's "Old Violin," and stated that this had stimulated his own interest in trompe l'oeil. Nevertheless, barring "Doughboy's Equipment" and some currency pictures that attracted the displeased attention of the Treasury Department, the bulk of Meurer's work is realistic rather than illusionistic.

356. *Richard La Barre Goodwin. Variation on* Theodore Roosevelt's Cabin Door. *New York, Collection Victor Spark*

357. *Richard La Barre Goodwin.* Kitchen Piece, *1890. Stanford, Calif., Stanford University Museum*

358. *Charles Meurer.* Doughboy's Equipment, *1921. Youngstown, Ohio, The Butler Institute of American Art*

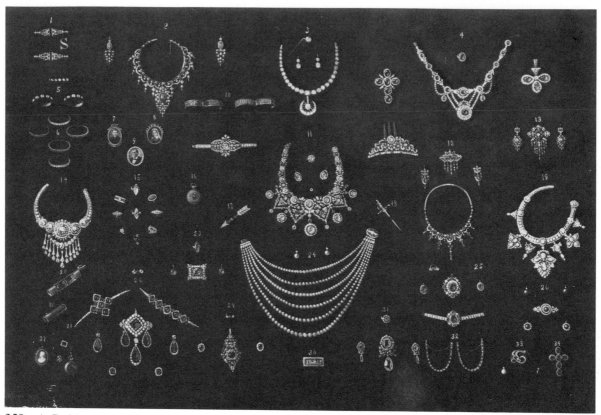

359. *A. D. M. Cooper. Mrs. Stanford's Jewel Collection, 1898. Stanford, Calif., Stanford University Museum*

Before abandoning the "trophy" theme, one should grant brief notice to what was in a sense its culmination: the unique trompe l'oeil done by A. M. D. Cooper of San Jose, California (pl. 359). "Mrs. Stanford's Jewel Collection" is a veritable panoply, whose purpose was to catalogue and immortalize the personal collection of jewels belonging to Mrs. Leland Stanford. In Frankenstein's matchless phrase, this goal was carried out "in imperishable impasto."

Like the hunting trophies, trompe l'oeil paintings of currency continued in great favor. There can be little doubt that there were practical reasons for the popularity of this theme, at least from the artist's viewpoint. Although such subjects were sure to attract wonder, they were also the easiest of all to render illusionistically, since the extreme flatness of a banknote calls for a minimum of optical adjustment and makes deception much easier. And in most examples, deception in a factual rather than an artistic sense was the goal. When the banknote is shown alone, and the painting is unsigned, there is generally a good reason for this anonymity: the trompe l'oeil was not intended as a work of art (although it may have been raised to that rank in modern times) but as a practical joke. It was intended to be inserted in a

314

counter top, or even in the flooring of a barroom, so as to trick a patron into attempting to pick it up surreptitiously, for the amusement of the onlookers. Not only would a signature have defeated the purpose, but such commissions were potboilers which no self-respecting artist was particularly anxious to acknowledge—let alone the very real risk of entanglement with the authorities. One should remember that even today, permission must be obtained from the Treasury Department for the reproduction of *any* painting depicting American currency.

It goes without saying that regardless of the skill that might be lavished on the execution of these "deceptions," they were far removed from the seriousness of paintings such as that of Nicholas Allen Brooks, where the representation of currency was always combined with other elements of special significance. In the example illustrated here (pl. 360), a five dollar bill appears together with a clipping from an auction catalogue referring to another painting of the same type, also by Brooks, that had actually been sold at the auction of the collection of William M. Shaw in March, 1890. The "printed" passage reads:

THE SHAW COLLECTION / N. A. BROOKS

Some alleged philosopher has stated that there is no really imperative necessity in life. I dispute this statement. Mr. Brooks paints this necessity in simple shape—in the shape of a five dollar note of common currency, to wit. He paints it, moreover, with an illusory power that is not at all common. There are a great many people who would try to pick up this bank bill if they saw it on the floor, and be astonished that it was the coinage of talent instead of the mint. . . .

360. *N. Allen Brooks.* Five Dollar Bill and Clipping. *New York, Courtesy of the Kennedy Galleries*

315

In the auction catalogue whence these lines were excerpted, the writer continued: ". . . It is but a counterfeit, but unlike most counterfeits, it may be said of this one that it is worth in the open market a great deal more than the original."[13]

Less thoughtful and subtle than Brooks, Victor Dubreuil (act. 1888–1900) was a blithe spirit who approached the sacrosanct theme of money in a highly irreverent spirit. He was seldom satisfied with the rendering of one puny bill: the greenbacks must overflow from crammed barrels with tops ripped off, as if in a modern cave of Ali Baba (pl. 361). Or else the currency is stuffed into a bank drawer—with holdup artists on the other side of the cage, filling up their bags (pl. 362); or packed neatly in tight wads in a safe with an ironic accounting of the company's profits (pl. 363). Obviously such improbable extravaganzas could not conceivably "deceive" anyone; nor did they qualify as trompe l'oeil even according to the most liberal standards. It

361. *Victor Dubreuil (act. 1880–1910).* Barrels of Money. *New York, Courtesy of the Kennedy Galleries*

316

362. *Victor Dubreuil.* Don't Make a Move. *New York, Courtesy of the Kennedy Galleries*

363. *Victor Dubreuil.* The Safe. *New York, Courtesy Kennedy Galleries*

364. *Victor Dubreuil.* Carte de Visite. *New York,*
Courtesy of the Kennedy Galleries

365. *Victor Dubreuil.* George Washington.
New York, Courtesy Kennedy Galleries

is hard to believe, therefore, that the U. S. Treasury Department took exception to this farcical counterfeiting and detained some works of this kind in their vaults for years. This may be taken as a tribute of sorts to Dubreuil's very real and eminent power as an illusionist—displayed, for example, in his renderings of visiting cards (pl. 364) which were then customarily embellished with portraits of famous figures, or in his trompe l'oeil of a print of Washington against a wooden background in the most orthodox illusionistic tradition (pl. 365). His "Declaration of War, 1898" depicts the official document signed by President McKinley displayed against a wooden background with a massive bevelled edge, i.e., on a plaque or table, eliminating all need for a frame.

The foremost master of the currency theme, however, acquired that status on the strength of a single performance: two trompe l'oeils in one, forever inseparable. In F. Danton, Jr.'s famous "Time Is Money" (pl. 366), the allegory is obvious, and all the subtlety and refinement are reserved for the illusionistic execution: the picture proper is painted on canvas, but there is a peripheral complement to it in the form of a wide frame painted to match the illusionistic background of the canvas. But as the frame necessarily projects somewhat beyond the canvas, it casts shadows. These the artist has nullified by means of several illusionistic devices. Further illusionistic "decoration" on the frame includes nail holes, some of which are real and others simulated. It all adds up to a dazzling tour de force.

366. *F. Danton, Jr.* Time Is Money. *Hartford, Courtesy Wadsworth Atheneum, E. G. Sumner and M. C. Sumner Collection*

Jefferson David Chalfant was until recently renowned primarily for a particularly acute deception involving not currency but postage stamps. "Which Is Which?" (pl. 367) displays an actual two-cent stamp pasted on a white enamelled metal ground immediately next to its painted counterpart, and below this a "printed" clipping defying the viewer to decide "which is which." Thus the original intention had been simply to incite wonder at the difficulties encountered in distinguishing illusion from reality. But in the course of time, the real stamp has become dull and lifeless while the deception still sparkles with pristine freshness. The present owner of "Which Is Which?" is a philatelist as well as an art lover and had considered replacement of the faded stamp with a fount-perfect issue from his collection, but was happily discouraged from this intent by Alfred Frankenstein, who commented that "there exists no more perfect demonstration of the relative permanence of reality and illusion than 'Which Is Which?' as it has been affected by 'the changes of time.' "[14] (The last phrase is an allusion to Haberle's famous painting bearing that title.)

A Pennsylvanian by birth, Chalfant at first followed his father's trade as a cabinetmaker. Entirely self-taught until 1890, Chalfant nevertheless achieved professional recognition on his own, but he was eventually sent to Paris to study with Bouguereau and Lefèbvre by an American art patron, Arthur Corning Clark. On his return, the artist decided to specialize in por-

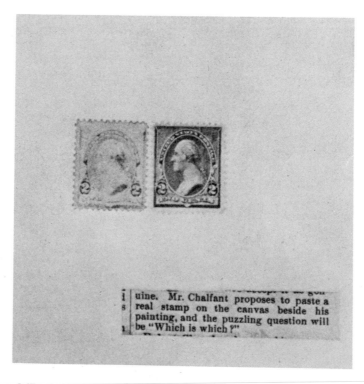

uine. Mr. Chalfant proposes to paste a
real stamp on the canvas beside his
painting, and the puzzling question will
be "Which is which?"

367. *Jefferson David Chalfant.* Which Is Which?, *c. 1890, Fort Lauderdale, Collection Ernest Jarvis*

trait painting. In his illusionistic work, however, Chalfant remained inspired by Harnett, whose themes he transposed in a minor key. "An Old Flintlock," for instance (pl. 368), lacks the smoldering drama of Harnett's "The Faithful Colt," even as the title itself has been toned down into hazy imprecision and impersonality (pl. 334). Similarly, Chalfant also produced his own version of "After the Hunt" (in this instance retaining the original title, in homage to Harnett), and even though the painting is known only through a photograph, it is clear that the same muting and taming process had taken place. In Chalfant's "The Old Violin," (pl. 369), the Harnettian values have actually been reversed: instead of emerging as a warm glow out of a mysteriously shadowy background, Chalfant's violin is a gracile dark shape silhouetted against a light wall.

368. *Jefferson David Chalfant.* An Old Flintlock. *Wilmington, Chalfant Collection*

369. *Jefferson David Chalfant.* The Old Violin, *1888. Wilmington, The Wilmington Society of the Fine Arts*

It is all to Chalfant's credit that he was able to maintain his own personality in the face of such a challenge. A conclusive tribute to Chalfant's technical virtuosity was paid by no less a judge than Marcel Duchamp: the French artist not only echoed the scepticism of Eastman Johnson in regard to Haberle's bill (see p. 305), but he too refused to believe that the musical score shown in "The Old Violin" was indeed painted and not collage.

Samuel Marsden Brookes, an English-born artist, was active in San Francisco from 1862 to 1892, and some of his still lifes were praised by a contemporary critic in terms that clearly indicate a trompe l'oeil style and intent. They are, we are told, "literal transcripts of nature. He takes a branch of a tree or vine, with all its fruits and leaves upon it, and paints that—nothing more—charming one with the mockery of reality."[15] A little farther on, however, the painter is chided for "fastening his cunning branches against bits of stuccoed brickwork and never composing his beautiful studies into a picture." Regrettably, none of these "uncomposed" pictures appear to have survived. That Brookes could, and occasionally did, "compose," is evidenced in his traditional trompe l'oeil of fish in a shallow, arched niche (pl. 370).

Some of the paintings of the German-born Joseph Decker (1853–1920), although not trompe l'oeil by definition, come very close to it indeed. In "Twenty-Three Pears" (pl. 371), branches are loaded with fruit, each one as carefully individualized as a portrait. Decker's vision is as modern as to-

370. *Samuel Marsden Brookes (1816–1892).* String of Fish, *1873. San Francisco, M. H. de Young Memorial Museum, Gift of C. P. Huntington, 1898*

322

371. *Joseph Decker.* Twenty-Three Pears. *Private Collection*

323

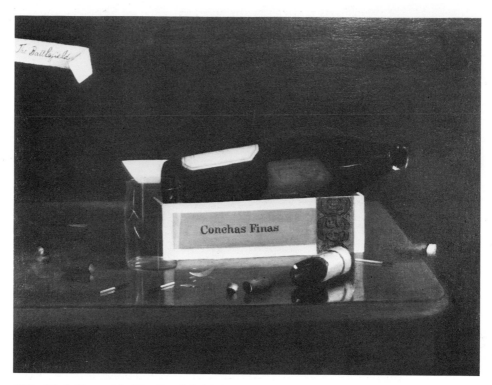

372. *W. S. Reynolds.* The Battlefield. *Bennington, Vt., Bennington Museum*

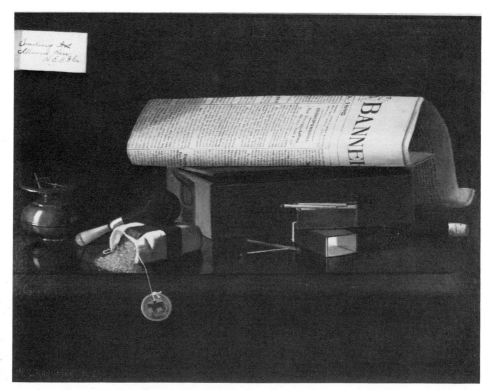

373. *W. S. Reynolds.* The Bennington Banner. *Bennington, Vt., Bennington Museum*

morrow—its cool precisionism suggests the work of Charles Sheeler—yet it is also oddly akin to the medieval spirit. The tall upright panel of "Twenty-Three Pears" evokes the narrow opening in Van Eyck's Ghent Altarpiece (pl. 59), and it could almost take a rightful place in such context.[16]

Another intriguing artist about whom little is known is W. S. Reynolds. This excellent still-life painter is registered in Frankenstein's *After the Hunt* solely on the strength of "one superb, eminently Harnettian still life."[17] But Reynolds' interest in trompe l'oeil is hinted at in two fine paintings (pls. 372–73) which, although they depict table-corners, contain *cartellini* rendered as if inserted between the frame and the canvas in the upper left corner. In one of these two, formally titled "The Bennington Banner," the *cartellino* reads "Smoking Not Allowed Here," while the other bears the inscription "The Battlefield," an allusion to the battle fought near Bennington, Vermont in August 1777. But the "battlefield" that the Vermont artist portrayed in clearly of quite another kind: both paintings together read as a kind of pictorial moralization against the evils of liquor and tobacco. The still lifes are, however, equally notable for their technical mastery. In keeping with its title, "The Bennington Banner" depicts newsprint—in so convincing a manner that one is tempted to seize a magnifying glass and acquaint oneself with the text. But such an attempt will reveal that the effect is achieved by meaningless strokes—only the headlines are readable. Yet, through subtle control of the density of the strokes, the impression of type is more real than reality. Such subtlety of technique brings Reynolds very close not only to Harnett but to Haberle as well. (For a comparable use of the *cartellino*, see pl. 295.)

A telling indicator of the universal popularity of trompe l'oeil in the United States during the late nineteenth century—particularly during the Centennial celebrations of 1876 and 1877 and well into the mid-1880's—is found in the trade cards and other business ephemera of the period. These reveal not only a strong partiality towards illusionistic themes but, even more important, a much greater familiarity with the classical repertory of trompe l'oeil than was believed to have existed. In an especially intriguing example, copyrighted in 1884, we find the theme of the life-sized fly (pl. 374), combined with a fantastic Arcimboldesque array of intermingled forms: the conventional scene of a traveller and his dog trudging home on a country road

374. Shoo! Fly! *1884*

375. Card of George M. Williams, Artist, *c. 1877*

325

376. Pink Tiger Lily with Dragonfly and Wasp

377. Hunting Trophy, *c. 1880.*

378. Golden Horseshoe, *c. 1887*

(pl. 375) is composed of no less than 152 representations of figures and objects. Elsewhere, the fly is replaced by a bee hovering over blossoms (pl. 376), or by a wasp shown feasting on a luscious peach.

Appropriately, the message of the card that is probably the outstanding illusionistic performance in the field of American trade cards (color pl. 22) is "Beware of Imitations." This remarkable trompe l'oeil of a postmarked envelope, partly torn to reveal a letter, a photograph, and a lock of hair, was issued by a soap company in 1889 to warn against fraudulent imitations of their product. The illustrated "fraud" on the recto of the card, however, is carried out with unusual delicacy and skill, causing one to regret all the more the invariable anonymity. Another notable card uses the theme of the picture under a broken pane of glass (color pl. 22), attesting to familiarity with eighteenth-century achievements of this kind. One also finds recognizable echoes of more recent feats of illusionism: miniature game pieces (pl. 377), or a golden horseshoe (pl. 378) that may have been inspired by its famous namesake by Harnett, while the ribbon-tied dolls (pl. 379) suggest both "Torn in Transit" and "Pups in Transit" (pls. 351, 355). The "currency" theme is not missing either (pl. 380), and even postage stamps were reproduced in actual size in crude emulation of Chalfant's "Which is Which?" (pl. 367).

In addition to numerous variations on the envelope theme (with or without enclosure, open or closed, torn or sealed), one finds also a surprising variety of objects rendered independently as *chantourné* trompe l'oeils: a large clam shell bearing a menu on the reverse (pl. 381) was placed on the guest's plate at a seashore resort; the familiar Union Army cap carried on the back the program for a G.A.R. function (pl. 382); for a bakery, an appetizing jelly roll, "even nicer on the other side," which carried an advertisement for other goodies; a medley of richly decorated eggs, presumably for the Easter trade (pl. 383); some ornate china cups; an envelope superimposed upon a sheet of stationery (pl. 384). It is surprising how faithfully the mood of the epoch is reflected in an assemblage of these make-believe objects.

379. The Twins, *c. 1885*

380. Mock Three-Dollar Bill, *1875*

381. Clam Shell, *1886. Die cut*

382. Union Cap, *1882. Die cut. Bearing on the reverse Order of Exercises for a G. A. R. function*

383. Oval Plate with Egg, Chick, and Fuchsia Bloom. *Sample card, c. 1880*

384. Letter and Envelope with Red Blooms, *early 20th century*

327

385. Needlebook *(verso)*.
*Recto (not illustrated) depicts a card
slipped in a pocket, reading "Try Parker's Ague Insoles and Parker's Rheu-
matic Liniment"*

Many objects, such as the outstanding needlecase with a banknote (pl. 385), illusionistic on the verso as well as recto—or kindred *chantourné* renderings of a penknife, watchcase, playing card, and even a fine-toothed comb—inevitably suggest the familiar repertory of trompe l'oeil. They could, with the greatest of ease, be compositioned in *quod libet* arrangements. "Papyromania" survived similarly in a somewhat debased form. At times, it was combined with sentimental or comical elements: a child's head peeping out; the fierce head of a watchdog through a torn screen (pl. 386); a "Cheshire" cat irrupting from a cigar box (color pl. 22).

One may even find occasional traces of illusionistic devices presented in miniature format, as if at the other end of a spyglass, but which would in fact have been suited to illusionistic schemes in the grand manner: the paw of a dog transcending the picture plane ("Go and Get a Gold Neck Chain for Baby," pl. 388); the boughs arching over and shadowing the roadway poster (pl. 389); the illusionistic bevel of a picture frame ("Reward of Merit," pl. 390); or, most effective of all perhaps, the use of the deep margin of the oval "portholes" so dear to the formal portraitists of the seventeenth and eighteenth centuries (cf. color pl. 13; pl. 324). Slight though such indications are of themselves, when gathered together they point to an intriguing social phenomenon: while the cultural elite was already looking down with undisguised scorn upon trompe l'oeil as an art form, it had by no means relinquished its ancient hold upon the popular imagination, where it would lie dormant, its prestige undimmed until our own days.

386. Bulldog Bursting through Paper Screen. *Embossed. Late 19th-century sample or album card*

387. Dog with Frog, *1893. Advertisement for Chicago Sewing Machine Company*

388. Go to Wood Bros. and Get a Gold Neck Chain for Baby, *1876*

389. Christmas Night, *1876*

390. Reward of Merit, *1880. Illusionistically bevelled frame*

391. Dog with Flower Basket, *c. 1890. Amusing parody of 17th- and 18th century "porthole" portraiture*

329

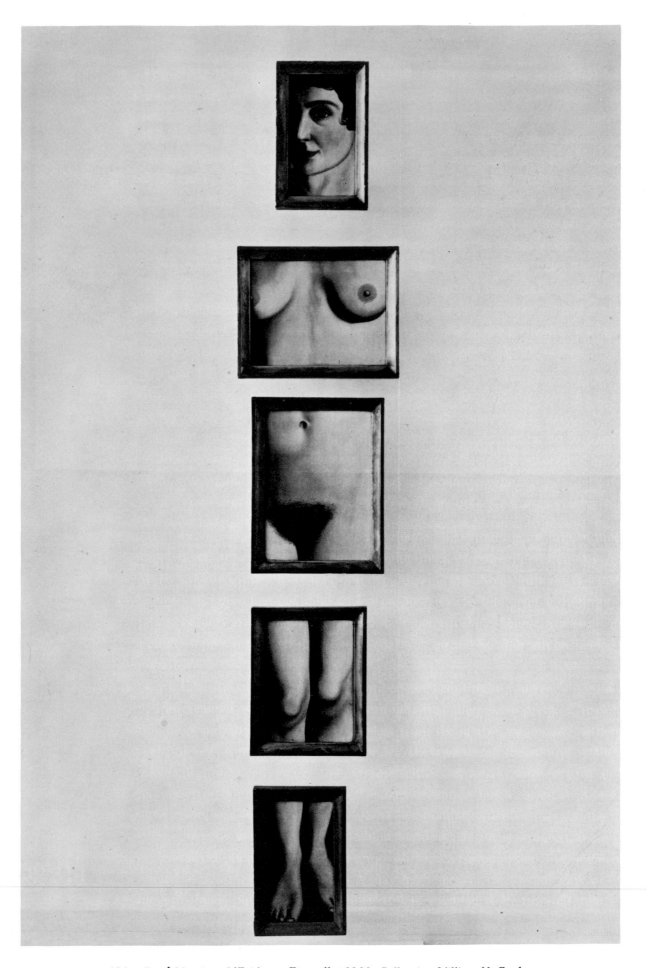

392. *René Magritte*, L'Evidence Eternelle, *1930. Collection William N. Copley*

9

Illusionism Plus

Present Trends

The few spasmodic manifestations of illusionism at the beginning of the twentieth century might reasonably have been considered its death throes. Just as its great rival, impressionism, had long run its course and had been replaced by other powerful currents—expressionism, cubism, dadaism—it seemed likely that illusionism, too, would be swept away by the tide of modernity.

Yet, counter to all such expectations, one of the new artistic creeds was destined not only to rejoin illusionism but even to transcend it. This was surrealism, whose initial goal was an intransigent questioning of the ambiguity of reality. While illusionism, as we have seen, had been content with intensification of reality, surrealism strove for the outer reality *plus* the inner reality. The new theory was perhaps not quite as revolutionary as its exponents believed: the "realists" of the past, inasmuch as they had been artists worthy of that title, had also been "*sur*realist," and the best illusionists were not exceptions to that rule. The revolution was highly beneficial nevertheless, for it was literally a turn of the wheel by means of which the circle was not closed but enlarged and released into an upward spiral.

The onset of the phenomenon probably occurred at the precise moment when, in the words of a modern critic, the practitioners of cubism first "realized that they were beginning to indulge in an aesthetic exercise [i.e., the analysis and reconstruction of forms in accordance with geometric formulas] which was approaching abstraction rather than reality, *even though their compositions always had their origin in definite objects.*"[1]

393. *Joan Miro.* Collage, *1931.*
Art Market

The solution to the dilemma was collage and the *objet trouvé*, which is of course equivalent to saying that during what André Breton called "la crise de l'objet," literal realism, that dread antagonist of liberated art, once more raised its abominated head over the horizon. Certainly the foremost artists of the early twentieth century stooped to subterfuges of the sort one deplores in a Bettera or an early Harnett: the imprinting of textures in fresh paint; the building up of impastos into relief effects; or even the incorporation of alien elements into the surface of the canvas. The most famous examples of such practices are Picasso's use of oilcloth printed in a pattern imitating rush caning in his "Still Life with Chair Caning" (1911) and the inclusion by Giorgio de Chirico of actual biscuits in his "Intérieur Métaphysique" (1916). Such artifices were not presented facetiously, but with deadly seriousness.[2] Collage, still relatively flat, was often superseded by assemblage—frankly three-dimensional and more sculptural than pictorial, as in the example by Miro (pl. 393).

In the wake of these transcendental experiments, surrealists of the orthodox denomination—such artists as Pierre Roy, Yves Tanguy, and eventually René Magritte—sublimated trompe l'oeil. Yves Tanguy, in particular, may be looked upon as the pioneer of an illusionism of the fourth dimension (pl. 394). His exquisitly precise style is the vehicle (the "time machine," as it were) by means of which he transports us into a supra-terrestrial world. The impeccable syntax of this visual idiom makes it all surprisingly plausible and acceptable.

Another one of the founding fathers of surrealism, Pierre Roy, startles us by juxtaposing the least likely elements, while apparently remaining on the conventional plane of everyday reality. Yet a lapse of taste is as unthinkable as in a Mozart concerto. It was perhaps this unusually delicate sense of balance that predisposed the artist to trompe l'oeil, as in his well-known "Daylight Saving Time" (pl. 395), which is a lyrical counterpart to the matter-of-fact "Time Is Money" by F. Danton (pl. 366).

394. *Yves Tanguy*. Gouache, *1942. New York, Pierre Natisse Gallery*

395. *Pierre Roy*. Daylight Savings Time, *1929. New York, The Museum of Modern Art*

333

René Magritte does not place a spell over us by transmuting the commonplace into something rich and strange; on the contrary, no painter ever showed more scrupulous respect for the humblest identity. "The Alphabet of Revelations" (pl. 396), an undoubted trompe l'oeil, is particularly notable in this regard. But Magritte's Flemish respect for details was often put to the service of metaphysical flights of fancy. The result was "magic realism." The enigmatic theme of "The Human Condition" (pl. 397), first encountered in 1934, is recurrent under various guises throughout the artist's career. Happily, the artist has defined the purpose of this extraordinary superimposition of several strata of reality:

> In front of a window as seen from the interior of a room, I
> placed a picture which represented precisely the portion of land-
> scape blotted out by the picture. For instance, the tree represent-
> ed in the picture displaced the tree situated behind it, outside the
> room. For the spectator, it was simultaneously inside the room, in
> the picture, and outside, in the real landscape, in thought. Which
> is how we see the world, namely outside of us, though having only
> one representation of it within us.[3]

A second picture on the same theme, "The Human Condition II," paint-ed in 1935 (pl. 398), may be looked upon as a perfect allegory of pictorial il-lusionism with the vista seen through the tall arch, whereas trompe l'oeil is more specifically represented by the seascape on the easel, a portion of the larger view. In "The Promenades of Euclid," 1955 (pl. 399), the artist illus-trates the optical ambiguity of reality: the conical roof of a turret in the fore-ground is exactly duplicated by the triangular perspective of the wide avenue in the distance.

396. *René Magritte.* The Alphabet of Revelations, *1935. Private Collection*

334

397. *René Magritte.* The Human Condition I, *1934.*
Paris, Private Collection

398. *René Magritte.* The Human Condition II, *1935.*
Brussels, Collection of Mme. Happé-Lorge

399. *René Magritte.* The Prominades of Euclid, *1955.*
Private Collection

400. *René Magritte.* The Memoirs of a Saint, *1960. Houston,*
University of St. Thomas

Again, in "The Memoirs of a Saint" (pl. 400), we are not quite certain
what the central object represents—a scroll or curtain, or something unknown
to our terrestial world. But what we do know is that we are face to face with
quintessential reality. This is certainly not illusionism in the conventional sense,
yet it comes very close. A painting such as "Personal Values" (1952) achieves
deception in a more subtle but traditional way: we feel that we have been mag-
ically transported into some hyperspace where it seems entirely normal and acceptable that common utensils should, with monstrous impudence, loom gigan-
tically against the tolerant heaven, which, paradoxically, has been dwarfed to
the compass of a cubbyhole (pl. 401). Here, admittedly, we do cross the fron-
tiers of trompe l'oeil into a far vaster domain, but realism, or better, precisionism, is nevertheless the gateway to both.

"L'Evidence Eternelle" (pl. 392) is not a single work but instead an inseparable group of five small paintings which together represent the nude body
of a woman as reflected in five mirrors. The first effect therefore is of illusionism pure and simple. It is only after a second (or third, or fourth) look that
one begins to puzzle over a subtle discrepancy, a disturbing sense of disproportion, and to ask whether this is due to some defect in the "mirrors"—
which are plainly framed and obviously a cheap kind of goods—or if the un-
easiness is due to a more mysterious cause. The feet of the figure are small
and the head is overly large, which can only be explained by supposing our-
selves to be looking down at it. This in turn implies that we are situated, not
at ground level as we believed, but at a great height, and also that the figure

401. *René Magritte.* Personal Values,
1952. Private Collection

is of giant stature in proportion to our own size. We are no more looking at the fly of early trompe l'oeil; we *are* that fly. The "mirrors" are not nearly as ordinary and innocuous as we thought them to be: this is indeed "illusionism plus."

Another illusionistic aspect of Magritte's oeuvre that appears at first conventional is the "calcification," or petrifaction, that was the culmination of Magritte's "passion for rock formations. It is notable that the founder of surrealism, André Breton, had a Celt's inborn love of stone, and that this was also the birthright of Yves Tanguy, whose work is haunted by memories of the menhirs and dolmens of his Brittany childhood. If Magritte, in turn, inherited this trait from his Flemish forebears of the Ages of Faith, he bypassed the intervening Age of Reason and its suavely civilized productions. In "Memory of a Voyage III," 1951 (pl. 402), the grim Walloon instantly crushes all the ancient grace of grisaille as if it were a mouse under the mighty paw of a couchant Belgian lion.

402. *René Magritte.* Memory of a Voyage III,
1951. New York, Collection Adelaide de Menil

403. *Eliot Hodgkin.* Spiked Papers, *1963. Collection of the artist*

The example of Magritte, however, remained an isolated case, and surrealism did not in fact galvanize illusionism into new life. Can the failure have come about in part because of the counter influence of what our Latin American neighbors are said to refer to *in petto* as the "Frigidaire School?"[4] Contrary to what one might logically suppose, American precisionism may not have been beneficent to illusionism. Demuth and Sheeler hovered on the brink of illusionism but never quite crossed over. The same is true in our own days of Andrew Wyeth and his numerous imitators. Ivan Le Lorraine Albright and his gifted twin brother, who chose to be known as "Zsissly," certainly possessed the necessary technical mastery, but not the essential detachment. Similarly, one can cite a number of artists who are undoubted precisionists but by no means illusionists: Gerald Brockhurst, Pietro Anigoni, Eduardo Malta, Cecil Kennedy, Charles Spencelay, Tristram Hillier, Edward Wadsworth, to name but a few.

Among those artists who do qualify as illusionists, we find Eliot Hodgkin, a skillful technician in the ancient medium of tempera on gesso ground. "Spiked Papers" and "Feathers" (pls. 403–404) are representative of the discrete excellence of his style. The first inevitably suggests the "Documents" by Cornelisz Brize (pl. 177). Another reference to earlier art is found in two decorative panels by Martin Battersby (pl. 405) which bring to mind eighteenth-

404. *Eliot Hodgkin.* Feathers, *1960. Collection Mrs. Van Raalte*

405. *Martin Battersby.* Trompe l'oeil panels. Artist's collection

406. *Martin Battersby.* The Fortune Teller, *1961.*
Collection of His Grace the Duke of Bedford

century prototypes, such as illusionistic cabinets. Battersby's "The Fortune Teller" (pl. 406) is at once more archaic and more modern in mood; it may owe something in the way of inspiration to the Ferrarese Madonna of the quattrocento (pl. 42a) but is also clearly indebted to the surrealists.

English illusionists often work closely with interior decorators, with results that vary widely both in mood and in artistic merit. Roy Alderson has made a specialty of architectural trompe l'oeil, including what might be called the garden variety: camouflaging unsatisfactory vistas on terraces of city dwellings (pl. 407). His whimsical decoration of his own motor car (pl. 408) should perhaps be described, with tongue in cheek, as "ambulatory trompe l'oeil." Yet, there is nothing truly new, for horse-drawn coaches were frequently decorated in this guise.

Then as now, however, "ambulatory trompe l'oeil" was visible to all. Architectural illusionism on the contrary has usually been the privilege of the moneyed elite and therefore viewed only by relatively few. Even in our own days, such creations are not likely to receive widespread publicity, unless executed by artists whose names are household words. One example of this kind is the Royal Hour Ceiling of the Palacetta de Albeñez in Barcelona, decorated by Salvador Dali (pl. 409). We have here again a famed surrealist naturally and effortlessly adopting the illusionistic discipline. However, while it is indubitably a brilliant conception—coloristically as well as compositionally—the Dali cupola in Barcelona is by no means original. It patently proceeds in direct line from Mantegna (pl. 85), Correggio (pl. 106), and their innumerable imitators through the ages. This is a constatation, not a criticism, since the formula has never yet been surpassed.

340

407. *Roy Alderson. Trompe l'oeil staircase, architecture, and plants in the garden of the artist's house in Chelsea*

408. *Roy Anderson. Decoration of the artist's automobile*

409. *Salvador Dali. The Royal Hour Ceiling, 1969, Barcelona, Alleusis Palace*

In contrast to the dazzling acrobatics of the Spanish master, a simple gridlike scheme of facetted panels was chosen for the decoration of the restored old Meeting House, at the Shelburne Museum (pl. 410). In keeping with the architecturally severe character of the room and its dedication as a place of worship, the decoration repeats that of the actual mouldings surviving on the opposite wall. The chief consideration of the artist, Duncan Munro, was to duplicate faithfully the play of shadows on the feigned mouldings according to the light conditions prevailing in the room at the time of day when it was most frequently in use. The effect achieved is austere, of great dignity and clarity.

Like the muralists, present-day practitioners of easel trompe l'oeil have continued to uphold the ancient traditions. The French artist, François Renard, for instance, acknowledges his indebtness to the seventeenth-century *petits maîtres de la réalité*. Like the works of his great predecessors, Renard's own poetic and exquisitely faithful still lifes are generally of the table-top variety, with the result that they are not trompe l'oeil in the strictest sense.

In another series of works, however, clearly inspired by the eighteenth-century examples, Renard does achieve undoubted illusionism. The familiar device of the broken glass pane suffices to endow with the allure of trompe l'oeil some otherwise rather unpretending still lifes (pl. 411). In one instance, as the subject shown under the glass purports to be a period picture, the artist has not appended his own signature, since this would negate the deception (pl. 412).

410. *Duncan Munro. Painted architectural decoration in the Meeting House. Shelburne Museum, Vermont*

411. *François Renard.* Still Life. *Collection Frederick P. Victoria*

412. *François Renard.* Les Tours de Cartes. *Collection Frederick P. Victoria*

343

413. *Rolf Hölter.* Anklage *(Accusation).*
Hamburg-Oberalster, Museum Rade

Other European exponents of traditional trompe l'oeil are Lucien Mathelin, Roger Natter, Georges Spiro, and Sougez, in France; the brothers Bueno in Spain; Fabrizio Clerici and Gregory Sciltan, in Italy; and Spiros Vassiliou, in Greece.

There can be little doubt that, given the traditionally diffident manner of trompe l'oeil artists, many other painters are presently active in this field but neither seek nor receive wide publicity. To these "hidden violets" should be added isolated performances by gifted amateurs—as that by the German mine worker and "Sunday painter" Rolf Hölter, who has made use of traditional trompe l'oeil idiom and repertory to express a message of social revolt (pl. 413).

As we have seen in the preceding chapter, illusionism in America never went out of favor. In our own day, it was given new impetus not only by the prestige of surrealsim but by the sensational revival of the Second School of Philadelphia. Traces of both these elements are found combined in varying proportions in the works of artists who in other respects stand poles apart.

The Chicago artist Aaron Bohrod was a pupil of John Sloan and began his career by painting cityscapes in the manner of the Ashcan School. A staunch opponent of the modern fallacy that the camera is able not only to replace but even to surpass the greatest achievements of painted realism, Bohrod has defined his own style as "distillation" rather than duplication. He is at his best when he submits to the ancient discipline of trompe l'oeil, thereby attaining far more serenity than in his somewhat turbulent still lifes with surrealist undertones. An admirable example is "The Shepherd" (pl. 414), particularly notable for its blend of the very old and the very new as subject matter: the aniline tints of the skeins of wool and the milky filminess of the transparent plastic wrap contrast with the archaism of the shepherd's portrait.

344

414. *Aaron Bohrod.* The Shepherd. *New York, Courtesy Hammer Galleries*

415. *Aaron Bohrod.* Still Life with Ballet Slippers, *1969. Southfield Michigan, Collection Mr. & Mrs. J. Bienenstock*

In the same spirit, Kenneth Davies never fails to include modern touches. "The Bookcase" (pl. 416) would indeed be difficult to date but for such revealing details as jacket covers, cigarette stubs, and the like. In another work, entitled "Pocusmania," an overflowing cupboard filled with miscellany is at first sight reminiscent of the Gysbrechts cupboards (pls. 150–52), but Davis' supposed door of a cabinet is actually a carpentered door, specifically a narrow bathroom door, reduced to miniature proportion, while the long-handled bath brush against it appears monstrously enlarged. This surrealistic reversal of facts brings to mind Magritte's "Personal Values" (pl. 401). Elsewhere, the artist is content to display miscellaneous objects against an old-fashioned slate without altering their proportions ("The Blackboard," pl. 417). Some words and num-

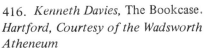

416. *Kenneth Davies,* The Bookcase. *Hartford, Courtesy of the Wadsworth Atheneum*

345

417. *Kenneth Davies.* The Blackboard, *1950. New York, Formerly Collection Joseph Verner Reed*

bers appear as if scribbled with chalk on the feigned slate. This, however, is far from being an innovation. We recall its use by Harnett, Peto, and Haberle—while the same irreverent device of grafitti had furnished Hondecoeter with a glint of humor in his famous study of a dishevelled cock hung against some wooden planks (pl. 173).

Kennard Harris's "Arrangement on Gray" (pl. 418) is perhaps his outstanding illusionistic achievement not only for the harmonious balance of the compositional elements but for its unusual coloristic refinement. It is worthy of notice that preeminence in trompe l'oeil should have been achieved by an artist who is primarily concerned with *form* rather than with texture for its own sake. The lure of tactile values has proven a fatal snare for many apprentice illusionists—conducive to a kind of myopia that deprived them of the necessary perspective. The golden mean, one is tempted to believe, must lie halfway between entanglement and estrangement. One might perhaps define it as detachment.

At the other end of the spectrum, Hananiah Harari has expressed frank delight in the purely sensuous aspect of the painter's craft:

> The subject matter of these paintings is of importance to me because I must love those things which I paint. The eye caresses the object, the craftsman's hand refines the surface of the canvas to create a new object of intrinsic beauty. Employing the close-up view reveals the delights inherent in flyspecks, dust, cracks, scalings, rips, dents, etc.[5]

418. *Kennard Harris.* Arrangement on
Gray. *Los Angeles, Salzer Collection*

420. *Ben-Hur Baz.* Mexican Paper Mask.
Formerly New York

It is notable that Harari should make use of the term "close-up," which is far
more appropriate than "trompe l'oeil" to a work such as "The Old Valentine"
(pl. 419). Earlier the artist also referred to the *Index of American Design,* a WPA
project employing artists, as an influence in the direction of "hyper-realism." It
was indeed the best school for learning to depict precise fragments of reality, unimpeachably faithful but totally devoid of the enigmatic appeal of trompe l'oeil.
On the contrary, "Mexican Paper Mask" (pl. 420) by Ben-Hur Baz is perfectly
self-contained and self-explanatory. It depicts with dramatic plasticity a macabre / humorous accoutrement worn on the Mexican equivalent of our Hal-
loween and is a not unworthy pendant to an ancient Vanitas.

The considerable role of illusionism in American commercial art of the

419. *Hananiah Harari.* The Old Valentine,
1941. Collection of the artist

347

twentieth century should by no means be minimized. In modern advertising— the equivalent of the nineteenth-century "trade cards"—trompe l'oeil wields unquestioned prestige and is almost always the choice when the effect striven for is, in art director's parlance, "class"--substance *cum* elegance—as in the discrete but unquestionably impressive advertisement for the St. Regis company by Certchik (pl. 421).

There is a sound reason for this, since the cool precisionist technique of topnotch commercial artists is particularly well suited to illusionistic renderings. This is demonstrated, for instance, in the series of panels executed for the U. S. Air Force Academy by Robert Geissmann, where the artist has combined trompe l'oeil framing devices and illusionistic vistas of the actual surroundings (pl. 422).

Trompe l'oeil has long been felt to be the perfect vehicle for themes of historical retrospection. In 1961, a design in honor of the Civil War Centennial was created for the cover of the magazine section of *The New York Herald Tribune* by William C. Kautz.[5a] The inspiration clearly stemmed from Harnett and Peto, but the picture does not achieve illusionism because the rifle at bottom and the attached leather strap are shown only in part. Similarly, "Fragments of History," 1974, by George H. MacLean (pl. 423) is an engaging, lively *quod libet.* The row of eyes at bottom (belonging to familiar Presidential faces) adds an intriguing element to the composition; but at the same time, because of its fragmentary nature, precludes acceptance of the picture as a trompe l'oeil.

421. *Certchik. Advertisement for the St. Regis Paper Company*

422. *Robert Geissmann. Illusionist panel for the U. S. Air Force Academy, Colorado Springs*

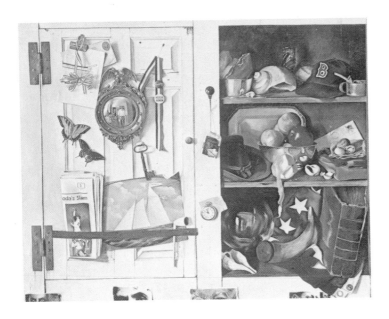

423. *George H. MacLean.* Fragments of History, *1974.*

One must place in a special category by themselves two masterly mystifications which have been dubbed "Picture A" and "Picture B" by Alfred Frankenstein. The eminent critic has demonstrated that most of the objects depicted in these two examples, both signed "A. Bianchi," were lifted from illustrations of earlier trompe l'oeil paintings reproduced in the first edition of his book *After the Hunt.* The tongue-in-cheek choice was truly eclectic, ranging all the way from Wallerant Vaillant, through various works by Harnett, Peto, and Haberle, to envelopes dated 1896.[6]

In a kindred pseudoarchaic mood, a Long Island artist, Ned La Roche, titled his charming little trompe l'oeil "Time Flies" (pl. 424) because it shows a pocket watch, the word "Times" (from the bannerhead of *The New York Times*), and some flies—a disarming pun, which Haberle would have truly savored.

424. *Ned La Roche.* Time Flies. *Oyster Bay, New York, Collection James Abbe*

425. *Howard Kanovitz.* The Radiator, *1968. New York, Waddell Gallery*

Pleasing and diverting as all of this is, one longs for illusionism (and trompe l'oeil as well) that would be truly representative of our own age rather than a nostalgic reflection of the past or a half-hearted adaptation of superannuated formulas.

Pop Art, though it was originally known as New Realism, has not furnished the solution, perhaps because, notwithstanding the legions of soup cans and the hosts of triangular cake portions, realism new or old was never its true goal. It is not surprising, therefore, that as far back as 1968 an article in *New York* magazine already heralded the advent of a new wave of photorealists under the sensational banner of "Super Reality."[7] "Infra-reality" might in fact have tallied better with the subtitle of the article: "The Inhumanists." The painters categorized there included one neoillusionist, Howard Kanowitz, the author of assemblages of hard-edge photographic likenesses. These semblances however were as yet still part of an orthodox rectangular painting surface. A year later, Kanowitz carried the formula to a logical conclusion with a show of cutout subjects—dummy boards—human as well as inanimate, over which, one critic remarked, "a cataleptic calm" reigned (pl. 425).[8] This effect is recognizable as the sense of unbalance that results from a subconscious awareness that the laws governing binocular vision are being trespassed. The only possible comparison is with the Dutch *chantourné* figures of the seventeenth century afflicted with the same kind of painterly rigor mortis. (See p. 164 and, for an early American example, pl. 309.) In these modern counterparts, the images are photographically projected onto the canvas, the faces and limbs are later livened with a neuter flesh tone, and the heads are topped with auburn hair in varying tints. The shadows have the soulless monotony of air-brush work—and for good reason, since that is precisely what they are. In a later show that same year, images of basketball players in congealed frenzy did not differ basically from the earlier cast of Kanowitz characters.

From the "Frigidaire School" to this Orwellian world of cataleptic robots was a sad progress indeed, holding out but little prospect for the future of illusionism. Yet there are rays of hope. The brightest perhaps was offered at a remarkable show held at The New York Cultural Center in the summer of 1973: "Reality and Trompe-l'oeil by French New Real Painters." The group on view consisted of only four artists: Claude Yvel, Pierre Ducordeau, Henri Cadiou, and Jean Malice. The technical proficiency of the quartet aroused the admiration of the art critic John Canaday, who commented (*The New York Times,* August 7, 1973) that Claude Yvel in particular "manages to suggest a degree of depth and richness beneath his meticulously detailed surfaces that—here and there, and just now and then—can even remind you of Chardin."

The subject matter of the four illusionists varied from the frankly archaic, as in Ducordeau's "Diploma" under broken glass (pl. 426), or Cadiou's masterly "Kitchen Shelf" (pl. 427), to Yvel's sardonic "Contemporary Art—All

426. *Pierre Ducordeau.* Diploma, *1963. Private Collection.*

427. *Henri Cadiou.* Kitchen Shelf, *1963. Private Collection*

428. *Claude Yvel.* Contemporary Art—All Wrapped Up, *1973. Private Collection*

Wrapped Up" (pl. 428), where a cover of transparent plastic echoes Bohrod's cellophane wrap (pl. 414). This, incidentally, can only have been a coincidence, since the French painter indicates in his foreword to the catalogue that he and his colleagues were totally unacquainted with American illusionism—more particularly, the work of Harnett, Peto, and Haberle—until publication of Frankenstein's catalogue *The Reality of Appearance* in 1970, and therefore also, one infers, with contemporary American examples of illusionism.

The "New Real" painters uncompromisingly refuse to use photography, even as a tool, because they believe that this expedient deprives the artist of the painstakingly acquired intimacy with his subject. From the start, their goal has been "integral trompe l'oeil," and they recall proudly that "a trompe l'oeil of a slit canvas was exhibited in the Paris Museum of Art at the same time as works by Fontana, as was a trompe l'oeil of a collage at the same time as Hains' and Rotella's poster collages, and a trompe l'oeil of a shipping crate opposite a real one."[9] All this indeed epochal, if only because it was done, as the writer also indicates, "during the triumphant reign of Abstract Expressionism."

Meanwhile, in America, the most telling indices of contemporary interest in illusionism surfaced in the works not of painters but of the sculptors who were placing extraordinary emphasis on textural rather than on plastic values, particularly on the frankly tactile appeal of wood fibers. The foremost example that comes to mind is, of course, Louise Nevelson, and also the Long Island artist Hubert Lang (pl. 429). One thinks also of the "boxes" of Joseph Cornell and, more recently, of Aline Porter (pl. 430). It is difficult to escape the conviction that these assemblages of objects—definitely "chosen," rather than found—represent a kind of vicarious illusionistic painting at least as much as they represent sculpture.

352

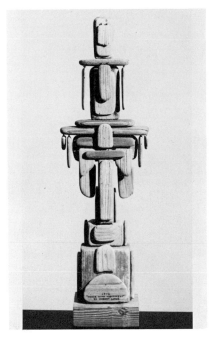

429. *Hubert Lang.* Cross with Movement, *1972. New York, Andrew Crispo Gallery*

430. *Arline Porter.* Saw, *1973, New York, Courtesy Betty Parsons Gallery*

It is undoubtedly an indication of the sentiments of the public at large on the subject of illusionism that no fewer than three American stamps reproducing trompe l'oeil paintings have been issued in recent years. First came, in 1968, the "Daniel Boone" stamp, evocative of frontier life (pl. 431), by the San Francisco artist Louis Macouillard. The next year appeared a coloristically simplified reproduction of the famous painting by Harnett in the Boston Museum, "Old Models" (pl. 339), issuance of which coincided with the Museum's centennial celebration. In 1974, Peto's "Old Time Letter Rack" (pl. 341) was similarly honored, being shown, however, in a slightly curtailed version because of the need to fit the image within a more elongated space.

It would seem therefore that, at this stage, the future of illusionism as a whole, and of trompe l'oeil more specifically, depends not so much on the readiness of the art public to receive it as on the willingness of modern practitioners to meet the unchanging standards of the art. More than two decades after the stirrings of the "New Real" movement in Paris, Claude Yvel, who

431. *Louis Macouillard.* The Daniel Boone stamp, *1968*

353

432. *Richard Haas. Painted building, Corner Greene and Prince Streets, New York, 1975*

should probably be looked upon as the foremost contemporary exponent of illusionism, was still querying, "Is the art world ready to admit a new realism that is both *rigorous* and *emotionally involved*?"[10] It seems as though the answer to this question might now be given in the affirmative.

One of the most significant manifestations in this respect has been the application of pictorial illusionism to the outside decoration of buildings. As demonstrated in Richard Haas' simulated architecture on a large side wall at "Corner Greene and Prince Street" (pl. 432) in New York's ebullient Soho district, the spirit of the movement has indeed been *rigorous* in design conception as well as means of execution. The effect has been achieved by the use of the simplest perspectival devices, such as can easily be carried out by a crew of artisans. It is just as certainly *emotionally involved,* and that in a dual sense: the artist has expressed eloquently his appreciation of the architectural style of a vanished era (the painted wall duplicates the original facade of the tall, narrow building), but he has also made a socially motivated gesture: the improvement of an environment.

In spite of the use of modern painting media, which certainly give it a longer lease on life than Holbein's "House of the Dance" (see pl. 104 and p. 117), such outside decoration is nevertheless of its very nature ephemeral. However, in our age of photography, at least a record will be preserved, as has already been done of similar accomplishments under the generic title of "street art." But one would wish for even more complete records, allowing for future restoration or duplication—for instance, of the monumental mural "People of Lakewood Together" (painted in Chicago, under the direction of John Weber), which is notable for the symbolic figures in superhuman scale and in a pictorial idiom frankly reminiscent of Léger's, but achieving illusionism because of the manner in which they appear detached from the homely background. Or of "Wall of Choices" painted by a young Chinese member of Cityarts Workshop in New York City, where two young Chinese-Americans, a boy and a girl, are shown striding forward into our plane out of a triangular street perspective, stretching uncluttered to the vanishing point.[11]

In even such a summary survey of contemporary American illusionism as this must necessarily be, it would seem advisable at the very outset to differentiate between traditional practitioners of the art (regardless of the modernity of their subject matter) and others who attempt to combine precisionism of technique with the liberating influences of surrealism and abstract expressionism. Such adventurousness is entirely in keeping with the

355

433. *Titian.* Filippo Archinto. *Philadelphia, John G. Johnson Collection*

434. *Angelo de Moro [?].*Vision of the Holy Family near Verona, *1581. Oberlin, Allen Memorial Art Museum, Oberlin College*

true spirit of illusionism—in fact, as we hope to have shown, it was undertaken far earlier than is always realized (pls. 42a, 433—34). It is encountered nowadays in the paintings of Jack Lembeck (pls. 435—36), where the illusionistic effect is undeniable, but what we are faced with is a sort of hyperspace fairyland for children of the Atomic Age. The appearance of double and triple tiering brings about an impression of considerable depth yet, at the same time, we are made aware that the superimposed layers are flat partitions: it is our imagination that supplies the intervening chasms. Dangling between these, basic forms—triangles and rectangles—suggest nothing so much as the cutout paper pennants of kindergarten windows. In fact,

435. *Jack Lembeck.* Lamb's Garden, *1975. New York, Courtesy Louis K. Meisel Gallery*

they are supplemented by amorphous blobs of clay, the productions, apparently, of young unskilled fingers. The shadows cast by these shapes are deceptively convincing exact reproductions of the objects. But this, one realizes on second thought, is of itself an impossibility: the supposed shadows are really "echoes," as the artist terms them, so that the delusion is itself a delusion, and the supposed trompe l'oeil is even more eminently *trompe l'esprit*. It is presented to the viewer as the most basic reality of all, that of a child's world—even the graffiti on the "walls" are puerile.

357

436. *Jack Lembeck.* Busy Corners, *1975. New York, Courtesy Louis K. Meisel Gallery*

437. *Juan Gonzalez.* La Misa Blanca, *1974. New York, Courtesy Nancy Hoffman Gallery*

Surrealism of the more familiar breed has left a clear spoor in the works of Cuban-born Juan Gonzales, together with a Latin flair for Romantic drama. In "La Misa Blanca" (pl. 437), the creased and puckered piece of rather ordinary stuff is transpierced with unnaturally elongated, stiletto-like tips of pencils. It also assumes most unordinary importance not only because of the exquisite skill of its rendering (one thinks of Raphaelle Peale's *After the Bath,* pl. 308) but because it unexpectedly rises, like a stage curtain, upon a weirdly grandiose seascape. Peopled by furtive, ghostly white beasts, this might serve as an illustration for Poe's mysterious "Narrative of Arthur Gordon Pym." Yet, its modest scale is candidly revealed by the inclusion of the pencils, the flower, and the moth. In final analysis, the overriding impression the artist wishes us to take away is the "reality" of the curtain. All else is presented with undeniable glamour, but as unmitigated make believe.

An even more patently single-minded insistence on the deceptive duplication of reality is the goal of the Oregon artist John Clem Clarke, whose study of great bare sheets of that most unromantic of subjects, plywood, nevertheless may well qualify as the *nec plus ultra* of present-day "deception." The painting is actual size, and viewed in the denuded, loftlike settings of the new galleries in Soho, it is completely and absolutely deceptive. It is safe to premise that, even in very widely different surroundings, it will always produce the same impression: some carpentry is in process, and the sheets have been left there for the workman. Needless to say, "Plywood"

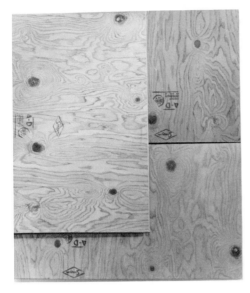

438. *John Clem Clarke.* Plywood, *1974.*
New York, Collection Richard Himmel

(pl. 438) is not framed, and as it is perfectly rectangular and the painting extends to the very edge of the canvas on its stretcher, it is also a completely orthodox *chantourné* trompe l'oeil, in direct filiation of Gysbrechts' "Turned-Over Canvas" (pl. 154) and its American variant by William Davis (pl. 327) done in the Civil War period. In one's own "museum without walls," one would certainly wish to place these next to Clark's display of hypermodern traditionalism.

In contrast, Frank Litto's archaic "Wheel" (pl. 439), while also an undoubted trompe l'oeil of the *chantourné* variety, seems to echo rather the intarsia of the Renaissance (pls. 50–53). In fact, at times the artist does not reproduce wood textures pictorially but instead creates collages and découpages, laminating to that end the weather-beaten timber of which he is enamored. In our age of permissiveness, this, like the "boxes" that are now riding the wave of a fad, should probably be recognized as trompe l'oeil in effect and intention, if no more. There are instances when it is very hard indeed to draw the demarcation line—as when Tony King endows his fantastic kaleidoscopic games with a sense of reality, if not of realism, by the use of newspaper print: "Wheel I" (pl. 440).

439. *Frank Litto.* Wheel. *Chantourné. New York, Courtesy Louis K. Meisel Gallery*

440. *Tony King.* Wheel I, *1972. New York, Saul Steinberg Collection*

359

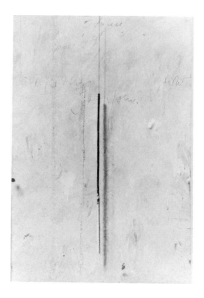

441. *Jorge Stevens.* Homage to Jasper Johns
New York, Ordover Collection

It is with unimpeachable pictorial legerdemain, however, that Jorge Stevens renders, on his canvas titled "Homage to Jasper Johns" (pl. 441), the texture of a plaster wall. The stylus that hangs before this scratched and maculated surface casts a perfectly perpendicular shadow. Comparison is inevitable with Haberle's "Leave Your Order Here" (pl. 348) and its variant, "Memoranda" (in the De Young Museum, San Francisco).

The love of texture for its own sake can hardly be brought further than by Frank Anthony Smith in his baffling "Condemned Painting, 1974" (pl. 442). It would be difficult to think of a more perfect instance of artistic abnegation: it is all too easy to accept the masterly simulation as reality, instead of as the ultimate display of painterly skill it actually is. The

360

442. *Frank Anthony Smith.* Condemned Painting, *1974. New York*

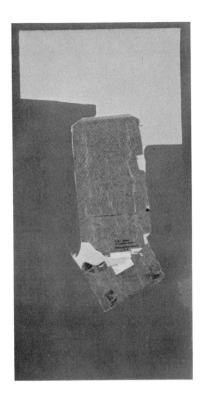

443. *Robert Motherwell.* Geneva Collage, *1974.*
New York

444. *Paul Sarkisian.* Untitled, *1974. New York,*
Courtesy Michael Walls Gallery

gloss and viscosity of the paint drippings, the finely differentiated degrees
of transparency or opacity of the various pigments, the feigned nails that
apparently secure the strips of heavy impasto to the background (the irony
of that detail is so subtle that it goes largely unnoticed), the whimsical triangle of string from which hangs the pale blue "element" (so like a pendant
jewel), all these factors, once fully appreciated, convince one that trompe
l'oeil has indeed attained here its final goal: the eye refuses to be *undeceived,*
even at the urging of reason.

A far more familiar, and therefore more easily understandable, form
of trompe l'oeil is that for which the term "papyromania" was coined earlier
(pp. 208–11). Modern art has been by no means lacking in sympathy with
this theme. One finds echoes of the letter racks of old (pls. 272–75) in
such a modern interpretation as Robert Motherwell's "Geneva Collage, 1974"
(pl. 443). It has been treated by aquarellists and draftsmen: Paul Sarkisian's
"Untitled" (pl. 444) and Dalia Ramanauskas' "Carton" and "Union Carbide"

361

445. *Dalia Ramanauskas.* Carton, *1974. New York, Courtesy Hundred Acres Gallery*

446. *Dalia Ramanauskas.* Union Carbide, *1974. Greensboro, N. C., Weatherspoon Art Gallery*

(pls. 445–46). This is something of a paradox, since watercolor and pen and pencil are undoubtedly the most difficult media for illusionistic purposes. Ramanauskas evinces particular sympathy with the texture and the utilitarian shapes of corrugated cardboard containers, but also, as well as Sarkisian, with the brown Manila paper and gummed tape which are staples of modern daily life. These artists rejoin the Old Masters in consummate skill, but their subject matter is unmistakably modern, revealed by such details as machine-typed addresses, postal-meter bands, et al.

Postage stamps, from their inception, have been part of the repertory of trompe l'oeil. In America, their inclusion took the form of such impeccable duplication as Chalfant's "Which Is Which?" (pl. 367)—that is, which is truer, or at least more enduring than reality (see p. 320)—while, on a more human level, the illustrators of trade cards (pls. 374–91) aimed instead at conveying a sense of alien glamor, the thrill of far-off voyaging. But the subject has now been given an unprecedented dimension by the modern American artist, Donald Evans, who might well be called the Baron Munchausen of philatelic art. The handsome stamps he "reproduces" with fidelity that deceives

362

447. *Donald Evans.* Katibo, *1974. Collection of the artist. Courtesy Fischbach Gallery*

experts—at least temporarily, and "at a distance," as the *Petit Larousse* so sagely stipulated (p. 20)—exist only in his imagination. He is not the copyist but the creator of designs which cleverly ape to perfection the subjects and decorative style of conventional postage stamps: miniature engravings of landscapes and historical buildings, of portrait heads of national figures, of native flora and fauna, all suitably framed in prim arabesques. Furthermore, the countries, from which the stamps issue are also of his invention: "Katibo"; "Nadorp" (capital: "Adelshoeve"), situated in the Third World; or "Yteke," a Northern dominion on the periphery of the Arctic circle. (One series, "Mangiare," while devoted to the utopian state by that name, is actually a gastronomical tribute to Italy; color pl. 24.) What truly matters is the driving tenacity that led this sensitive artist to deceive himself even more than us by creation of this, his own personal world, pictured in a unique color scheme of muted colors, glowing softly against the conventional background of a philatelist's album pages (pl. 447, color pl. 23).

363

448. *Michael Ponce de Leon.* Echo, *1962. Washington, D. C., Smithsonian Institution, Courtesy of the artist*

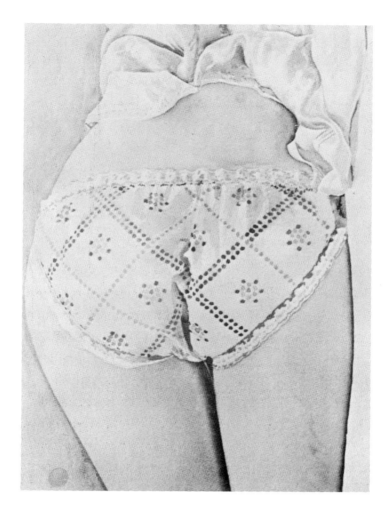

449. *John Kacere.*
Derrière, *1974,*
New York

In addition to their artistic merit, the Evans miniatures have the value of contributing a much needed element of scale to modern illusionism, which so many practitioners either "see big" or are prone to disregard entirely. While it is not actually trompe l'oeil, the air-mail stamp, depicted not actual size but approximately twenty times that, does not appear "unreal." We are struck by no incongruity, warned by no instinctive doubt, so used have we grown to photographic enlargement on a monstrous scale (pl. 448). The way was prepared in the thirties, first by the development of cinematographic art, and also by productions of the fine arts, such as the well-familiar giant petunia blossoms and bleached skulls on desert sands of Georgia O'Keefe. We now have the derrières of John Kacere (shades of Boucher and of "La Morphy")—callipygian Venuses turned in series off some cyclopean assembly line (pl. **449**).

The constatation is vaguely disturbing, for it means that we have let go of one of our trusted anchor lines to reality. There are absolutely no

364

guiding marks of any kind, for instance, in Stephen Posen's study of a tri-color drapery (pl. 450). When Dürer lavished his skill in depicting the myriad pleats and creases of a garment, it was primarily—we understood—because it clothed, i.e. half hid and half revealed, a human form. And a curtain, whether Botticelli's (pl. 49) or Gysbrechts' (pl.151), might tease, but it never shut us off entirely in this virtually inhuman manner. If illusionism of the past embodied one message above all others, it was perhaps the ancient philosophical dictum "Man is the measure of all things." Illusionism of the present has overthrown this hitherto firm foundation. Leon Battista Alberti once defined painting as "a window into space"; this should now perhaps be changed to "a window into hyperspace." We may be standing on the threshold of an age when pictorial deception will be expected to reflect much that lies beyond the reality of a man-scaled world, to encompass the macrocosm as well as the microcosm. As Magritte hinted in "L'Evidence Eternelle" (pl. 392), trompe l'oeil, which traditionally started with depiction of a fly, seems now to have appropriated the vision of that very fly.

450. *Stephen Posen.* Untitled ["Final Curtain"].
New York, Chase Manhattan Bank. N. A.

451. Nile Scene. *American Illusionistic Mirror Frame, c. 1870.*
Private Collection, New York

This unique American example of earlier date by an anonymous artist of the Centennial era daringly combines illusionism and surrealism. Reversing the usual formula of containing an imaginary vision within a framework of reality, the artist has chosen to depict his painted illusion as circumventing reality. The very large painted "frame" is actually the painting itself, and the viewer sees himself at the very core of it in a small mirror pane. The scene depicted is a Nilotic landscape; such subjects were at the height of their popularity in the 1870's, but the choice appears particularly appropriate here in this context of "magic realism," linking the mirror of the anonymous painter of that era with that of Van Eyck (color pl. 2), of Parmigianino (color pl. 8) in the past, as well as of Magritte in the future (pl. 392).

Footnotes

Chapter 1

1   According to E. H. Gombrich (*Illusion in Nature and Art* [New York: 1973], p. 195), the term "illusionism" in art-historical parlance "was introduced by Franz Wickhoff in 1895 in his famous publication of the *Vienna Genesis,* an early Christian manuscript, to characterize the deft style of brushwork which had survived from Hellenistic times." In modern times, however, the term has assumed far wider connotations: *vide* "Illusionism and Trompe l'Oeil," title of both the exhibition of pictorial illusionism and of its catalogue, held in 1949 at the California Palace of the Legion of Honor, San Francisco.

2   These studies are to be found in the bibliography beginning on p. 377.

2a   Faré 1962, p. 43. The first lexicographic recognition of the term "trompe l'oeil" is found in the 1803 edition of Claude Boiste's *Dictionnaire universel de la langue française* (first edition published in Paris in 1800; succeeding editions were issued during the nineteenth century). Paul Robert, *Dictionnaire alphabétique et analytique de la langue française* (Paris: 1973), defines trompe l'oeil as *"peinture visant essentiellement à créer par des artifices de perspective l'illusion d'objects réels et en relief."*

3   Sterling 1952, p. 34.

4   D. Mac Agy 1949.

5   Sir Joshua Reynolds, A Journey to Flanders and Holland, in *The Works of Sir Joshua Reynolds, Containing His Discourses, Idlers, A Journey to Flanders and Holland,* . . . 4th ed. (London:1809), p. 355

6   Troubnikoff 1938, p. 11.

7   Howe 1949.

8   Gilson 1959, p. 228.

9   Cited in Kahnweiler 1947, pp. 138 ff (app. A, no. 4); also in Gilson 1959, p. 295, n. 1.

10   See Ivins 1938, p. 348.

11   Hans Rupprich, Die kunsttheoretischen Schriften L. B. Albertis und ihre Nachwirkung bei Dürer, *Schweitzer Beiträge zur Allgemeinen Geschichte* (1960–61), pp. 219–39.

12   Ivins, op. cit. pp. 42–43.

13   Fassmann 1971, pp. 601–603.

Chapter 2

1   Gaston Maspero, *Guide to the Cairo Museum,* translated by J. E and A. A. Quibell. 3d ed. (Cairo: 1905), p. 40.

2   Ibid., p. 13.

3   Georges Posener, *Dictionary of Egyptian Civilization* (New York: n.d.), p. 156.

4   S. G. F. Brandon, *Man, Myth and Magic. Encyclopedia of the Supernatural,* pt. 28 (New York: 1974), p. 793.

5   Homer, *Iliad* 5. Andrew Lang, M. A. and Walter Leaf, Litt.D., *The Iliad of Homer.* Abridged edition (New York–London: 1912), pp. 238–42.

6   Vitruvius, *De Architectura* 5. 3 (Loeb Classical Library, translated by Frank Granger [London: 1970]).

7   Pliny, *Natural History* 35. 61 (Loeb Classical Library, vol. 9, translated by H. Rackham [Cambridge, Mass.: 1968], p. 311.

8   Ibid. Also Gombrich 1960 (rev. ed. 1972), pp. 101 ff, 412 n.

9   Pliny, *Nat. Hist.* 35. 65 (Loeb edition: vol. 9, p. 311).

10   Ibid.

11   Pliny, *Nat. Hist.* 35. 85 (Loeb edition: vol. 9, p. 325).

12   Pliny, *Nat. Hist.* 35. 92 (Loeb edition: vol. 9, p. 331).

12a   Illusionistic effects in mosaic works were made possible by the use of minute free-form fragments. "The Unswept Floor" (pl. 19) averages 120 tesserae to the square inch, a record that was bettered in another famous surviving example, the panel of "The Doves" from Hadrian's villa, with 160 pieces to the square inch. The technique used was known as *opus vermiculatum*—"inlaid in a pattern resembling the sinuous movements or tracks of worms" (The Oxford English Dictionary)—a graphic name that faithfully reflects the extreme flexibility of this medium as opposed to the coarser *opus tesselatum*, composed of particles that were not only of larger size but uniformly geometrical in shape.

13   Plutarch, *Lives.*

14   Pliny, *Nat. Hist.* 35 (Loeb edition: vol. 9).

15   Petronius Arbiter, *Satyricon,* Loeb Classical Library, translated by Michael Heseltine, (Cambridge, Mass.: 1969), p. 83.

16   Pliny, *Nat. Hist.* 35 (Loeb edition: vol. 9).

17   Sterling 1952, p. 13.

18   Arthur Fairbanks, trans., *Philostratus' Imagines—Callistratus' Descriptions,* Loeb Classical Library (London-New York: 1931), p. xviii.

19   Ibid., p. xxvi.

20   Philostratus, *Imagines* 1 (Loeb edition: p. 3).

21   Callistratus, *Descriptions,* chap. 5 (Loeb edition: pp. 391–92).

22   Callistratus, *Descriptions,* chap. 8 (Loeb edition: p. 405).

23   Callistratus, *Descriptions,* chap. 14 (Loeb edition: p. 423).

24   Philostratus the Younger, *Imagines,* Proemium (Loeb edition: p. 283).

25   Philostratus the Elder, *Imagines* 1. 31 (Loeb edition: p. 123).

26   Philostratus the Elder, *Imagines* 2. 1 (Loeb edition: p. 129).

27   Philostratus the Elder, *Imagines* 1. 28 (Loeb edition: p. 109).

28   Philostratus the Elder, *Imagines,* Proemium (Loeb edition: p. 285).

29   Philostratus the Younger, *Imagines* 2. 28 (Loeb edition: p. 249).

30   Quoted in D. Mac Agy 1949.

Chapter 3

1   The same effect was achieved in an illustration for a calendar manuscript made between 1137 and 1147: "Sts. Gereon, Willimarus, Gall, and the Martyrdom of St. Ursula and Her Eleven Thousand Maidens" (Stuttgart, Landesbibliothek). Perhaps inspired by the exceptional fantasticality of the subject, the anonymous artist included two figures shown as trespassing the rectangular border of the picture plane, or "space curtain." A reproduction appears on page 135 of E. H. Gombrich's *History of Painting* (reprint ed. New York: 1973).

2   This naive ancient device of figures protruding into the text space of the page

was also applied to objects. A miniature from the *Chroniques* of Froissart depicts the "Departure from Paris for England of Raymond de Montault, Seigneur de Mussidan" (Pierpont Morgan Library, M.804). In this lively little tableau, attributed to Guillaume de Bailly and assistants (probably at Toyes, circa 1400), some square banners flown atop the towers are shown as trespassing onto the page, precisely as did the wings of the mythical Flying Fish of Tyre (pl. 3).

2a   David M. Robb, *The Harper History of Painting* (New York: 1957), p. 128

3   Victor W. von Hagen, *Realm of the Incas* (New York: 1957), p. 15.

4   Sterling 1952, pp. 17–18.

5   Charles de Tolnay, quoted by Sterling, op. cit. p. 125.

6   For example, in the lunette mosaic of the Good Shepherd in the mausoleum of Galla Placidia, Ravenna.

7   Vasari, op. cit. p. 194.

8   Max J. Friedländer, *Landscape, Portrait, Still Life* (New York: 1963), p. 236.

9   For a detailed study of the instruments and other objects portrayed, see Emmanuel Winternitz, Quattrocento Science in the Gubbio Study, *Metropolitan Museum of Art Bulletin*, Oct. 1942.

10   Half-open closet doors are depicted illusionistically on the dado of the Segna della Signatura at the Vatican.

11   Gavelle 1938, pp. 231 ff.

12   Panofsky 1934, pp. 117 ff.

13   Smart 1972, p. 40; Bergström 1953, pp. 30, 40.

14   Other striking instances of effective illusionism abound in this volume. Among these: a border of peapods, with stems apparently passed through slots in the vellum of the page (G-f.11); a sumptuously jewelled neckband seemingly laid down on the page (M. p.300); and most effective of all perhaps the border surrounding an image of St. Nicholas (M.-p.280), where sturdily sculptural "cloud" forms suggest rather a gadrooned piecrust. All these are far removed in mood from the lacy arabesques that frequently supply the undeniably flat surround of medieval illuminations. It is notable, furthermore, that in the same volume a border to a Crucifixion scene includes several panels of intarsialike designs, one of which corresponds very closely to the illusionistic cubical pattern from Antioch (frontispiece illustration).

Chapter 4

1   Robb 1957, p. 242.

2   Alfred M. Frankfurter, Interpreting Masterpieces, *Art News Annual* 21 (1952): 92.

3   It has now been demonstrated that this second door was added in 1572 to facilitate the flow of traffic in and out of the room. See David Rosand, Titian's "Presentation of the Virgin": The Second Door, *The Burlington Magazine* 115 (1973): 603.

4   See P. B. Hetherington, *Mosaics* (London: n.d.).

5   Two other more attempts at pictorial illusionism are cited by Vasari: the depiction of "a bowl of water with some marvellous flowers; the dew upon them seeming actually to be there, so that they look more real than reality itself"; and a second painting of a Medusa head, begun but never finished (Vasari 1967, p. 190). It is intriguing to wonder if this lost Medusa, which Vasari said belonged

to Duke Cosimo, may not have inspired the famous illusionistic tondo on the same theme by Caravaggio—either because he was familiar with the tale or may even have still seen the Leonardo original.

6 Ibid., pp. 189–90. Vasari writes further that Leonardo made a living trompe l'oeil of a small reptile: "A gardener from Belvedere one day brought in a curious lizard, for which Leonardo made wings from the skins of other lizards. In these wings he put quicksilver, so that, when the animal walked, the wings moved with a tremulous motion. He then made eyes, horns, and beard for the creature, which he tamed and kept in a cage. He showed it to his visitors, and all who saw it ran away terrified." Ibid., p. 195.

7 The illusionistic intent is also clearly evident in another famous work by Hobein: his "Christ in the Tomb" depicts the life-sized body in profile, laid out in a low, narrow niche strongly evocative of the catacombs. It provides a stark Northern equivalent to Mantegna's "Dead Christ" (pl. 88) and is fully its rival as a masterly display of "anatomical architecture."

   For an interesting study of the "House of the Dance," see Bergström 1957.

8 Faré 1962, vol. 1, p. 24.

9 Nicholas Loyr and Louis Testelin are discussed in Faré 1962, vol. 1, p. 126; vol. 2, pls. 1–9.

10 The landscapes are described in Piganiol de la Force, *Description de la Ville de Paris et de ses environs,* vol. 9 (Paris: 1745), p. 105.

11 Joseph Pernéty, *Dictionnaire portatif de la peinture, sculpture et gravure* (Paris: 1757), pp. xvii–xix. Author's translation.

12 In Verrio's graceful design for the oval cupola of the ceiling of the White Closet at Ham House, the feature of the putti shown climbing over a feigned railing inevitably recalls Mantegna's primal treatment of the same theme in the Camera degli Sposi (pl. 85).

13 See Fitzgerald 1969, p. 146.

14 Samuel Coumen in Louis Hourticq et al, *The New Standard Encyclopedia of Art* (New York: 1939), p. 39.

15 Ibid., p. 33.

Chapter 5

1 The anecdote is told in Joachim Camerarius' posthumous Latin translation of Dürer's *Vier Bücher von menschlicher Proportion*, published in Nuremberg in 1532.

2 Hans Rupprich, *Dürers schriftlicher Nachlass,* 3 vols. (Berlin: 1956–59), 1: 308; translation is from Walter L. Strauss, *The Complete Drawings of Albrecht Dürer,* 6 vols. (New York: 1974), 2: 906.

3 Strauss, loc. cit. p. 714.

4 J. Mac Agy 1949.

5 Wolfgang Born, *Still-Life Painting in America* (New York: 1947), reprint ed. 1973, pp. 6–7. The italics are those of the present author.

6 The most important work on the two Gysbrechts was published by Poul Gammelbo, *Study on the Gysbrechts* (Copenhagen: Kunstmuseet, 1955). His book includes a catalogue raisonne of fifty-eight works (fifty-one by Cornelis and seven by Franciscus). More than half of the works by Cornelis Gysbrechts are in Denmark, where the artist spent his longest period of activity.

7 This point was made by Georges Marlier, C. N. Gysbrechts, l'illusioniste,

Connaissance des Arts 145 (March 1964): pp. 96–105.

8 Ibid.

9 A close equivalent of this second term was indeed suggested by Louis Cheronnet in his article "Le trompe l'oeil," which appeared in *Marianne*, 18 Nov. 1937: *"On peut affirmer que le trompe-l'oeil est en quelque sorte l'inquiètant sublime de la nature morte."* The suggestive term *"inquiètant"* is well nigh untranslatable in this context, however.

10 Bergström 1956.

11 Roger de Piles. *The Principles of Painting* (London: 1743), p. 10.

12 Roger de Piles. *Dialogue sur le coloris* (Paris: 1673), p. 69.

12a According to tradition, Mabuse has once placed his illusionistic skill to practical use. As court painter, he had been allotted a stipend for suitable habiliments, and the emperor Charles V was struck by the splendor of the painter's garments. But on closer view, they were found to consist of painted paper: the artist had squandered the sum on feasting and gambling.

13 Faré 1962, vol 1, p. 126.

14 D'Argenville, *Abrégé de la vie des plus fameux peintres.* (Paris: 1762), vol. 1, p. 80. Hurtaut and Magny, *Dictionnaire historique de la Ville de Paris* (Paris: 1779), vol. 3, p. 494.

15 Abbé de Monville, *La Vie de Mignard* (Paris: 1730), p. 29.

16 Pater Orlandi, author of *Abecedario Pittorico* (1733), is cited in Clerici 1954.

Chapter 6

1 Among Charles de Brosses' published books are the first work on Herculaneum, *Lettres sur l'état actuel de la ville souterraine d'Herculée* (1750); *Histoire des navigations aux terres australes* (1756), which for the first time laid down the geographical divisions of Australia and Polynesia; *Traité de la formation mécanique des langues* (1765), still a classic of philology; and *L'Histoire du septième siècle de la république romaine* (1777), which included a life of Sallust. De Brosses was also a magistrate, the first president of the Dijon Parliament, and a keen *amateur d'art.*

2 *Lettres familières écrites d'Italie en 1739 et 1740* (Paris: 1858), p. 117, published by R. Colomb.

3 According to Faré (1962 vol. 1, p. 231), the painting is now in the collection of Baron Henri de Rothschild.

4 The Brunetti Chapel has been described at length by Yvan Christ, Un Décor d'Opéra dans une petite église, *Connaissance des Arts* 72 (Feb. 1958): 18–21.

5 See Evelyne Schlumberger, Le Pavillon de musique de Madame, l'infortunée comtesse de Provence, *Connaissance des Arts* 145 (March 1964): 88–92.

6 The fascinating history of the *devant de cheminée*—the many examples that have survived as well as those known only from descriptions—is discussed by M. G. Lastic Saint-Jal, Les Devants de Cheminée, *Connaissance des Arts* 39 (May 1955): 26–31.

7 Faré, op. cit. p. 126.

8 It also trespasses another rule: that objects must be shown in their entirety.

9 Tessier's *devant de cheminée* was recently discovered by Faré, op. cit. p. 230. The papers shown as if tossed away in the porcelain bucket is the artist's own petition to the powerful minister for a commission.

10 Marandel 1973, pp. 13 ff. This scholarly assumption, however, seems somewhat

farfetched in view of the fact that architectural grisaille was used for wall decoration of medieval and Renaissance churches throughout Europe. In England, examples are found in the chapel of Eton College and the cathedral of Winchester (the Lady's Chapel). Permanent use of this kind certainly bore no relation to the liturgical calendar. Nor were the small easel grisailles on religious subjects reserved for use solely on the Lenten, or mourning, days.

10a The catalogues of the various salons (Salon de l'Académie de Saint-Luc, Salon de l'Académie, Salon de la Correspondance) supply the manes of artists officially known as *grisaillistes*: Simon-Michel Liègeois (1751); Marcenay de Ghuy (1762); Plauger (1779); François Vavocque (1782); Guillaume Bertrand (1765); Jean-François Garnery (1799). While in sales catalogues appear the names of: Bounieu, Peyron, Charles Coypel, Jean-Baptiste Dusillon. Schemes of grisaille architectural decoration were carried out by Durameau, Marcenay, Eisen the Elder (at Lyon), and Lajoue (at the Bibliothèque Sainte Geneviève).

11 Sauvage may have originated some of his grisaille themes, but it is also known that he made copies of Clodion bas-reliefs.

12 Gaston Schefer, *Chardin* (Paris: 1904), p. 47.

13 Faré (op. cit. p. 233) cites a number of such works, which were illustrated in Georges Wildenstein's *Chardin,* a catalogue raisonné published in Paris in 1921: i.e., numbers 1152, 1157, 1157 *bis* to 1207, 1208, 1208 *bis*; also numbers 1144, 1144 *bis* of the sale of November 5, 1832.

14 A trompe l'oeil practitioner known only as "Salvet" worked in a style and mood remarkably similar to Penot's.

15 The painting was sold at Christie's on October 29, 1965 for what was noted as an unusually high price for a trompe l'oeil but justified by the high quality. See *Connaissance des Arts* (Nov. 1965), p. 91.

16 Other tiled kitchens with illusionistic decorations in the same mood are found *in situ* in the region of Valencia in the palaces of the Barons of Llauri and of Vallvert and in that of the Marqués of Benicarló.

17 Dominique de Menil in Marandel, op. cit. p. 104.

Chapter 7

1 Richardson 1956, p. 70.

2 Sellers 1952, p. 4.

3 Ibid., p. 6.

4 Rembrandt Peale in *Crayon* 3 (Apr. 1856): 100.

5 The "Staircase Group" must have been seen by George Washington sometime before the opening of the Columbianum since Rembrandt Peale reports that it had been "just finished." He could not have seen it, as Sellers suggests, early in 1797 because by then the painting would have been too well known to deceive anyone.

6 Cited in Faré 1962, vol. 1, p. 326, fn. 408. Also Wilhelm 1947.

7 Both letters are quoted in Sellers, op. cit. p. 162.

8 Ibid., p. 161.

9 Barker 1950, p. 307. According to E. P. Richardson (op. cit. p. 180), "The models for these early examples and for those of the first specialists in still life after 1800 were Flemish and Dutch still lifes by the little masters of the early seventeenth century, like Van Hulsdonck, Boschaert, and their compeers. Du Simitière wrote in 1779 to Governor Clinton in Philadelphia offering for sale a

group of pictures: ' . . . pictures chiefly painted in oyl, on boards, in black ebony frames highly polished, of these kinds the Dutch settlers brought a great many with their other furniture . . . I pikt them up in New York, where they had been confined as unfashionable when that city was modernized.' "

Barker (op. cit. pp. 295–96) writes of a tongue-in-cheek tale with significant illusionistic overtones told of Bass Otis, the scythemaker turned artist, who became a successful portraitist of the Federal era, as well as the teacher of John Neagle and John Inman. Otis, it appears, was not above accepting commissions for "mortuary portraits," i.e., posthumous likenesses. In making these "from a quick sketch or even a verbal description, he would borrow the deceased person's clothes and paint them so 'like' that the facial resemblance proved acceptable too." In this instance at least, the clothes did make the man—and Bass Otis practiced what one might term psychological illusionism.

9a   In a letter to the author, dated August 29, 1669, Mr. James O. Peale, a descendant of the artist, commented: "At the top of the photo [of Margaretta Angelica Peale's deceptive "catalogue"] you will see the nail hole, worn through over the course of many years when the painting hung just inside the door of the Peale's Museum. The family legend is that many visitors attempted to consult the 'Catalogue.' Possibly they were very nearsighted! The painting was cleaned for the recent Peale shows in Detroit, which improved the details considerably."

10   Nazman H. Keyser et al., *History of Old Germantown* (Philadelphia: 1907), pp. 262–65. The information was furnished by Mr. John D. Kilbourne, Curator, The Historical Society of Pennsylvania.

11   Ibid.

12   Born 1947, p. 28.

13   The "Fraser Gallery" appears to have been considerably more than a studio. The full title of the exhibition catalogue (of which an exemplar is available at the Frick Library, New York) reads: *"Catalogue of Miniatures, Portraits, Landscapes, and other Pieces Exhibited at the Fraser Gallery, Charleston, during the Months of February and March 1857–Accompanied by Occasional Quotations and a Compendious Sketch of the Life and Career of the Artist.* Charleston, South Carolina. James and Williams, Printers, 16 State Street. 1857."

14   Charles Fraser may well have been the author of an approving comment that appeared in the *Charleston Mercury* of 16 February 1859: ". . . that rising young artist [is] still gratifying the attention of every lover of art." See M.-L. d'Otrange Mastai, William Aiken Walker, Painter of "The Land of Cotton," *The Connoisseur Year Book*, 1964, p. 78.

14a   Born, op. cit. p. 29.

15   Information regarding the attribution of the lower part to Church was supplied by the owner of the picture, Dr. Irving F. Burton.

16   Frankenstein 1969, p. 53.

17   Philostratus the Elder, *Imagines* 2. 1. Arthur Fairbanks, trans. *Philostratus Imagines–Callistratus Descriptions* (London–New York: 1931), p. 129.

18   Frankenstein 1969, p. xiii. Also Frankenstein 1970, p. 54.

19   Frankenstein 1969, p. xiii.

20   Ibid.

21   Frankenstein (Ibid., p. 158) notes that two other trompe l'oeils by De Scott Evans are known, both showing fruit hanging by strings against a wooden background.

Chapter 8

1 Frankenstein (1969, p. 55) cites an undated Harnett interview with a reporter from the New York *News.*

2 Ibid., pp. 55, 90.

3 Ibid., p. 53.

4 Ibid., p. ix.

5 Ibid., p. 80. Frankenstein cites George Inness, Jr., *The Life, Art, and Letters of George Inness* (New York: 1917), p. 124.

6 Ibid., p. 81.

7 Ibid., p. 78.

8 The relationship between music and mathematics is well known; something of the same kind perhaps links illusionism with both mathematics and music. At any rate, while as we have seen that Harnett was an amateur musician, Peto actually derived at least part of his income from musical performance: he played the cornet in camp meetings. It is intriguing to conjecture not only on the role music may have played in his life and art but also whether the revival meetings did not in some measure color his outlook, which is marked by a consistent sympathy with the lonely and downtrodden.

   Frankenstein (Ibid., pp. 41, 74) also points out that while Harnett made no mistakes in depicting musical scores or in rendering the flute, his own instrument, his violins were incorrectly strung.

9 Frankenstein 1970, p. 124.

10 Ibid., p. 116.

11 Alfred Frankenstein (1969, p. 121) has pointed out that the greater part of "Torn in Transit," a supremely illusionistic work, was nevertheless necessarily done in a nonillusionistic style. This refers to the mediocre landscape that Haberle has purposefully "portrayed" as a true sidewalk piece of art, a miserable daub. Equally interesting, however, is the superimposition of dual strata of reality: (1.) the fictitious landscape; and over it (2.) the damaged wrapping with the loose string, which one is irresistibly tempted to twang. And one wonders also if it is merely a coincidence that the waterfall should stop at the very edge of the appointed space—inevitably suggesting "Gremlin in the Studio" (pl. 317).

11a Ibid., p. 156, pl. 70.

12 Frankenstein 1970, p. 150.

13 See Frankenstein 1969, pls. 119–121.

14 Frankenstein, op. cit. pp. 127–28. A recent exhibition (summer, 1975) at The Metropolitan Museum of Art, New York—"George Washington: Icon for America" —included a pair of painted enamel cuff links of the same period in the shape and actual size of postage stamps. The popularity of the illusionistic postage stamp is also attested by the use in trade cards (see color pl. 22 and p. 326).

   A number of paintings listed (though not reproduced) as American still lifes by Alfred Frankenstein (Ibid., pp. 157–58, 159–60) belong equally in the roster of American trompe l'oeil: a rack picture by Ben Austrian, a Pennsylvania artist (illustrated in *The Old Print Shop Portfolio,* August-September, 1952); "A Feather Duster Hanging against a Door," by J. Henry Burnett (formerly in the Edwin Hewitt Collection); "A Dollar Bill," by John Califano; "A Whisk Broom Hanging against a Door," by G. Keil, Collection Mrs. John Barnes; "Doves," by J. M. Lawler; "Grapes and Papers on Board," by Thomas Pope; and finally another rack picture by Ben Cohen.

15 Ibid., p. 148.

16 The paradox is that Joseph Decker also painted rather tame landscapes, echoing the themes of Inness. We may believe, however, that these were merely potboilers.

17 Frankenstein 1969, p. 160 n.

Chapter 9

1 Roland Penrose, *Illusion in Nature and Art*, edited by R. L. Gregory and E. H. Gombrich (New York: 1973), p. 250. Emphasis added.

2 For an analysis of the profound psychological and metaphysical considerations by which these artists appear to have been motivated, the reader is referred to the specialized treatises listed in the bibliography: Gombrich 1956 and 1973.

Illusionistic subterfuge, collage, or assemblage, however we call it, is an old, old thing under a new name. The demarcation between pictorial and sculptural illusionism has always been tenuous. Without harking back to ancient polychrome statuary, nearer to us, during the Italian Renaissance, the versatile Milanese Gaudenzio Ferrari (friend of Raphael and follower of Leonardo) plied his dual talents as sculptor and as painter in his illusionistic schemes. Besides combining tridimensional elements in his pictorial representations, he even went so far as to use silver and gold pigments in depicting metal. In the same mood, two centuries later, the collaborators of Tiepolo incorporated actual objects in the decoration of palazzos: for exemple, a metal chain as leash for the simulacrum of a pet monkey.

3 "La Ligne de Vie," lecture given by Magritte on November 20, 1938, at the Musée des Beaux-Arts, Antwerp. Quoted in James Thrall Soby, *René Magritte* (New York: The Museum of Modern Art, 1965), p. 14

4 Lincoln Kirstein, Introduction to *American Realists and Magic Realists*, edited by Dorothy C. Miller and Alfred H. Barr, Jr. Reprint ed. (New York: The Museum of Modern Art, 1969), 1969, p. 8.

5 Quoted in Miller and Barr 1969, p. 40.

5a *The New York Herald Tribune*, sec. 7 (Jan. 8, 1961).

6 In the second edition of *After the Hunt* (1969, pp. xi–xii), Mr. Frankenstein describes but does not illustrate the paintings. He expresses a hope that the artist would get in touch with him.

7 Rosalind Constable, Style of the Year: The Inhumanists, *New York Magazine* (Dec. 16, 1968), pp. 44–50.

8 Sam Hunter, Foreword to the catalogue of the Waddell Gallery's Kanowitz exhibition held in New York City in 1969.

9 Claude Evel, Foreword to *Reality and Trompe l'Oeil by French New Real Painters*. Exhibition catalogue (New York: The New York Cultural Center, 1973).

10 Ibid. Emphasis added.

11 Robert Sommer, *Street Art* (New York: 1975). Professor Sommer (University of California) devoted ten years to the compilation of this photographic documentary.

Bibliography

A

Arnheim, Rudolph. 1954. *Art and Visual Perception.* Berkeley.

Art Forum, 1966. Special issue on Surrealism. Sept. 1966.

Arthur Jeffress Galleries. 1955. *Trompe l'Oeil from the 18th Century to the Present Day.* Exhibition catalogue: (Jan.–Feb. 1955; A. Jeffress Galleries). London.

B

Barker, Virgil. 1950. *American Painting History and Interpretation.* New York.

Battersby, Martin. 1974. *Trompe l'Oeil: The Eye Deceived.* New York.

Berenson, Bernard. 1896. *The Florentine Painters of the Renaissance.* New York–London.

Bergström, Ingvar. 1956. *Dutch Still-Life Painting in the Seventeenth Century.* New York.

———. 1957. The Revival of Antique Illusionistic Painting in Renaissance Art. *Gøtesborg Universitets Aarskrift 63.*

Bialostoki, Jan. 1958. Les Bêtes et les humains de Roelandt Savery. *Bulletin des Musées Royaux de Belgique,* p. 76. Brussels.

Billeter, E. 1968. *Die Geschichte des Collage.* Zürich.

Bogaerts, Theo. 1958. *Kunst der Illusie.* The Hague.

Born, Wolfgang. 1947. *Still-Life Painting in America.* New York. Reprint New York: 1973.

Breasted, James Henry. 1964. *A History of Egypt.* New York.

C

Cary, Joyce. 1958. *Art and Reality.* New York–Cambridge, Mass.

Christensen, Erwin O. 1950. *The Index of American Design.* New York.

Clerici, Fabrizio. 1954. The Grand Illusion. *Art News Annual* 2:99–122.

Coletti, Luigi. 1954. *Pisanello.* Milan.

D

D'Argenville. 1762. *Abrégé de la vie des plus fameux peintres.* Paris.

Dauzat, Albert. 1964. *Nouveau dictionnaire étymologique.* Paris.

Deonna, Waldemar. 1945–1948. *Du miracle grec au miracle chrétien.* Basel.

Dimier, Louis, 1925. *Histoire de la peinture française.* Paris.

———. 1925a. La perspective des peintres et les amusements d'optique dans l'ancienne école de peinture. *Bulletin de la société de l'histoire de l'art français* 1:7–22.

———. 1928. *Le Primatice.* Paris.

F

Fairman, Charles. E. 1927. *Art and Artists of the Capitol.* Washington, D.C.

Faré, Michel. 1962. *La Nature morte en France.* 2 vols. Geneva.

———. 1975. *Le Grand siècle de la nature morte en France: le 17ème siècle.* Paris.

Fassmann, Dr. Kurt. 1971. Article on Trompe l'Oeil. In: *Kindlers Malerei Lexikon* 6: 601–603. Zürich.

Faure, Elie. 1926. *Histoire de l'art.* Paris.

Félibien, André. 1725. *Entretiens sur les vies et sur les ouvrages des plus excellents peintres anciens et modernes.* Trévoux.

Feliskenian, Luisa Marzoli. 1955. *Pittori italiani del sesto al ventesimo secolo.* Milan.

Fiocco, Giuseppe. 1953. *Mantegna.* Milan.

Fitzgerald, Desmond. 1969. The Mural at 44 Grosvenor Square. *The Victoria and Albert Yearbook,* pp. 143 ff.

Frankenstein, Alfred. 1948. Haberle, or the Illusion of the Real. *The Magazine of Art.* Oct. issue.

———. 1950. *John F. Peto.* Exhibition catalogue (Smith College Museum).

of Art). Northhampton, Mass.

———. 1965. *The Reminiscent Object: Paintings by William Michael Harnett, John Frederick Peto and John Haberle.* Exhibition catalogue (La Jolla Museum of Art–Santa Barbara Museum of Art). La Jolla–Santa Barbara.

———. 1965a. Harnett, Peto, Haberle. *Art Forum* 4.

———. 1966. American Art and American Moods. *Art in America* 54 (March/April).

———. 1969. *After the Hunt.* Rev. ed. Berkeley–Los Angeles.

———. 1970. *The Reality of Appearance.* New York.

G

Gammelbo, Poul. 1955. *Study on the Gysbrechts.* Copenhagen.

Gavelle, Robert. 1938. Aspects du Trompe l'oeil. *L'Amour de l'Art* 19 (no. 6): 231 ff.

Gilson, Etienne. 1959. *Painting and Reality.* New York. [Originally given in 1955 as part of the A. W. Mellon Lectures in the Fine Arts. Bollingen Series 35. 2d rev. ed.,

Gloton, Marie-Christine. 1965. *Trompe-l'oeil et le décor plafonnant dans les eglises romaines de l'âge baroque,* pp. 191–203. Rome.

Goldscheider, Ludwig. 1937. *Botticelli.* Vienna.

———. 1943. *Leonardo da Vinci.* London.

Gombrich, E. H. 1950. *The Story of Art.* London–New York.

———. 1956. *Art and Illusion: A Study in the Psychology of Pictorial Representation.* A. W. Mellon Lectures in the Fine Arts. Bollingen Series 35. 2d rev. ed., 1972. Princeton. [Chapters 3 and 4 are particularly relevant to this subject.]

———. 1973. *The History of Painting.* Reprint ed. New York.

Goncourt, Edmond de, and Goncourt, Jules de. 1948. *French Eighteenth-Century Painters.* New York.

Gregory, R. L., and Gombrich, E. H. 1973. *Illusion in Nature and Art.* New York.

Grosser, Maurice. 1955. *The Painter's Eye.* New York.

H

Hamlin, Talbot. 1940. *Architecture through the Ages.* New York.

Hartman, Sadakichi. 1902. *A History of American Art.* Boston.

Hetherton, P. B. N.d. Mosaics. London.

Hourticq, Louis, ed. 1939. *The New Standard Encyclopedia of Art.* Garden City, L. I.

Howe, Thomas Carr, Jr. 1949. Foreword to *Illusionism and Trompe l'Oeil.* Exhibition catalogue (California Palace of the Legion of Honor: May–June 1949). San Francisco.

Hurtaut and Magny. 1779. *Dictionnaire historique de la Ville de Paris.* Paris.

I

Institute of the Arts, Rice Univ. 1973 *Gray is the Color: An Exhibition of Grisaille Painting XIIth to XXth Centuries.* Exhibition catalogue (Institute of the Arts: 13 Oct. 1973–19 Jan. 1974). Houston.

Isham, Samuel. 1927. *A History of American Painting* [with additional chapters by Royal Cortissoz]. New York.

Ivins, William M., Jr. 1938. *On the Rationalization of Sight, with an Examination of Three Renaissance Texts on Perspective.* Metropolitan Museum of Art *Papers,* no. 8. New York. Reprint New York: 1973.

K

Kahnweiler, Daniel-Henry. 1947. *Juan Gris. His Life and Work,* trans. Douglas Cooper. New York.

Kansas University, Museum of. 1964. *The Salzer Collection: Trompe l'Oeil and Still-Life Painting.* Exhibition catalogue (Oct.–Nov., 1964). Lawrence, Ka.

Koller, H. 1934. *Die Mimesis in der Antike.* Berne.

L

Lehmann, Phyllis Williams. 1953. *Roman Wall Paintings from Boscoreale in the Metropolitan Museum.* Cambridge, Mass.

Liotard, Jean Etienne. 1781. *Traité des principes et des règles de la peinture.* Geneva. Reprint ed. 1945.

377

Lorant, Stefan. 1946. *The New World: The First Pictures of America*. New York.

M

Mac Agy, Douglas. 1949. Phantasy in Fact. In: *Illusionism and Trompe l'Oeil*. Exhibition catalogue (California Palace of the Legion of Honor: May–June 1949). San Francisco.

Mac Agy, Jermaine. 1949. The Advance of the Object. In: *Illusionism and Trompe l'Oeil*. Exhibition catalogue (California Palace of the Legion of Honor: May–June 1949). San Francisco.

Maiuri, Amedeo. 1953. *La Peinture romaine à Rome, Herculaneum, Statres, Paestum, Cumes et Pino*. Geneva-Paris-New York.

Malraux, André. 1952. *Les Voix du silence*. Paris.

———. 1967. *Museum without Walls*. Garden City, N.Y.

Marandel, J. Patrice. 1973. *Gray is the Color: An Exhibition of Grisaille Painting XIIth to XXth Centuries*. Foreword by Dominique de Menil. Exhibition catalogue (Institute of the Arts: 13 Oct. 1973–19 Jan. 1974). Houston.

Marlier, Georges. 1964. C. N. Gysbrechts, l'illusioniste. *Connaissance des Arts, no. 145* (March).

Mastai, M.-L. d'Otrange. 1957. William Merritt Chase—A Retrospective Exhibition. *Connoisseur* (June issue), p. 266.

———. 1957a. Introduction and chronology for *William Merritt Chase*. Exhibition catalogue (Parrish Art Museum). Southhampton, N.Y.

———. 1961. The World of William Aiken Walker. *Apollo* 74 (no. 436): 213–15.

———. 1963. Landscapists of the South Fork. *Connoisseur* (Aug. issue), pp. 281, 284.

———. 1963a. Primitive or Primaeval? *Connoisseur* (May issue), pp. 65–66.

———. 1963b. American Originality in Art and Antiques. *Connoisseur* (June issue), pp. 146–48.

———. 1964. American Seventeenth Century Masterpieces. *Connoisseur* (Oct. issue), pp 137–39.

———. 1964a. William Aiken Walker, Painter of "The Land of Cotton." *The Connoisseur Year Book* 78.

———. 1964b. The Morgan Wesson Collection. *Connoisseur* (June issue), p. 135.

———. 1965. An American Family Portrait. *Connoisseur* (March issue), pp. 208–9.

McMahon, A. Philip, ed. 1956. *Leonardo da Vinci: Treatise on Painting*. Princeton.

Miller, Dorothy C., and Barr, Alfred H. 1943. *American Realists and Magic Realists*. Exhibition catalogue (Museum of Modern Art). Reprint ed. 1969. New York.

Montet, Pierre. 1968. *Eternal Egypt*. New York.

Monville, Abbé de. 1730. *La Vie de Mignard*. Paris.

P

Panofsky, Erwin. 1934. Jan van Eyck's Arnolfini Portrait. *The Burlington Magazine* 64.

———. 1939. *Studies in Iconology*. Princeton.

Paul, Robert. 1973. *Dictionnaire alphabétique et analytique de la langue française*. Paris.

Piles, Roger de. 1699. *Abrégé de la vie de peintres. Avec leur réflexions sur leur ouvrages et un traité du peintre parfait et de l'utilité des estampes*. Paris.

———. 1743. *The Principles of Painting*. London.

Plummer, John. 1966. *The Hours of Catherine of Clèves*. New York.

Posener, Georges. 1959. *Dictionnaire de la civilisation égyptienne*. Paris.

Puyvelde, Leo van. 1946. *Van Eyck—L'Agneau mystique*. Brussels.

R

Réau, Louis. 1939. *French Painting of the XIVth, XVth, and XVIth Centuries*. Paris.

Reynolds, Sir Joshua. 1928. *Discourses*. New York–London.

Richardson, E. P. 1956. *Painting in America: The Story of 450 Years*. New York.

Robb, David M. 1957. *The Harper History of Painting.* New York.

Roof, Katherine Metcalf. 1917. *The Life and Art of William Merritt Chase.* New York.

S

Sandström, Sven. 1963. *Levels of Unreality.* Uppsala.

Schéfer, Gaston. 1904. *Chardin.* Paris.

Schnapper, Antoine. 1966. Colonna et la "quadratura" en France à l'époque de Louis XIV' *Bulletin de la Société de l'Histoire de l'Art Français.*

Sellers, Charles Coleman. 1952. Portraits and Miniatures by Charles Willson Peale. *Transactions of the American Philosophical Society* 42.

———. 1959. *The World of Raphaelle Peale.* Exhibition catalogue (Milwaukee Art Center: Jan.–Feb. 1959). Milwaukee–New York.

Shipp, Horace. 1959. The Art of Trompe l'Oeil. In: *The Concise Encyclopedia of Antiques* 4:124.

Smart, Alastair. 1972. *The Renaissance and Mannerism in Northern Europe and Spain.* London.

Sterling, Charles. 1950. *French Painting, 1100–1900.* Exhibition catalogue (Carnegie Institute). Pittsburgh.

———. 1952. *La Nature morte de l'antiquité à nos jours.* Paris.

———. 1952a. *Catalogue de l'exposition de la nature morte.* Exhibition catalogue: l'Orangerie, Paris.

T

Troubnikoff, A. 1938. Trompe l'Oeil. *Illustrated London News,* Christmas 1938 issue. London.

V

Vasari, Giorgio. 1967. *Vasari's Lives of the Artists,* abridged and edited with commentary by Betty Burroughs. New York.

W

Wildenstein, Georges. 1921. *Chardin.* Catalogue raisonné. Paris.

———. *Chardin.* Catalogue raisonné, revised and enlarged by Daniel Wildenstein. Oxford.

Wilhelm, Jacques. 1947. Magie du trompe-l'oeil. *Plaisir de France,* pp. 21–27.

Index

I. General

Index
II. Works